EXPLORING SOUTHERN CALIFORNIA:
80 Outings for the Urban Adventurer

William A. Hoffman, MA, PhD

Founder and CEO of Hoffy Tours, LLC

hoffytours.com

Special thanks to Russell Pierce, whose design made every outing a fun visual adventure, and to my wonderful wife, Maria, and my dear friend and business partner, David Bratton-Kearns, whose editing skills prevented me from calling every place the most beautiful, the most famous, and the best!

www.mascotbooks.com

For more information, please contact:
Mascot Books, an imprint of Amplify Publishing Group
620 Herndon Parkway, Suite 220
Herndon, VA 20170
info@mascotbooks.com

Library of Congress Control Number: 2025916198
CPSIA Code: PRV0925A
ISBN: 979-8-9925701-0-6

Printed in the United States

CELEBRATING SOUTHERN CALIFORNIA...

County by County

LOS ANGELES

Diverse and exciting describe LA County. Downtown LA has over ten specialty districts, cutting edge architecture, historic movie palaces, and world class museums. Moving west, you'll find the glamour of Hollywood and Beverly Hills along with the famous beach areas of Santa Monica, Venice and Malibu. To the east are the graceful cities of Pasadena and Claremont, famous for craftsman bungalows, art and learning.

ORANGE

Orange County is known for its famous beach towns—artful Laguna Beach, sparkling Newport Beach, and Surf City Huntington Beach. You'll also find much to explore inland—a burgeoning art scene, historic San Juan Capistrano, quaint Orange, and creative Santa Ana. Discover new food halls, history trails, ethnic enclaves, famous planned communities, and a presidential library.

RIVERSIDE/SAN BERNARDINO

Downtown Riverside is a historic jewel with a new museum of Chicano art next to the landmark Mission Inn. Nearby you'll find the 220-acre Citrus State Historic Park and the stately mansions of beautiful Redlands. Farther east is the desert resort of Palm Springs with its mid-century modern architecture and new Agua Caliente Cultural Museum. One hour north is the high desert majesty of Joshua Tree National Park.

SAN DIEGO

No wonder they call San Diego - "America's Finest City." Along the Harbor find Little Italy, Gaslamp Quarter, Liberty Station, and the USS Midway Museum. Just up the hill is stunning Balboa Park. Cruising north through the coastal cities of Del Mar, Encinitas, Solana Beach, and Carlsbad is a real treat, offering scenic beaches, flower fields, nature preserves, and fun downtowns.

SANTA BARBARA

The City of Santa Barbara is the most beautiful of Spanish Colonial towns. The downtown Mission, Presidio, historic County Courthouse and Red Tile Walk are not to be missed. The County offers the gorgeously preserved Danish village of Solvang and the quaint wine-country towns of Los Olivos and Los Alamos.

VENTURA

Downtown Ventura is a delight with its walkable and historic main street, famous city hall, and mission. Nearby Ojai is an enchanting city of health, history, and art, and Simi Valley boasts the largest presidential library in the nation.

80 OUTINGS FOR THE URBAN ADVENTURER

Practical Itineraries for Lots of Fun Places

TABLE OF CONTENTS

DOWNTOWN LA

GREATER LA

PASADENA/CLAREMONT/EAST LA COUNTY

ORANGE COUNTY

INTRODUCTION

A Guide for the Urban Adventurer

This local road map is a bit different from your typical travel guide. It focuses less on the well-known tourist spots and instead introduces interesting, historic, lively and fun places. It's for curious people who like to explore the best in cities - architecture, historic districts, museums, neighborhoods, and landmarks. *Exploring Southern California: 80 Outings for the Urban Adventurer* encourages the reader to take a second look at places that they may have heard about, but never really explored or observed. It represents what I consider to be the best in Southern California.

My book has four goals: **1)** to give you numerous options for fun outings and interesting places to explore; **2)** to save you time in planning day trips; **3)** to compile the best of Southern California in one reference book that you can use time and time again; and **4)** to provide background information that enriches the urban experience. Finding great ideas online or from an article is fine, but it's nice to have your options organized in one place. And, of course, I hope the book increases your appreciation of this amazing region where we live.

Southern California has more museums than any other region in the country.

Southern California might be the most diverse region in the world – geographically, culturally and architecturally – and, as a tour guide, I'm quite happy about it. There's never a shortage of places to go or activities to pursue. With a huge and diverse population, with landforms that range from deserts to mountains to beaches, and with more museums than any US city, Southern California has something for almost everyone. Being home to Los Angeles, the nation's second largest city, along with its world-famous entertainment industry, is a huge bonus.

Piazza della Famiglia in Little Italy, San Diego, is a great example of pedestrian-friendly development.

I have nothing against the megapopular theme parks such as Disneyland, Universal Studios, or LEGOLAND, but I have little to offer the reader here. Instead, this book focuses on places you can learn from, that can teach you something that you didn't already know. Some of the places I've chosen are quite popular and, for these, I've tried to add new perspectives. After all, famous places are popular for a reason—they are interesting! Also, I'm attracted to places where people are encouraged to walk around and explore. Because so much of Southern California was built for the convenience of the car, I like to focus on places that are pedestrian-friendly. I'm a strong proponent of the "new urbanism" movement in planning cities that supports walkable and mixed-use development.

Happily, I've noticed that over time, cities are becoming more and more interesting. They are capitalizing on their unique identities and strengthening those qualities that set them apart. Whether it be unique signage, street-spanning arches, historic preservation, walking tours, or distinctive museums, cities are capturing what makes them special and fun to visit. With over three hundred cities, eight metropolitan areas, and over twenty-three million people, Southern California makes for a lot of potential outings!!

The geographic diversity of Southern California is unparalleled.

80 Outings is not meant to be an exhaustive guide of everything there is to see and do in Southern California. The region is simply too large to include everything, so I've had to be selective. It's one urban appreciator's best day adventures. It skews towards architecture, historic preservation, art, coastal spots and the desert more than the mountains. By describing places and a suggested order of activities, it's on you – the explorer – to fill in the blanks, to decide where to eat and where to turn. Consider it a motivating guide, not a complete treatise. Use your Google Maps to orient yourself, but drive carefully and go with a friend.

In summary, each day trip is meant to fill one day, but certainly the tours can be extended or shortened. Each description gives you a suggested itinerary and order of activities, but nothing is cast in stone. You can mix and match the destinations as you choose. The guide sometimes suggests places to park, eat and walk, but much is left to the traveler. Each day trip format is as follows:

1. **Short Summary:** Describes the outing in a nutshell and helps you decide if it's for you.
2. **Background:** Provides you with information describing why the area is unique and what you'll expect to find and do there. This is where the facts and history are presented.
3. **Suggested Itinerary:** Gives a recommended order of activities and practical information on parking, access, timing and even places to eat. A careful reading of this section should really help you get the most out of your outing.
4. **Map:** You gotta have a map, for heaven's sake!
5. **Nearby Attractions:** These are add-on visits that are close by to provide variety to the day trip.

This book is born out of my love for cities. I hope you enjoy this celebration of the diversity of Southern California as much as I have enjoyed compiling this book. And, yes, despite all the crowds, traffic, and great distances, there is so much of interest and beauty to explore in this amazing Southern California!

Southern California is one of the most culturally diverse regions in the world.

OUTING #1: LA SMORGASBORD

A Driving Tour of Downtown Los Angeles

Downtown LA has tons to see in a fairly small area, and this driving tour hits many of the highlights. It's way too much for one day, so pick and choose your favorite stops. Driving in DTLA is not difficult, although parking is quite expensive. Make sure you have a good navigator with you and drive carefully. You may consider hiring an Uber or Lyft driver, instructing them to stop along the way. If you embark on this outing in the late afternoon into the evening, take advantage of the many rooftop bars and restaurants of historic and modern hotels.

Background: DTLA is bounded by four freeways and, in this relatively small area (see map, page 9), you have world-class museums (the Broad, MOCA), vibrant ethnic enclaves (**Chinatown**, **Olvera Street**, **Little Tokyo**), world-class architecture, a historic core, numerous **specialty districts** (Fashion, Arts, Flower, Toy, Produce, to name a few) and **LA Live** with its sports arena, convention center, and hotel complex. DTLA used to be somewhat of a ghost town at night, but now, thanks largely to a change in the zoning code – the **Adaptive Reuse Program** - over 80,000 people live downtown. Sadly, though, downtown is also home to Skid Row and the largest homeless population in the state.

One $2 gets you into both LA Flower Markets. $1 on Saturdays.

Apple's meticulous restoration of a 1927 theater.

Riding Angel's Flight to the top of Bunker Hill is a DTLA must-do!

Itinerary:

1. 4th Street Bridge - Start your day by crossing the historic, gothic-style 4th Street Bridge from the 101 Freeway into downtown. You'll cross the LA River and get a good view of the skyline. Lots of car commercials are filmed here.

2. Flower District - Make a left on Alameda (south) to Olympic Avenue (right) and drive through the Produce and Pinata Districts to the Flower District. You'll want to park near Wall Street and cruise the two huge flower markets – **The Original Los Angeles Flower Market** (754 Wall St.) and the **Southern California Flower Market** - that face each other on either side of Wall Street. It's best to go early for fresher flowers and a greater selection.

3. Fashion District - After your floral adventure, cruise south on Maple Street into the heart of the Fashion District. The amount of merchandise in the street is a colorful mind-blower. You may want to park and walk the famous **Santee Alley** – a five-block narrow pedestrian street with discount apparel. The Fashion District is huge and you'll want to do some research if you're a true fashionista. Next stop – LA Live.

4. LA Live - From Maple Ave., turn right on Pico, then a right on Figueroa Ave. You'll soon see the Crypto.com Arena – home of the Lakers basketball team on your left. Just past **Chick Hearn Drive**, you'll see the **Grammy Museum** – a great stop for music lovers with tons of video clips and interactive displays. This entertainment district – part of the South Park district - is the glitziest part of downtown LA with its huge, high-resolution digital displays, trendy stores and restaurants, modern skyscrapers and famous hotels.

5. Historic Core - Make a right on Olympic and then right on Broadway St. to enter the **Historic Theater District** – the greatest concentration of pre-1931 movie palaces in the US. Notice the marquee of the former United Artists Theatre, a Gothic-revival beauty. A cool stop is the **Apple Tower Theater** at the corner of Broadway and 8th Street, Apple Corporation took a deteriorating 1927 Renaissance Revival theater and renovated it to create an Apple Store. The original balcony, ceiling oval skylight, lobby and proscenium are all still here in their cleaned-up, terra-cotta glory! And you can buy an iPhone! This is adaptive reuse at its finest!

6. Consider lunch at Grand Central Market – a DTLA favorite since 1917 and home to over twenty food vendors. After lunch, walk across Broadway and enter the famous **Bradbury Building** (corner of Broadway and 3rd). This famous office building from 1893 has a stunning skylit atrium surrounded by stairways, elevators and walkways of ornate ironwork. No wonder it's a National Historic Landmark (notice the plaque to the right of the front entrance). You can also exit the back of the market and take a steep ride on the historic **Angel's Flight Funicular Railway** to the California Plaza on top of Bunker Hill and its skyscrapers.

7. Little Tokyo - After grabbing a bite, head east on Broadway to 1st Street (right) and in three blocks you're in Little Tokyo's **Historic Landmark District**. Park your car and find the large, red wooden tower – the entrance to the **Japanese Village Plaza**. You can cruise this beautiful pedestrian street or go across the street to the **Japanese American National Museum** or the **Geffen Contemporary at MOCA Museum**. The original buildings of the historic district survive on the east side of 1st Street between Central and San Pedro Streets. **Koyasan Buddhist Temple** (1912), also on 1st Street is one of the oldest in North America.

The Fire Tower is Little Tokyo's most visible landmark and the entrance to Japanese Village Plaza.

8. Olvera St. & El Pueblo de Los Angeles - Go north on 1st Street, make a right on Main, cross the freeway, park your car and enter the birthplace of LA - Olvera Street and El Pueblo de Los Angeles. This beautiful plaza area with its huge Moreton Bay fig trees was founded in 1781 by the Spanish. You have lots of options here. You can cruise the tight street of colorful shops and Mexican curios, or you can get more serious and visit one of the many **museums** – **Chinese American**, **Italian American**, **Avila Adobe**, **La Plaza de Art y Cultural** or **America Tropical** (which tells the story of a very controversial mural from 1932). Whatever you do, have a taquito slathered in green avocado sauce at **Cielito Lindo** – an LA tradition!

Olvera St. is more than a colorful Mexican market street. It has three interesting museums.

9. Chinatown is right around the corner. Make a left on Cesar Chavez and then right on Broadway. As you pass under the **Dragon Gateway**, you'll notice four blocks of crowded sidewalks, shops and restaurants. Prices are great, by the way! The most scenic area is the historic **Central Plaza** with its ornate gateway, fountains and statues – particularly beautiful with neon lights at night. Try to visit nearby **Homeboy Industries** and **Homegirl Café** (130 W. Bruno St.) - an inspiring national model of gang intervention.

10. Bunker Hill - Leaving Chinatown en route to Bunker Hill, go southwest on Broadway, turn right on Temple. You may want to stop at the distinctive **Our Lady of the Angels Cathedral** (2002), the metropolitan museum of the Catholic Church in LA with its famous tapestries and extensive use of the translucent stone, alabaster. As you reach the top of Bunker Hill, make a left on Grand Ave. In a half block, with the 1960s Music Center to the right, stop at the steps marking the entrance to **Grand Park**. Look to your left to the art moderne City Hall (1928); and to your right to the mid-century modern **Department of Water and Power Building** (1965). How cool it is that LA created this linear park for its downtown celebrations and relaxation!

LA's Grand Park is a breath of fresh air in DTLA. Love the magenta chairs and tables!

The rest of Grand Ave. is indeed grand, with world-famous architecture and cultural attractions. One block ahead is the famous **Disney Concert Hall** (2003) by Frank Gehry. Its whimsical, stainless-steel walls are complemented across the street by the stacked, modernist towers of **The Grand LA**, a mixed-use project also by Gehry . Next door is the contemporary art **Broad Museum**, with a squarish-honeycomb exterior that allows natural light into the galleries. Farther down on the left is the postmodern **Museum of Contemporary Art** (1979), another of LA's world-class museums. With all these spectacular venues, let's hope that Grand Avenue becomes a pedestrian mecca day and night.

Frank Gehry's deconstructivist, lyrical modern Disney Concert Hall set the stage for Grand Avenue's transformation.

11. Sixth Street Viaduct - By now, you've seen much of the diversity of Downtown LA. Finish your tour in dramatic fashion by crossing the **LA River** on the Sixth Street Viaduct (2022). The popular bridge, with ten pairs of rising and falling arches, connects the **Arts District** with **Boyle Heights**. This bridge is proof that infrastructure can be both functional and beautiful.

The Sixth Street Viaduct is the coolest bridge in an LA century!

Murals seem to be on every wall in the Arts District.

12. Arts District - We'll finish our driving tour of DTLA at the Arts District. As Grand Ave. descends Bunker Hill, turn left on 6th St. Take 6th St. through the **Jewelry District** and Skid Row to Alameda, where you will make a left. You could avoid Skid Row by going east, but why not see the city as it is? The Arts District, bordered by Alameda and the LA River between 1st and 7th Sts., is LA's best example of adaptive reuse; abandoned manufacturing buildings and warehouses have been transformed into creative uses of all types. And the area has the greatest concentration of murals anywhere in the city. If you have time to stop, make a right on Traction and explore the area around 3rd Street. See **Hauser & Wirth** on 3rd Street, a modern art gallery located in a former flour mill. The relentless coolness of the Arts District is around every corner.

HOFFYTOURS™
UNIQUE URBAN ADVENTURES

Los Angeles

Location Legend

1. 4th Street Bridge
2. Flower District
3. Fashion District
4. LA Live
5. Historic Core
6. Grand Central Market
7. Little Tokyo
8. Olvera St.
9. Chinatown
10. Bunker Hill
11. 6th St. Viaduct
12. Arts District

101
110
10
Bunker Hill
Civic Center
El Pueblo
Financial District
Historic Core
Gallery Row
Little Tokyo
Toy District
Arts District
South Park
Fashion District

Nearby Attractions:

- California Science Center with Oschin Air & Space Center
- Lucas Museum of Narrative Art
- < Natural History Museum
- California African American Museum

OUTING #2: BECOME A BUILDING WATCHER!

Skyscraper Walk

Let's crane our necks and go 'scraper gazing! Skyscraper design has undergone noticeable style periods, and it's fun to guess when a particular building was built. LA's skyline may not compare to that of New York or Chicago, but it represents over one hundred years of skyscraper evolution in a fairly small area. From Beaux Art (1900s) to Art Deco (1920s to 1930s) to modernism (1950s to 1970s) to post-modernism (1980s and 1990s) and beyond, LA's got it all.

Length: 2 to 2.5 hours

Background: A skyscraper's shape can often tell its style and date. Here's your tutorial before you begin your "skyscraper walk."

Beaux Arts
1880s - 1920
Building as three-part classical column: base, shaft, capital.

Art Deco/Art Moderne
1925 - 1935
Stepped-up, decorative "wedding cake" look.

Modernism
1950 - 1970
Simplified volumes, rectangular shapes, flat tops.

Expressive Modernism
1970 - 1985
Architects break up the box; new abstract shapes emerge.

Postmodern
1975 - 1990
Playful buildings with cultural references/historic symbols.

New, High-Tech Modernism
1995 - on
Energy-efficient, translucent glass, interesting tops.

Itinerary:

1. Start at the Jerry Moss Plaza above the Gloria Molina Grand Park in front of the **Music Center**. Look north to the Department of Water and Power Building for a great example of modernism (1964) and then south to the beautiful LA City Hall (1928) for an example of Art Moderne/Deco style. Notice how the building narrows as it rises.

2. Continue west one block on Grand Avenue to **Disney Concert Hall**. Although the fanciful concert hall doesn't qualify as a skyscraper, you could call its style "lyrical modernism" or "deconstructivism." Notice the Conrad Hotel and residential tower (2022), called The Grand LA, across the street. Their interesting shapes and translucent facades are hard to classify but qualify as "ultramodern deconstructivism"!

3. Continue west two blocks on Grand Avenue to the **Wells Fargo Center** towers. These fifty-story, reddish-brown granite towers (1980-81) with their tapered shapes would qualify as "expressive modernism." Go to the plaza area to the right and look up – this is ground zero for skyscraper viewing in LA.

4. Walk to the bottom of Bunker Hill and make a right on 5th Ave. Stop in front of LA Central Library. It doesn't get better than this for viewing four generations of skyscraper design. The **US Bank Tower** across the street is an understated example of postmodernism with its nod to Art Deco. To the right, the tower addition to the **Biltmore Hotel** is postmodern as well. The Union Bank Building (1968), behind and to the north of the US Bank Tower, is a classic example of modernism, sometimes called "International Style" since skyscrapers of that period looked the same all over the world. On the corner of 5th and Grand – the Torrey Pines Bank – you'll find another great example of the Art Deco style. Check out the Art Deco bas relief patterns above the entry and try to visit the ornate lobby. Finally, notice the **Bonaventure Hotel** to the northeast with its cylindrical, reflective glass – very popular in the 1970s.

5. Walk south on 5th Avenue three blocks to Broadway Street. As you walk past **Pershing Square** at the corner of Hill Street, stop and take in the view. The Biltmore Hotel is a fine example of Beaux Arts design (1923) with some Italian Renaissance thrown in. If you have time, the lobby and conference rooms are stunningly decorated with Art Deco and renaissance detailing. No wonder so many movies were filmed here. Around the Square you'll see reflective glass, Art Deco and modern 'scrapers. Wowzer!

6. Turn left on Broadway Street, go one block and look south towards Spring Street. At the corner of Spring and 5th Street you'll see LA's most famous early skyscraper – the **Continental Building** (1903). This is a classic example of Beaux Arts design with its richly detailed capital, simplified shaft and substantial base. Building as column – there it is! And it's one of LA's over 1200 **Cultural Heritage Landmarks**.

7. Continue down Broadway two more blocks to Grand Central Market. You've gotta be hungry by now and this has been LA's vintage food hall since 1917. I love the neon signs and the great variety of food vendors. After you've had a drink and a snack, cross the street to the **Bradbury Building** at the corner of Broadway and 3rd Street. Unassuming on the front, it's the stunning interior of wrought-iron balconies in the atrium space that earned this 1893 office building designation as a National Historic Landmark.

8. Take Angel's Flight back to Grand Avenue! When you're finished with your snack, walk through the back of Grand Central to Hill Street and catch the historic Angel's Flight Funicular Railway to the top of Bunker Hill and Grand Avenue. The train lets you off in a beautiful corporate plaza among the skyscrapers. It's a short walk back to Grand Avenue. and your car.

Note: A really nice option for this walking tour is to sign up for the LA Conservancy's Saturday walking tours. "LA's Evolving Skyline" is one of the many great walking tours you'll find on the website of this historic preservation advocacy group. Finally consider arriving in LA via train. From Union Station, take the Red Line subway two stops to the Pershing Square Metro Station. As you exit the station, you'll be in skyscraper heaven!

OUTING #3: FLOWER, FASHION & ARTS DISTRICTS

Specialty Districts Galore!

Downtown LA has over eleven specialty districts, and this tour takes you to three very lively ones. This is an outing focusing on aesthetics – flowers, fashion, and art – rather than architecture or history. Plan an early departure to buy some flowers followed by a cruise through the vibrant Fashion District. After lunch, enjoy LA's hip Arts District with a visit to a renowned art gallery and a brief walking tour of its neighborhood. Parking can be a challenge, so make sure to go with family and friends to help you navigate.

Background: The two largest flower markets – the **Original Los Angeles Flower Market** and the **Southern California Flower Market** - are conveniently located right across from one another on Wall St. between 7th and 8th Streets. The prices are great, the fragrances sweet, and the selection is delightfully massive. The Fashion District, formerly known as the Garment District, is huge, covering 100 blocks in DTLA. You could use the Fashion District website **(fashiondistrict.org)** to locate your shopping preferences, but this outing takes you to the popular and crowded **Santee Alley** – a three-blocks-long outdoor market with lots of junky treasures. Finally, the Arts District is a great example of urban evolution – originally an industrial and warehouse district, it is now a creative hub of restaurants, lofts, galleries and small businesses, and its many murals make it an outdoor gallery of color. You could spend a whole day here, but this outing will take you to its most walkable neighborhood.

Succulents abound and at great prices!

Itinerary:

1. AM: Start at Original Flower Market – Walking into two huge flower markets is a sweet smelling way to start the day. I recommend you arrive no later than 9:00 a.m. to get the best selection. Park your car near Wall or Maple Street, and pay the $2 entry fee. Remember that you will be exploring two large markets separated by Wall Street. You may be overwhelmed by the choices, but you'll soon find cut flowers, potted plants, succulents and more. If you need a coffee or snack, consider Poppy and Rose on Wall St. Happy shopping!

2. Cruise the Fashion District – Part of the fun here is driving the streets and seeing all the colorful merchandise lining the streets. This area is huge so make sure to download a map before taking off. Go south on Maple Street from the Flower Market and park anywhere between 9th and 11th Streets. Your two stops are going to be **Michael Levine Fabrics** at 920 Maple St. and Santee Alley, both close together. Levine Fabrics is one of the oldest fabric stores in the district where you can buy a huge variety of fabric by the pound. Enter the bustling promenade of Santee Alley at Olympic Boulevard for the three-block-walk fashion gauntlet to Pico Boulevard. It's colorful, tight, and very affordable. This is not high-end fashion, but quite an experience. As you leave the Fashion District, drive northeast on Los Angeles Street to get more of the flavor of the immensity of this area.

3. Lunch – You have lots of downtown lunch options. Here are a few of my favorites: **San Antonio Winery** – LA's wonderful, historic winery; **Sonoratown** – casual eatery with award-winning Northern Mexico-style tacos; **Grand Central Market** – the go-to historic food hall with more than two dozen floor vendors; and **Wurstkuche** – the Arts District sausage and beer hall with exotic choices including rabbit and snake!

4. PM: Explore the Arts District – This area is LA's best example of adaptive reuse, where abandoned manufacturing buildings and warehouses have been transformed into creative uses of all types. And the place is overflowing with murals, making it one of the most interesting neighborhoods to walk or drive. In addition, some of LA's best restaurants and hippest shops are here, and new places open up all the time. Since the District is large – bordered on the west by Alameda St., the east by the LA River, the north by 1st Street, and the south by 7th Street – use the website below.

LA is a city of murals and you'll find the best concentration and variety in the Arts District.

Discoverlosangeles.com is a wonderful website for exploring the city. Use the search bar and type your preferences such as "arts district" or "rooftop bars."

The most walkable neighborhood is in the north part of the Arts District at the corner of 3rd Street and Traction Avenue just east of Alameda St. On Traction, you'll find the Angel City Brewery, The Pie Hole, Wurstküche, the Arts District Brewing Company and tons of murals. Walking east along 3rd Street, don't miss **Hauser & Wirth** a **contemporary and modern art gallery** occupying a former flour mill. This gallery sponsors art exhibitions and events in a vibrant architectural space with a restaurant, bookstore and urban garden. Don't miss it. Also, continue walking east on 3rd Street and make a right on Santa Fe Ave. Check out the huge, linear mixed-use project – **One Santa Fe** – that borders the adjacent MTA rail yard, LA River, and **SCI-Arc** – the **Southern California Institute of Architecture**, housed in a former rail freight depot. This white and red, 438-unit development - more than ¼ mile long - contains a few eateries and shops, my favorite being **Hennessey + Ingalls Bookstore** specializing in art and architecture. You gotta love the Arts District with its creative surprises.

Stamped crosswalks mark the Fashion District; Bob confronts too many choices.

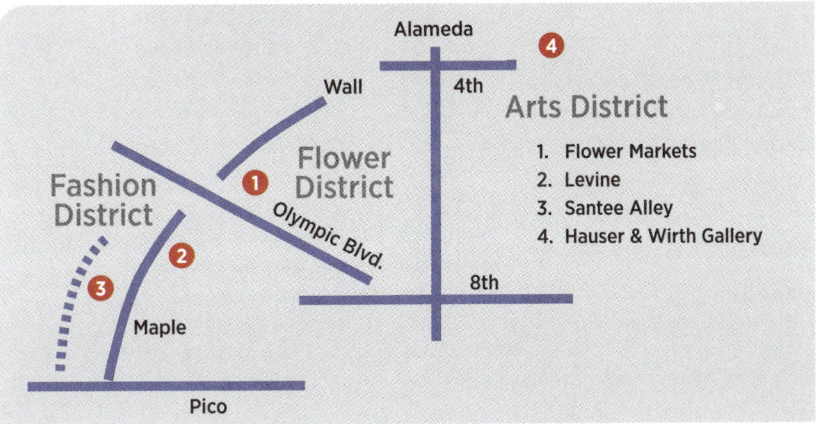

OUTING #4: TWO SLICES OF MULTICULTURAL LA

Little Tokyo and Chinatown

Los Angeles is one of the most multicultural cities in the world, with numerous ethnic enclaves - Chinatown, the Byzantine-Latino Quarter, Historic Filipinotown, Thai Town, Little Armenia, Little Ethiopia, Little Bangladesh, Little Tokyo, Koreatown and many others. This outing introduces two of them - Little Tokyo and Chinatown - located within two miles of each other in Downtown Los Angeles. You can focus on one or both of them, depending on your time. Historically, both of these Asian communities suffered tremendous discrimination and have demonstrated remarkable resilience. To explore the Mexican American legacy district and LA's birthplace - El Pueblo de Los Angeles and Olvera Street - see Outing 9. You will start this outing in Little Tokyo.

Little Tokyo Background: Japanese immigrants began arriving in Los Angeles in the late 1800s, and before World War II, Little Tokyo was the largest Japanese community in the US. World War II forced the relocation of 120,000 Japanese Americans to concentration camps in isolated areas in the US. Two camps were in Arkansas. After the war, Little Tokyo bounced back with new businesses and was declared a **National Historic Landmark District** in 1995. It is a vibrant district today, but rising rents and an aging population pose definite challenges.

Little Tokyo Walking Tour

The heart of Little Tokyo is First Street, between Alameda and Judge John Aiso Streets. Use the tall, red **Fire Tower** as your point of reference.

1. Start your walking tour at the Japanese American National Museum. Here you will learn 130 years of Japanese American history, starting with the first Issei generation of immigrants. A good part of the museum focuses on the resilience of the Japanese community after their forced relocation to concentration camps in isolated areas of the US. Numerous special exhibits, art installations and educational programs make this an excellent two-hour visit. Turn right as you exit the museum and walk two hundred yards to the **Go For Broke Monument**, honoring the more than 16,000 Japanese American men and women who served during WWII. Next to the monument is the **Geffen Contemporary at MOCA** - a 40,000 square foot exhibition space for modern art installations.

2. Historic First Street - Double back to First Street and walk the short commercial block between Central Avenue and Judge John Aiso Street. This is the last intact block of historic Little Tokyo with its restaurants and legacy businesses. You might notice the brass plaques and images placed in the concrete sidewalks that tell part of the Japanese American experience.

This mural on Alameda Street displays the pride and resilience of Little Tokyo.

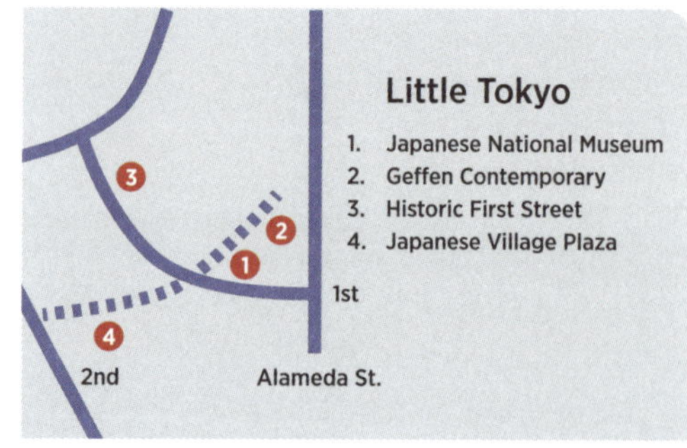

3. Stroll the Japanese Village Plaza - Look for the fifty-five-foot-tall **Japanese Fire Tower** with its red beams and blue tiled top. This symbol marks the entrance to a colorful outdoor shopping street (opened in 1978) where you'll find iconic Japanese fashion brands, art supplies, a bakery, restaurants and supermarket. With gingko trees and paper lanterns, this beautifully scaled plaza is a stroller's and shopper's delight.

Chinatown's East Gate marks the entrance to the Central Plaza.

4. Other sights - You can experience the peace and beauty of two **Buddhist Temples** - **Koyasan** and **Higashi Honganji** - or savor the Japanese rooftop garden at the Hilton Kyoto DoubleTree Hotel. The cascading water provides a respite from the city below. A favorite store for affordable Japanese gifts and knickknacks is Bunkado on First Street near the Fire Tower.

Chinatown Background: The Chinese in Los Angeles established a strong presence in the downtown area around La Plaza since 1870 despite the Chinese Exclusion Act and laws that prevented property ownership. Construction of Union Station dislocated the community to its present location along Broadway Street. The **New Chinatown** had a gala opening in 1938 followed by major construction near the famed **Broadway Gate**. Although LA's Chinatown is rated one of the most interesting in the US, the majority of Chinese Americans have moved east to suburban areas in the San Gabriel Valley which some call the Chinese "food mecca" of the US (Do we sense another tour?).

Chinatown Walking Tour

Chinatown is quite walkable and can be reached without a car from Union Station. Take the **Metro Gold Line** to the Chinatown Station and walk 1.5 blocks west to the bustling stores on Broadway. The area has become quite a foodie destination as well as a bargain shopper's paradise. The four-block stretch of North Broadway, between Cesar Chavez Boulevard and Bernard Street, is where you'll find most of the shops, restaurants and plazas. The **West Plaza**, just west of Hill St., also has restaurants and art galleries. The district has done a great job with its Chinese-themed urban design. Notice the upturned, flying eaves, even on the corner gas station!

1. Chinese American Museum - A good place to start your tour is here in El Pueblo de Los Angeles Historic Monument, the site of the original Chinatown. The entrance is very understated, located just west of La Plaza in the brick Garnier Building (1890). The two-story museum does an excellent job documenting the history of the Chinese American community from the late 1800s on. This is an LA hidden gem!

2. Continue to North Broadway Street to the Chinatown Gateway Dragon Monument just beyond Cesar Chavez Boulevard. This marks the south entrance to Chinatown.

3. Continue on Broadway to the Far East Plaza Building (727 N. Broadway). This 1979 food court and mall has some of Chinatown's best eateries. You'll find delicious, quick food but not formal seating here. Continue down Broadway and browse colorful gift shops selling plants, herbs, paper lanterns, clothing and all sorts of affordable knickknacks. Continue two blocks to Chinatown's Central Plaza just beyond College Ave.

4. Central Plaza - This ornate gateway and outdoor shopping area was opened in the 1930s as part of the "new Chinatown." Here you will find statues of Sun Yat-Sen, the first president of the Republic of China, and Bruce Lee, the famous actor and martial artist. The plaza is a beautiful public space with colorful themed buildings and paper lanterns. Although not as bustling as it once was, the plaza is particularly gorgeous at night with its extensive neon lights. Just up the street is Phoenix Bakery, a Chinatown classic.

5. Continue through the Central Plaza to the beautiful West Gate built in 1938. Cross Hill Street to **Chung King Road and Court**. This forty-foot-wide pedestrian street, also built in the 1930s and '40s, transitioned from a traditional Chinese retail street to contemporary art galleries and studios. Although quiet during the day, the area has enjoyed a nighttime revival and its urban spaces are very picturesque and fun to explore.

OUTING #5: ART, WINE & SONG

The Broad, San Antonio Winery and Grammy Museum

This downtown outing combines two of LA's specialties: contemporary art and music. Oh, yeah, and wine too! In the morning, you'll visit the wonderful Broad Museum on Bunker Hill, a unique architectural experience and a stunning collection! Make a morning, timed reservation for this free museum. Enjoy a delicious, buffet-style lunch at an LA treasure - the San Antonio Winery - and the City's only operating winery. The location might fool you, though, as it is found just east of the LA River in a semi-industrial zone. After lunch, make the fifteen-minute drive to the Grammy Museum in the exciting entertainment district - LA Live. This four-story museum has great interactive exhibits on the history and winners of the Grammy Awards.

The fiberglass-reinforced concrete panels form the "veil" or outer shell of the Broad.

Itinerary:

1. Broad Museum - The architecture of this world-class contemporary art museum (2015) is a big part of the experience. You enter under the building's honeycomb outer shell, called the "veil," and take an escalator through a smooth cave to the third floor of the galleries. As you ascend, watch carefully for glimpses of the second floor "vault," where hundreds of artworks are stored for later showing. As you enter the galleries, the natural light emanating from the openings in the "veil" creates an openness and clarity rarely experienced in many museums.

The Broad's collection is a literal "who's who" of famous contemporary artists. You'll see **Warhol's** and **Lichtenstein's** Pop Art and **Koon's** famous *Balloon Dog*, along with works by **Braque**, **Calder**, **Diebenkorn**, **Francis**, **Johns**, **Matisse**, **Miro**, **Picasso**, **Rauschenberg**, **Ruscha**, **Basquiat**, and **Stella**. Of course, works of art are added and moved, and you'll find special exhibitions on the first floor. Take a break at the **Broad Plaza** with its century-old olive trees on the west side of the building on **Grand Avenue**.

Option - Take a Walk on Grand! Grand Ave. has a stunning collection of contemporary architecture. Within two blocks you'll see the Museum of Contemporary Art (MOCA - 1976); the Grand LA (2022) and Disney Concert Hall (2003), both by Frank Gehry and the Music Center Plaza and Grand Park. Hopefully, Grand Avenue will become a pedestrian-friendly, mixed-use mecca!

2. Lunch at San Antonio Winery – San Antonio is where downtown LA comes to drink wine. This family business, under the Riboli family, first opened in 1917 and was declared **Historic Cultural Monument #42** in the early '60s. It's a beautiful facility with a long tasting bar, an extensive gift shop, tasty buffet-style entrees, and an attractive dining room. The winery makes a wide selection of varietals from their vineyards in Napa, Monterey and San Luis Obispo counties. Take a tour of the winery, check out the historic photo gallery and learn how it survived during Prohibition by selling sacramental wine. With luck, you'll meet the owner - Santo Riboli. No wonder San Antonio won **Winery of the Year** in 2018!

Spacious tasting areas, tours, and great food make this winery a joy to visit.

Fun interactive exhibits are a big draw at the Grammy Museum.

3. Grammy Museum - Spend your afternoon exploring your favorite music. The Grammy Museum is located in the heart of the **LA Live Entertainment District**, close to numerous restaurants, the Convention Center and Crypto.com Arena. There are four floors of interactive music exhibits along with video clips of your favorite music stars and concerts. Permanent exhibits include *On the Red Carpet, Michael Jackson, Grammy Moments, Latin Music highlights,* and *From Mono to Immersive*, an experience room that traces the evolution of sound from gramophones to surround sound. Watch for rotating exhibits of your favorite music and time your visit to experience a concert or film screening in the 200-seat **Clive Davis Theater**. Go to the fifth floor's Ray Charles Terrace for a drink and great views of this colorful and modern part of downtown LA. What a fun way to rock on in the rock 'n' roll capital of the world!

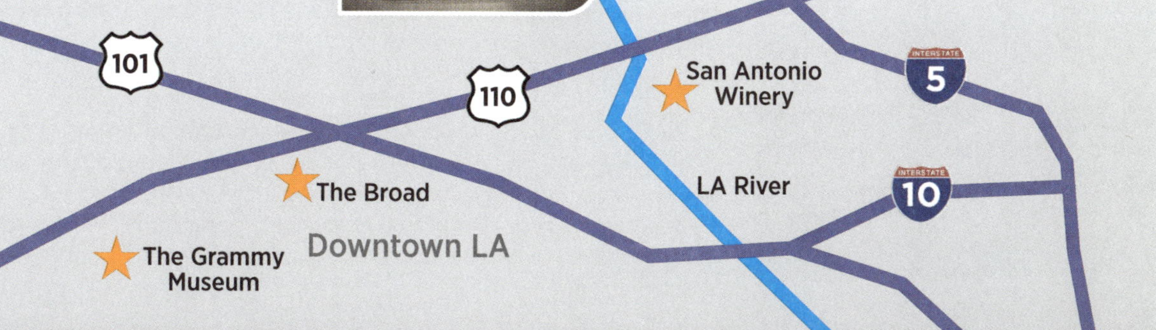

Optional Walk: Explore LA Live on foot. Walk one block down Figueroa St. to Chick Hearn Ct. in front of the Crypto.com Arena - home of the Lakers and Kings. See the statues of Kareem Abdul-Jabbar, Magic Johnson, Jerry West, Kobe Bryant, Luc Robitaille and more. This area is LA's version of Times Square - pulsing with huge video screens, restaurants, hotels and entertainment options.

OUTING #6: MOVIE PALACES, ART DECO & MORE

Historic Core Highlights Walk

LA's historic core is intense and gritty, but also contains the best concentration of large, dramatic, and historic buildings anywhere on the West Coast. You'll see ornate movie palaces, Art Deco styling, and, thankfully, vibrant street life. Downtown LA has been making a comeback, and you'll see it here in a big way. This outing requires quite a bit of walking, so choose the places that most interest you. A good option for this area is to sign up for one of the LA Conservancy Historic Downtown Walking Tours on Saturday mornings. The two applicable tours are the Broadway Historic Theater and Commercial District and Art Deco Tours.

Downtown's Broadway Street was built before parking requirements, creating very urban, vertical public spaces.

Background: Downtown LA's Historic Core was largely abandoned with the post-World War II suburban boom. Theaters closed and department stores moved out. But by the 1980s, things began to change. Both Broadway and Spring Streets were designated as **National Register Historic Districts**. The City passed an **Adaptive Reuse Ordinance**, making the zoning code more flexible to convert older commercial buildings to residential uses. More than 80,000 people now live in Downtown Los Angeles. Broadway St. has more movie palaces than any street in the US, and Spring Street has an impressive concentration of beautiful early 1900s, Beaux Arts buildings.

View of Bunker Hill skyline from the observation deck of City Hall.

Walking Tour

1. Start your adventure at LA's gorgeous 1928 City Hall. This Art Moderne masterpiece features a beautiful rotunda and extensive tile work. For the best view of DTLA, take two elevators to the **Observation Deck** where you will find portraits of all of LA's past mayors. From here, twenty-eight floors up, you'll have a 360-degree view.

2. Walk one block west on Main St. to the Vibiana, an event space fashioned from the former St. Vibiana's Cathedral, one of LA's oldest buildings from 1876. The cathedral was about to be demolished, but when it was declared a **Historic-Cultural Monument**, preservation efforts and tax incentives gave the landmark new life. Walk two blocks north to Broadway Street and 3rd.

3. Grand Central Market, the Bradbury Building and Angel's Flight. There's lots of action at the corner of Broadway and 3rd. Grand Central Market, open since 1917, is LA's most famous food hall with over 20 food vendors and vintage neon signage. Don't miss the famous Bradbury Building (corner of Broadway and 3rd) across the street. This office building from 1893 has a stunning skylit atrium surrounded by stairways, elevators and walkways of ornate ironwork. No wonder it's a **National Historic Landmark** (notice the plaque to the right of the front entrance) and a favorite for movie shoots. Before you leave, make sure to ride Angel's Flight (located on Hill St. in back of the market) - the funicular railway that climbs to the **California Plaza** atop Bunker Hill. Here you'll enjoy great views of the Historic Core amid 50-story modern skyscrapers.

4. Continental Building and The Last Book Store. For a good feel of the revitalization of Spring Street, cut over one block south to Spring Street and check out the Continental Building (408 Spring St.), LA's first skyscraper. Built in 1903, this 13-story building is a classic example of the Beaux Arts style with a three-part design: ornate base, elongated shaft and richly-detailed capital. This style was popular for bank and government buildings throughout the US.

A visit to The Last Book Store is one of DTLA's most unique stops.

Walk one block west to the corner of Spring and 5th Street to the wonderfully quirky **Last Book Store** (453 Spring St.). At 22,000 square feet, this is California's largest new and used book and record store. Located in a century-old commercial building, you'll love exploring the two-story space, including a mezzanine level with artwork and creative displays. This is a book lover's dream and a truly unique place to visit.

5. Historic Theater District and the Apple Tower Theater. Walk one half block west to the Spring Street Arcade. Cut through the historic arcade to Broadway Street and head west. You'll notice the ornate **Los Angeles Theater** just beyond 6th Street. This was the last of the great movie palaces (1931) and a favorite for filming. The interior is a recreation of the Hall of Mirrors at Versailles and the rococo bathroom lobby has to be seen to be believed! Broadway St. certainly put the palace in movie design. To explore inside this gem, you can sign up for an **LA Conservancy Walking Tour** or buy a ticket to their annual Last Remaining Seats program where the historic theaters are opened for vintage films.

The LA Theater's ornate French baroque interior is the most lavish of Broadway's movie palaces.

Don't fail to see the impressive **Apple Tower Theater** at the corner of Broadway and 8th St. Apple Corporation took a deteriorating 1927 Renaissance Revival theater and adaptively reused it to create an Apple Store. The original balcony, ceiling oval skylight, lobby and proscenium are all still here in their cleaned-up, terra-cotta glory! And you can buy an iPhone! This is adaptive reuse at its best and a wonderful example of the revitalization of LA's Historic Core! The staff is friendly and welcoming. Make sure to go downstairs to see the before-and-after photos.

Farther down Broadway, you'll notice an Urban Outfitters inside of the original 1917 Rialto Theater and the **Orpheum Theater** beautifully restored for live performances. At Broadway and Ninth, you'll find the largest Art Deco building on the West Coast - the green and gold terra cotta **Eastern Columbia Building**. You'll find yet another vintage theater reborn at 929 Broadway. The original 1927 Gothic Revival United Artists Theater became the Ace Hotel and then a limited-service, rooms-only operation. The original theater, in an almost spooky Spanish Gothic style, hosts live concerts and performances.

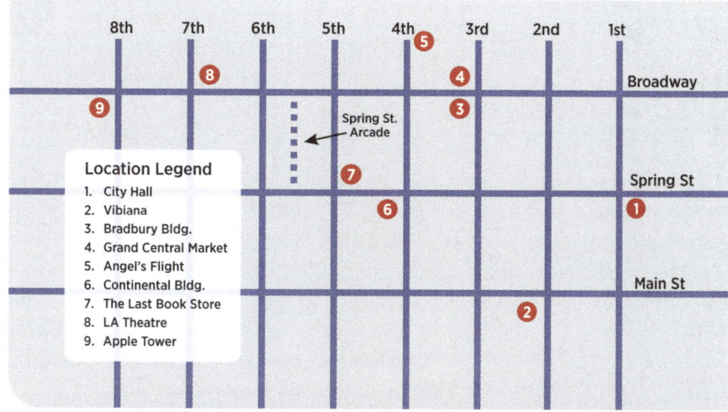

Nearby Attractions: Downtown LA has many other historic buildings and hotels. A good source for exploring more is to access the Los Angeles Conservancy website for walking tours. Other nearby notable historic buildings include: The Biltmore Hotel, Los Angeles Central Library, CalEdison, Eastern Columbia, Title Guarantee and Trust, and the Hoxton Hotel.

OUTING #7: THE LIBRARY TOUR

Historic Central Library and The Last Book Store

*This outing is not just for bookworms; it's for people who love libraries and want to explore a cherished historic building with a great story of survival. The library is an Art Deco masterpiece with murals, sculpture and an exciting new wing. You can take a docent, virtual or self-guided tour of the 1926 LA Central Library (***www.lapl.org/central-library/docent-tours***). Plan on at least a 90-minute visit followed by a stop at the Museum Store on the ground floor. The Library survived a devasting fire in 1986, which is chronicled in* The Library Book *(2018) by Susan Orlean. Round out your literary adventure with a visit to quirky and wonderful The Last Book Store on Sixth Street in the Historic Core.*

48 bulbs (one for each state in 1926) adorn the rotunda chandelier.

Background: In the early 1920s, LA was outgrowing its Central Library. The City chose New York architect **Bertram Goodhue** - famous for the ornate Spanish Colonial architecture of Balboa Park in San Diego and the semimodern Art Deco Nebraska State Capitol. Goodhue worked with **sculptor Lee Lawrie** to create an artistic and symbolic building capped with ***The Light of Learning*** sculpture atop the pyramidal mosaic tower. The interior rotunda and reading rooms have extensive murals and painted ceilings. The Library survived a suspicious 1986 fire and was given a burst of funds when developer **Robert Maguire** bought 40 floors of developable space above the Library for $125 million. Maguire then transferred these "air rights" to the US Bank Tower across the street, enabling it to reach a height of 73 stories. With its developable envelope gone, the Library was saved from overdevelopment. The funds from the sale of air rights allowed for the addition of the impressive, multilevel **Tom Bradley Wing**.

Itinerary:

1. LA Central Library - Before you enter the Library, walk to the top of the **Bunker Hills Steps** on 5th Street next to the **US Bank Building**. As you gaze down at the Central Library, picture the 40 stories of developable space that was purchased and transferred to the 73-story, cylindrical tower next to you.

Entering the Central Library from 5th Street, notice sculptures and inscriptions on the walls above inspiring visitors to read and learn. On the second floor find, the ***Statue of Civilization*** guarded by two sphinxes above the north staircase. There's lots of symbolism in this marble figure. Now enter the **rotunda** with its huge chandelier. The surrounding murals, created by magazine illustrator Dean Cornwell, depict the four great eras of California history. Now walk straight ahead into the **Children's Literature Department**. Its walls are adorned with murals of Spanish explorers of California - Juan Cabrillo and Gaspar de Portola.

As you walk back into the Rotunda, find the Annenberg Gallery to the left of the staircase. This leads to two rooms that usually have great rotating exhibits. Take the hallway to your right to view the new Tom Bradley Wing. The eight-story high atrium has three themed chandeliers by Therman Statom. The escalator lanterns, called *Illumination*, by Anne Preston, are in the shape of an upside-down human profile. Check out the historic Ivanhoe frieze by Garnsey and Parsons and ceiling decorations in the **International Languages Department**.

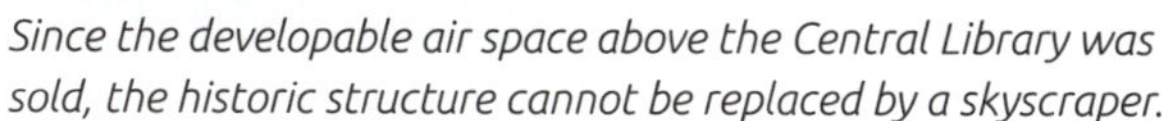

Since the developable air space above the Central Library was sold, the historic structure cannot be replaced by a skyscraper.

A visit to The Last Book Store is one of DTLA's most unique stops.

On the first floor, notice the modern ceiling mural featuring the names of Los Angeles novelists intertwined in the ceiling. Visit the small and interesting **Library Store** with proceeds benefiting the Library. Libraries are one of the few truly democratic places left in American cities, and the LA Central Library is a treasure.

2. The Last Book Store - At the corner of 5th and Spring Streets, the Last Book Store is a wonderful way to end your literary outing. This unique establishment is not really the last bookstore, but the largest new and used bookstore in California. The store has a record store, comic book store, 5 art studios, an epic yarn shop, a famous book tunnel, a mammoth head, local arts and crafts, and "unexpected nooks of funkiness." Since it is located in a hundred-year-old bank building, The Last Book Store has vaults and ghosts!

Maguire was able to add 33 stories to his Library Tower (right) from his purchase of air rights above the historic Central Library.

Fun Fact: Spring Street is one of the oldest streets in LA with over 23 historic bank buildings, including the City's first skyscraper. It is on the National Register of Historic Places and was once called "the Wall Street of the West." Thanks to LA's Adaptive Use Ordinance, many of these "Beaux Arts" style commercial buildings are now lofts and apartments. Downtown LA is no longer a ghost town after dark as it was in the 1960s. 80,000 people now live downtown.

OUTING #8: CUTTING - EDGE DESIGN ON BUNKER HILL

Grand Avenue Architecture Walk

Grand Avenue on Bunker Hill in DTLA is living up to its name. This three-block walk has three concert halls, two modern art museums, a new Frank Gehry-designed hotel and residential tower, some nice restaurants and cafés, lots of skyscrapers, and a Grand Park. If you like contemporary architecture, there's enough variety here to keep you engaged for an entire afternoon. The museums bring visitors during the day, and the concert halls attract the evening crowd. With the new mixed-use Grand LA project, it is hoped that Grand Avenue will become a vibrant area throughout the day.

The Grand Park is a much needed breath of fresh air and event space for DTLA.

Background: Bunker Hill, named for a street commemorating the famous battle, was the site of lavish, 2-story Victorian homes around the turn of the 20th century. However, in the '20s and '30s, wealthy residents left for enclaves such as Beverly Hills and Pasadena, and the area became blighted. As part of the controversial **"urban renewal"** process, the houses were cleared and the city's **Redevelopment Agency** sold the land to developers who built 40-to-50-story skyscrapers in the 1980s. LA now had a skyline! With the completion of Disney Concert Hall in 2003 and the Grand Park in 2012, Grand Avenue was off to the races.

Itinerary: This walk will start at the Music Center and Grand Park entrance and move westward.

1. Gloria Molina Grand Park - Stand at the entrance to the Grand Park and look down to **LA's iconic City Hall**, the tallest building allowed by earthquake codes in 1928. This 3-block linear park with sight lines between prominent landmarks is an example of the "City Beautiful Movement" of the early 1900s. The idea was to create linear parks, such as the Mall in Washington, DC, highlighting important civic buildings. The Grand Park has a wonderful landscape plan featuring five floristic kingdoms - Cape, Boreal, Neotropical, Paleotropical, and Australian. You can grow pretty much anything in LA's climate! As you descend into the park, take advantage of the numerous and movable magenta chairs and tables.

2. Music Center - Across from the entrance to the Grand Park, cross Grand Avenue and ascend the steps or the escalator into the **Jerry Moss Plaza** at the Music Center. Straight ahead is what many consider to be the most beautiful example of mid-century modern design in the city - Welton Becket's **Water and Power Building** (1965). This 17-story beauty has white, horizontal floors that cantilever twelve feet beyond the building, creating an elegant visual geometry. To your left is the famous **Dorothy Chandler Pavilion** - a New Formalist building with stylized columns and an overhanging flat roof. The Pavilion hosted many Academy Awards nights.

3. Disney Concert Hall - Proceed west on Grand Avenue to one of LA's most famous modern buildings - the magnificent Disney Concert Hall by **Frank Gehry**. Completed in 2003 at a cost of $274 million, the hall's style has been described as "deconstructivist, sculpturist and lyrical modernist." Whatever it is, this home to the **LA Philharmonic** has world-class acoustics. Find the stairway to the Blue Ribbon Garden - a tranquil and beautiful oasis of trees and sculpture nestled on the west and north sides of the building.

4. The Grand LA - Check out Gehry's mixed use Grand LA complex across the street (pictured top right). With a 45-story apartment tower and a 25-story hotel, the mixed-use development is the last piece of the Grand Avenue rebirth. Meant to complement Disney Hall, the two towers are stepped back from the street rising in building blocks slightly jostled out of alignment. Ground floor retail and a small park are intended to enliven Grand Avenue. Let's hope so. In the meantime, have a drink at the one of the **Conrad Hotel's** beautiful terraces with views the city and its surrounding mountains.

5. The Broad - Continue one block to the west to The Broad Museum. Looking like a rectangular honeycomb, this museum is as much about the architecture as the art. The architects - Diller Scofidio + Renfro - created an ingenious **"veil and vault"** concept. The veil is the exterior honeycomb, which allows natural light into the third-floor galleries. The vault is the second-floor storehouse for art, which is regularly recycled for viewing upstairs. As you enter the museum's cavernous lobby, take the escalator through the smooth, cavelike opening. As you ascend, look for views of the vault and its stored art. As you exit on the third floor, the contemporary art is beautifully illuminated through the veil's openings. This is architecture as its finest, and the museum is free.

The Broad's honeycomb veil, with its famous occulus, plops right down on the sidewalk.

6. Colburn School of Performing Arts - Across from The Broad, you'll see the Colburn School. A new one hundred thousand foot expansion (also by Frank Gehry) is planned along 2nd Street with a 1,000 seat performance hall. Long live the arts on Bunker Hill!

7. MOCA - Walking westward along Grand, notice the **Museum of Contemporary Art** (1986) by Japanese architect Arata Isozaki. With a design that is vaguely postmodern with its red sandstone and cluster of geometric forms, this museum is in stark contrast to the surrounding towers, with only four of its seven floors above street level. From the sunken courtyard entrance, world-class art awaits!

Gazing up at the skyscrapers makes you feel a little small!

8. California Plaza and the Wells Fargo Center - Complete your stroll at the west end of Grand Avenue. Here you'll find the gleaming skyscrapers of the Wells Fargo Center - trapezoids of marble and glass. Look up and feel small. To the south, check out the California Plaza with its fountains and sitting areas - a delightful respite from the bustle below. Fun restaurants abound one floor down.

9. Find the bright orange gateway of Angel's Flight - the famous funicular whose exciting and steep ride takes you down to lively **Grand Central Market**.

OUTING #9: TRAINS & TAQUITOS

Union Station & Olvera Street

Yes, you can have a grand adventure in LA without needing a car! Take the train, subway, light rail, or bus to Union Station and then simply walk across the street to Olvera Street and El Pueblo de Los Angeles Historical Monument. Union Station (1939) was the last great train station built in the US and was recently remodeled to host the 93rd Academy Awards. Olvera Street and El Pueblo are the birthplace of Los Angeles, containing the town's original plaza, six diverse museums and one of LA's best and most colorful pedestrian streets. Plan for three hours or more for this adventure.

Background: Stunning Union Station is still the most important transportation hub in the City of Angels with connections to trains, light rail, Metro buses and the subway. Architecturally, it is a beautiful blend of Art Deco, Spanish Colonial, and Mission Revival styles - so let's call it "Mission Moderne." It was built on the remains of the original Chinatown, which was forcibly moved four blocks to the northeast in 1938.

Olvera Street and **El Pueblo de Los Angeles** are the historical ground zero of the city. Founded In 1781 by the Spanish governor of California, it followed the strict urban planning laws of the King. Unlike the English colonies, Spanish settlements in the New World required a central plaza with accompanying church and civic buildings. Thankfully, **LA's original plaza** has been preserved and is the heart of the original "pueblo" or town. Olvera Street was a dusty alleyway off the plaza that was transformed into a quaint Mexican street by Christine Sterling in the late 1920s.

Years of smoke and grime had covered up these beautiful Southwestern-themed ceiling tiles.

Itinerary:

1. Union Station - As you enter the station, admire the huge Ticket Concourse to the left and the **Grand Waiting Room** straight ahead. Look up at the beautiful floral, Mission Revival ceiling tiles. They were recently cleaned in a painstaking restoration effort for the Station's 75th birthday. Walk through the Waiting Room with its Art Deco chandeliers and huge leather chairs, through the hallway past the train platforms to East Plaza. Here you'll find connections to **LA's Red Line Subway** and bus terminal. Notice the huge mural - *City of Dreams, River of History* - and the patterned glass half dome. Art is everywhere in this grand station!

As a final treat, on your way out to Olvera Street, visit another preservation success. Just south of the main entrance, you'll find another beautiful, high-ceilinged room, formerly a **Fred Harvey Restaurant** (opened 1941). The room was designed by Mary Colter, the architect of many of the rustic buildings of the Grand Canyon, including the Hopi House and Hermit's Rest. The design is Southwest Art Deco, with a zigzag marble floor resembling a Navajo rug! Have a beer, take a walk up to the mezzanine and take it all in.

2. Olvera Street and El Pueblo de Los Angeles Historical Monument

There's so much to see in this historic park. Here are your fun options:

"Lucha libre" masks are among the colorful items for sale by vendors on Olvera Street.

a) La Plaza - Everything starts here. Surrounded by huge **Moreton Bay fig trees** with a central bandstand, La Plaza is a wonderful gathering place. The statues of founding Spanish governor - Felipe de Neve - and his ing, Carlos III, are on opposite sides.

b) West of Plaza - The brick buildings directly west of the plaza were built by French settler Phillipe Garnier in 1890 for Chinese commercial tenants. Check out the excellent **Chinese American Museum** located at mid-block. It tells the important story of resilience in the face of tremendous discrimination. (Note: The small entrance sign doesn't do this jewel of a museum justice.) On the south corner, find the 1884 Victorian **Plaza Firehouse** - the City's first. Horses were stabled inside, and the round turntable floor enabled quick deployment of the wagon. Towards Main Street are two beautiful Italianate buildings: the larger **Pico House** and the smaller **Merced Theater** (1870).

A taquito at Cielito Lindo at the end of Olvera Street is a must! Notice the "papel picado" above the sign.

c) Across the Street - Looking north across Main Street, you'll see two ornate brick buildings which house **La Plaza de Artes y Cultura** - a museum and cultural center devoted to telling the history and stories of Mexicans, Mexican Americans and Latinx people in Southern California. Next door is the mission revival **La Placita Church**, LA's oldest (1822) and still an active parish.

d) East of the Plaza - As you enter the colorful and tight Olvera Street Mexican Marketplace - named one of the top five "Great Streets" in the US - you may just want to browse colorful stands of Mexican handicrafts and folk art. Amid the cheaper Mexican curios, you can find some high quality gifts here, especially in the stores on the north side. Halfway down the gauntlet of Mexican curios on the south side of the street, find the entrance to the **Avila Adobe**. Built in 1818, it's LA's oldest residence and is furnished in the 1840s, Mexican rancho period of California history. You'll love the tranquil courtyard with its pomegranate tree and prickly pear cactus.

On the opposite side of the street is the **America Tropical Interpretive Center** that tells the fascinating story of a highly controversial 1932 work painted here by the famous Mexican muralist David Siqueiros. The mural proved so contentious that it was quickly whitewashed, only to be restored 80 years later with funds from the Getty Foundation. You can still see the faded mural to this day after visiting the interpretive center on the first floor. Next door are the Sepulveda House, an 1887 Eastlake Victorian structure, and the **Italian American Museum of Los Angeles**.

Finish your visit at the bottom of Olvera Street with an LA tradition - a taquito plate from **Cielito Lindo Restaurant**. The line might be a bit long, but the taquitos, smothered in avocado sauce, are worth the wait! Also, a favorite purchase for many visitors is "papel picado" - the decorative, perforated paper banners thatadorn courtyards throughout Mexico, especially during "Dia de los Muertos."

OUTING #10: DINOSAURS, SPACE SHUTTLES & STAR WARS

Exposition Park Museums

Dinosaur bones, the Space Shuttle, IMAX theater, Star Wars *Museum—all within a ten-minute walk? Yes, if you want a wonderful day of science and learning, the California Science Center in Exposition Park near USC is your ticket. Here you'll find five world-class attractions – the California Science Center, the Samuel Oschin Air and Space Center, the Natural History Museum, the California African American Museum, and the Lucas Museum of Narrative Art. The sunken, 7-acre Exposition Park Rose Garden provides a beautiful walk between museum visits. Obviously, you can't do this all in one day, so follow your curiosity and use this guide to give you ideas. The California Science Center sponsors rotating exhibits combined with IMAX movies. Check with them before planning your visit.*

The ornate Beaux Arts style was popular for museums, train stations and other public buildings in the early 1900s.

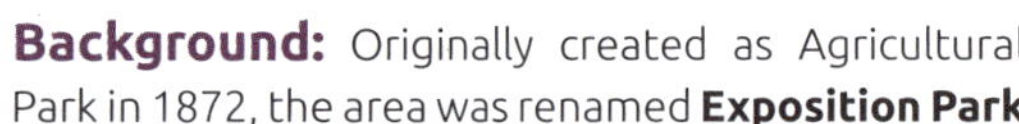

Background: Originally created as Agricultural Park in 1872, the area was renamed **Exposition Park** in 1910. The physical planning, with major museums separated by linear open space (the **Rose Garden**), was part of the "City Beautiful" trend of the era. The Natural History Museum (1913) is an excellent example of Beaux Arts architecture, and nearby **LA Coliseum** was completed in 1923 and renovated for the 1932 Olympics. This Art Moderne stadium, having hosted two Olympics, two Super Bowls, a World Series and numerous professional sports teams, was designated a National Historic Landmark.

Toothy dinosaurs and classic dioramas await you at the Natural History Museum.

Itinerary: Here are some cool highlights of each attraction. Plan your day your own way.

Natural History Museum – In addition to the many dinosaur bones, the North American and African dioramas are classics. Don't miss the stunning statue – *The Three Graces* (1914) – in the historic rotunda. Check out the new **Commons Wing** of the museum, a 70,000 sq. foot indoor/outdoor space, and the engaging Nature Lab, focusing on wildlife in urban settings.

California Science Center – This two-story center contains permanent and rotating exhibits, nature centers, a café and an **IMAX theater**. Special exhibits have included King Tut, Angkor Wat and the Maya.

Samuel Oschin Air and Space Center – This exciting expansion will add four floors of exhibit space on "Aviation, Space and Shuttle." The most exciting exhibit involves moving the **Space Shuttle Endeavor** to a vertical position within the Center, mated to real solid rocket boosters and attached to its huge flight-qualified external tank. Imagine seeing this complete and massive shuttle system from multiple angles and elevations. Sign me up!

California African American Museum – Opened in 1984, this museum contains over 5,000 objects from the 1800s to the present focusing primarily on the cultural contributions and history of African Americans in California and the western United States. Traditional art from Western, Central and Sub-Saharan Africa, as well examples from Jamaica, Haiti, and Brazil, are also included.

Exposition Park Rose Garden – Where else can you walk among seven acres of roses with views of an ornate, century-old Beaux Arts Museum? Located just north of the Science Center, this oasis of color was first opened in 1928 and placed on the National Register of Historic Places in 1991.

The USC Village is a beautiful public space with plenty of eateries and comfortable seating.

Lucas Museum of Narrative Art – LA leads the nation in number of museums, and here we get another one! The building looks like a space ship that landed just west of the Coliseum – appropriate for the creator of *Star Wars*! As the first museum dedicated to the art of storytelling through images, it will have galleries, two theaters, dining facilities, and event spaces in the 500,000 square foot building. Can't wait to check it out!

Suggestions for lunch: Several options here. You could eat in the café at the Science Center, pack your own lunch for a picnic around the Rose Garden, visit the hip Mexican food hall **Mercado La Paloma** (3655 S. Grand Ave.) or go to the interesting **USC Village**, only a half mile away. The Village (2017) is a dynamic mixed-use town center with a very well-designed plaza and a ton of lunch options.

Architectural/urban design note: The pedestrian activity, seating options and urban space of the USC Village are impressive examples of the planning trend – **"new urbanism"** – with the plaza serving as an outdoor living room for USC's more than 40,000 students. Wish we had more pedestrian-friendly areas like this in SoCal. Yes, it's crowded, but why not try it for lunch? My only complaint is not the quality of the buildings, but the "neo-Gothic" style with pointed arches. The adjoining USC campus employed a Romanesque style of rounded windows and arches since its inception in the 1920s. Picky, picky! It's still beautiful architecture and perhaps the best public space in Los Angeles.

The stunning 1913 rotunda of the NHM with The Three Graces *statue, marble columns, coffered ceilings and restored glass dome.*

OUTING #11: LA'S AMAZING MUSEUM ROW!

Petersen Automotive, Tar Pits, Academy Museum and LACMA

Four diverse, world-class museums within one block! That's Museum Row in Los Angeles, and aren't we lucky? This tour describes these four gems, and lets you choose which to visit and in what order. A good strategy is to pick one attraction in the morning and then go to lunch at nearby Farmers Market before your second choice. Not only do the museums have great collections, but they represent truly innovative, contemporary architecture.

Background: Happily for Southlanders, Los Angeles has more museums than any city in the US and ranks third in the world (**see Appendix C** for a list of the **top museums in the Southland**). All of these venues are located on Wilshire Boulevard between Fairfax and Curson Avenues, easily walkable from one to the other. The Tar Pits, Los Angeles County Museum of Art (LACMA) and the Academy Museum are all accessible through the walking paths of Hancock Park. Beginning at Fairfax Avenue and continuing east to La Brea, this stretch of Wilshire Boulevard is called the **"Miracle Mile"** and contains the highest concentration of Art Deco buildings in the city.

The earthquake-mitigating base isolators for all to see at the Academy Museum.

Itinerary:

La Brea Tar Pits & Museum – It's quite amazing that near downtown Los Angeles, we find the world's most famous extraction site for Ice Age mammals. With hundreds of saber-toothed cats, dire wolves, ground sloths, bison, elephants and other megafauna, it's no wonder that the site was named one of the top 100 **World Geological Heritage Sites**. For your visit, plan about one hour for the museum and another 30 minutes to cruise adjoining Hancock Park and its outdoor excavation pits. At the museum, don't miss the 3-D movie – *Titans of the Ice Age* – to get a vivid picture of how these poor animals became mired in the asphalt, and check out the **Fossil Lab** where scientists are cleaning and studying tiny and large fossils. As you explore the park, don't miss Excavation Pit 91 where you can see huge fossil bones in situ! Imagine 3,000-pound giant ground sloths that roamed the LA area as recently as 11,000 years ago!

Academy Museum of Motion Pictures: It's quite appropriate that LA would have the largest museum in the world devoted to moviemaking. During your visit, you will quickly see that the architecture itself is a big part of the experience. **Pritzker Prize-winning architect Renzo Piano** converted the 1933 Streamline Moderne May Company Building into four floors of exhibit space. The architects even restored the huge gold-leaf "perfume bottle" at the corner of Wilshire and Fairfax. Piano also added a huge sphere (please don't call it the "Death Star"!) whose lower portion houses the 1,000-seat **Geffen Theater**. Make sure to check out the sphere's earthquake shock absorbers – called base isolators – in plain view on the ground floor. The upper part of the sphere contains a glass-covered observation terrace with jaw-dropping views of the Hollywood Hills and more. This is not to be missed! Take the elevator to the fifth floor, walk across the skybridge, and you'll be in awe. Floors one to three are devoted to the museum's core exhibition - *Stories of Cinema* - and floor four is devoted to special exhibitions. For a nice respite, there's a nice restaurant and bar on the bottom floor.

Lunch Options

Chris Burden's Urban Light *- an assemblage of 1920s and 1930s LA street lamps - is one of the City's most popular pieces of public art.*

1. The Original Farmers Market (since 1934) is an LA favorite. Only half a mile north on Fairfax, it has dozens of restaurants, specialty shops and gourmet produce nestled together in a semicovered labyrinth of fun. Try to arrive before noon to beat the lunch crowd and grab a map as you enter. The choices of international cuisine are many, but don't overlook the simple pleasures at **Magee's House of Nuts**. Right next door to the market is the popular **Grove LA**, an open-air, upscale dining and shopping center by developer Rick Caruso (he also developed the Americana at Brand in downtown Glendale). The central pedestrian street is quite beautiful, flanked by two story shops with pseudo-Art Deco detailing and ending in a fountain area with ample seating. Caruso actually based these public space proportions on famous King's Street in Charleston. The street, which even has a colorful trolley, might be fake, but is gorgeous at every level and super popular.

2. Canter's Deli - A bit farther up Fairfax on the west side, you'll find this famous Jewish delicatessen. People love the **Pastrami Reuben sandwich** and the fact that this all-night diner is often frequented by famous rock bands in the wee hours. Check out the mural of LA Jewish history on the wall to the north of the parking lot.

The Petersen has one of the world's greatest collections of automobiles.

Petersen Automotive Museum – You don't even have to love cars to enjoy this great museum. And, once again, the architecture is stunning. The Petersen is wrapped in ribbons of stainless steel and red-painted aluminum that flow around the building on all sides. The design evokes speed and movement and some say it's a contemporary version of the space-age **"Googie" style** of architecture prevalent in LA in the '50s. Once inside, behold one of the world's best collections of famous and unusual cars. The museum even has a vault with over 250 vehicles from around the world. Like the Academy Museum, the Petersen is spread over four floors. There are **classic** and **experimental cars** of every style, from 1939 Art Deco Bugattis to supercharged Teslas. Famous cars from TV and film are on display along with major sports and race cars. The craftsmanship, styles and detailing of these cars will bring out a lot of oohhs and aahhs – even if you don't have a driver's license!

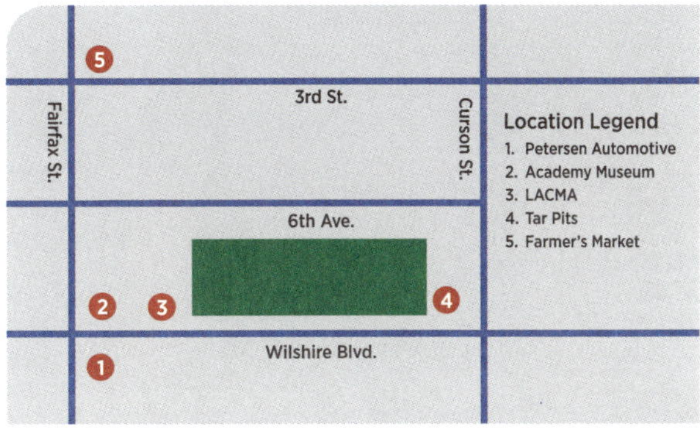

Los Angeles County Museum of Art (LACMA) – This is the fourth piece in the Museum Row mosaic! LACMA is the **largest art museum on the West Coast** with over 150,000 works from ancient to contemporary art. Here you'll find American, European, Latin American, Asian and Islamic art and sculpture with creative rotating exhibitions. The museum's architecture has undergone many transformations, and the latest is the most nontraditional. **Pritzker Prize-winning architect Peter Zumthor** has designed an elevated, organically shaped building that dramatically stretches over Wilshire Boulevard. With floor-to-ceiling glass and semitransparent concrete in a shape from above that resembles an amoeba, LACMA's new building will be a fantastic contribution to Museum Row and the Miracle Mile. Don't miss **Chris Burden's *Urban Light*** – one of LA's most popular public art installations featuring a forest of vintage streetlamps from 1920s and '30s Los Angeles. It's fun to see folks walking among the streetlamps which once lit the streets of LA.

OUTING #12: STARS & STARCHITECT

Hollyhock House and Griffith Observatory

This outing features Frank Lloyd Wright's Hollyhock House – his first LA commission and a UNESCO World Heritage Site, a visit to an Art Deco planetarium with amazing views, and a cruise down LA's most star-struck boulevard. These three places are among the top sights in the region and they are close together. Book your visit to the Hollyhock House in the morning, have lunch after you cruise Hollywood Boulevard's Walk of Fame, and spend part of your afternoon at the wonderful Griffith Observatory. The observatory's museum opens at noon on weekdays and 10:00 AM on weekends. Be prepared for huge crowds and difficult parking unless you visit on weekdays and by bus.

Background: Wow! The opportunity to tour a Frank Lloyd Wright house is a bucket-list experience for architecture lovers, and the Hollyhock House (1921) is the only one of his homes in the LA area open for tours. **Hollywood Boulevard's Walk of Fame** holds over 2,800 five-pointed terrazzo and brass stars embedded in 1.3 miles of sidewalk. The Boulevard hosts some of the most famous movie palaces in the nation as well as the **Academy Awards**. The 1933 Art Deco Griffith Park Observatory is a cherished landmark - sitting high enough above the city and near enough to the Hollywood Sign to make you want to shout! Many films have been shot here, and you'll soon see the *Rebel Without a Cause* monument.

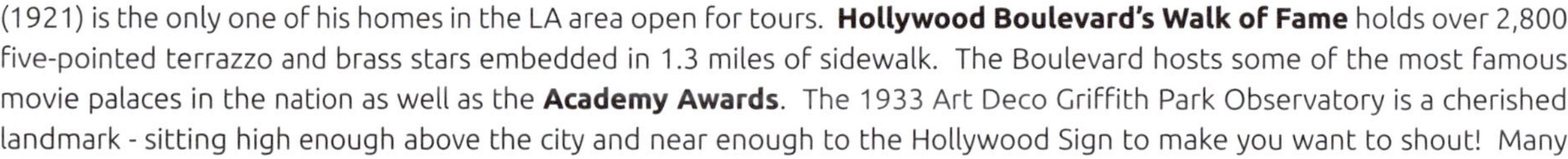

The style of this most famous of movie theaters is "Exotic Revival" like its nearby 1922 cousin - the Egyptian.

Itinerary:

AM: Hollyhock House – Sitting on Olive Hill with beautiful views of Hollywood and West LA is one of Frank Lloyd Wright's masterpieces – the Hollyhock House. Built between 1919 and 1921 for oil heiress Aline Barnsdall, the house has been variously described as Mayan, Egyptian, and "California Romanza" and represents a transitional design between the architect's **earlier prairie style** and later **textile block homes**. The interior is stunning with all the furniture, rugs, light fixtures and leaded windows reflecting the geometric patterns of Wright. The house is not large, and the self-guided tour will take you about 45 minutes. Knowledgeable docents and a small bookstore complete the experience. Take some time to enjoy the adjoining **Barnsdall Park** and its views. You can even see Wright's textile block Innes Home in the Hollywood Hills to the north.

Hollywood Boulevard's Walk of Fame Driving Tour – As you leave the Hollyhock House, turn left on Hollywood Boulevard and be prepared to experience LA's most famous street. First you'll drive through **Thai Town** (one of LA's many wonderful ethnic enclaves and a possible lunch stop). As you approach **Hollywood and Vine**, you'll notice the beginning of 15 blocks of terrazzo and brass sidewalk stars honoring actors, directors and producers in the entertainment industry. The real stars of the show are the movie palaces whose premieres made Hollywood famous. Highlights include the art deco **Pantages Theater**, the iconic **Capital Records Building** (turn right on Vine Street and then loop back to the boulevard), the newly renovated **Egyptian Theater**, and, the show-stopper, the **TCL Chinese Theater** (1927) where movie stars made hand- and footprints in the cement in the "Forecourt of the Stars." The crush of tourists can be stifling, but gazing up at the ornate façade is an LA sight to behold. Depending on time, book the tour of the lavish interior or buy tickets to the IMAX theater and see a movie in LA's most famous movie palace.

The 1934 Art Deco "Astronomer's Monument" was a Public Works of Art project awarded to six artists during the New Deal.

Lunch options:

Musso and Frank Grill - A Hollywood classic with great martinis

Figaro Bistrot - Los Feliz neighborhood

Thai Town - Lots of eateries along 3-block area east of Western Ave.

PM: Griffith Observatory – Double back to Vermont Ave. and take the short, scenic trip up the hill to Griffith Observatory. This art deco landmark is an "LA Top Five" highlight because of the amazing views of the LA Basin and the **Hollywood Sign**. The two-story museum has wonderful exhibits of the solar system. I especially like the Hugo Ballin murals in the entry hall above the pendulum exhibit. Try to buy tickets for one of the daily **planetarium shows**, which can only be purchased on site. Don't miss strolling the balcony walkway all the way around the Observatory as you try to comprehend the immensity of LA County and its 88 cities!

Look for the beautiful, stylized lamp posts announcing Thai Town on Hollywood Boulevard.

Nearby Attractions:

- < Hotel Roosevelt
- Canter's Deli
- Farmer's Market
- Academy Museum of Motion Pictures

OUTING #13: STARSTRUCK LA!

Hollywood's Walk of Fame

Hollywood Boulevard's Walk of Fame has tons of famous landmarks in a fairly small area. Yes, the crowds and tackiness can be overwhelming, but it's fun to see ground zero of the entertainment world. Follow this plan and you'll see the famous theaters around Hollywood and Highland in the morning and then have the afternoon for your favorite movie star activity.

The first version of this iconic sign, erected in 1923, originally spelled "Hollywoodland."

Background: The idea of a thriving theater district began in the 1920s with the opening of the Chinese, Egyptian and El Capitan Theaters. Starting in 1960, the famous five-pointed, terrazzo and brass stars were embedded in the sidewalk to honor achievement in the entertainment industry. Awarded by the **Hollywood Chamber of Commerce**, the stars are given in the categories of movies, television, radio, music, theater, and sports. You can now easily get to the Walk of Fame via the **Metro Red Line Subway** with connections at Vine St. and Highland Avenue. It is estimated that the Walk of Fame attracts ten million tourists per year!

Ovation Hollywood is a beautiful shopping and entertainment center tucked just above the famous boulevard.

Itinerary:

AM: Visit the Walk of Fame and Chinese Theater. This is the epicenter of Walk of Fame tourism, so enjoy and prepare for crowds. If you drive, park your car in the huge parking garage on Highland Ave. just above Hollywood Boulevard. Make your way to the courtyard of the new **Ovation Hollywood** - a multilevel dining and shopping center with a beautiful courtyard. Climb to the second floor under the arch to get a view of the Hollywood Sign (of course, you can hike to the sign: see below). Make your way down the stairs to the bustle of Hollywood Boulevard. You'll immediately see the famous terrazzo sidewalk stars (there are actually 2,783 of them along 15 blocks).

Across the street is the **El Capitan Theater**, a Spanish Colonial beauty run by the Disney Corporation. Make a right turn and walk about 300 yards to the **TCL Chinese Theater**. This is Hollywood's most famous theater with its famous forecourt of over 200 stars', footprints, and autographs. The Chinese has recently been upgraded to an IMAX theater. You might also try to book the 30-minute walking tour of the history and design of this ornate, Far Eastern Revival movie palace. You might consider visiting Madame Tussaud's Hollywood, which bills itself as the world's greatest wax museum. This is a very highly rated attraction for those who love the lore of Hollywood.

Cross the street and check out the **Roosevelt Hotel** (1927) - This landmark Hollywood hotel is a great place to stay, have a drink,

Embedded in black terrazzo tile, the famous stars number almost 3,000!

You can't beat the ambience or the martinis at Musso & Frank.

Orange Ave.
Highland Ave.
Hollywood Blvd.

Location Legend

1. Roosevelt Hotel
2. Wax Museum
3. TCL Chinese Theatre
4. Dolby Theatre
5. Ovation Hollywood
6. El Capitan Theatre
7. Egyptian Theatre

and check out the Blossom Room where the first Academy Awards were held. Double back to the north side of Hollywood Boulevard to the grand entrance of the **Dolby Theater** - the permanent home of the Academy Awards. Right here, along a one-block stretch of Hollywood Boulevard, is where the famous red carpet is rolled out. As you walk into the Dolby's entrance corridor and ascend the staircase, notice the side pillars where all the Best Picture Oscars are illustrated in chronological order. Make a right turn at the top of the stairs, go back to the Ovation Hollywood courtyard, enjoy a snack and then go retrieve your car.

Lunch or early dinner - Why not make a reservation or at least have a martini at **Musso & Frank Grill**, the oldest and most famous restaurant in Hollywood with its tuxedoed waiters, great martinis and plush leather booths?

PM: You choose your activity

Book a Hollywood Movie Star Home Tour - There are many companies along the boulevard that whisk you into the Hollywood Hills and through Beverly Hills to see movie star homes. The ride is quite exciting in open-air vans seating about 8 to 10 guests. The guides give you the latest Hollywood gossip and show you areas that you'd be hard-pressed to find on your own. Since Hollywood is the world epicenter of movie and TV entertainment, these tours are some of LA's most highly rated activities. There are many tour companies, including the famous Starline Tours, and I've had some great guides with the company, Ultimate Hollywood Tours.

Hike to the Hollywood Sign - For some great exercise and wonderful views of Los Angeles, consider hiking to one of the world's most famous signs atop **Mount Lee** (elevation - 1708 feet). There are three main routes to the top, but coming from the west is less crowded. Access Barnham Boulevard from the 101 Freeway. Connect to Lake Hollywood Drive and then to 3160 Canyon Lake Drive. The starting point for the hike is **Lake Hollywood Park**, but you can often drive up farther to the trailhead. The hike is 5.5 miles round trip, of average steepness, and will take you about 3 hours total. This trail actually winds around the back (north) of Mount Lee, giving you expansive views of the San Fernando Valley and several major movie studios. You'll let out an excited sigh when you turn the corner and see the sign right below you! The letters are fenced in, but you won't feel cheated when you gaze south and west over the City of Angels!

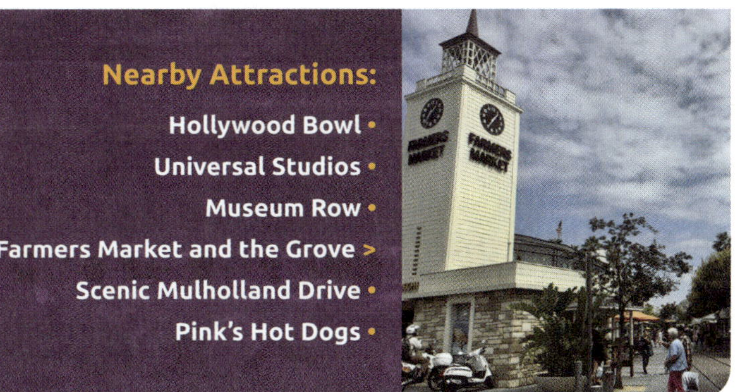

OUTING #14: STUDIOS & COWBOYS

Warner Brothers Studios and the Autry Museum of the American West

This outing takes in two great venues that are only 15 minutes apart – both on the edge of beautiful Griffith Park. You can book a two-hour tour at Warner Brothers Studio, have a lunch break, and then enjoy the Autry Museum of the American West.

Background: Warner Brothers Studio recently celebrated its 100th birthday and visiting this 110-acre facility is a "bucket list" LA experience. The Warner Brothers lot has 32 sound stages, extensive outdoor urban sets, and excellent interactive exhibits. The Autry Museum of the American West in nearby **Griffith Park** is one of the nation's best for this genre, with an impressive collection of art and artifacts about cowboys, settlers, and Native Americans. The Autry is located right across from the **LA Zoo** and there's a nice courtyard and nearby picnic tables if you want an informal lunch. The museum was opened in 1988 by actor and businessman Gene Autry.

You'll be whisked around the huge lot in an elongated golf cart. And the tour guides are fun and knowledgeable.

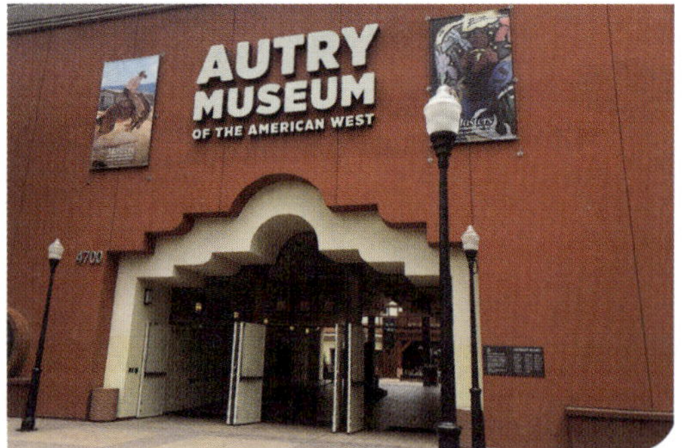

A great example of postmodern architecture of the 1980s. Western symbols, in this case the outline of a Mission gable, are represented with modern materials.

Itinerary:

AM: Warner Brothers Studio Tours, Burbank - I chose this outing over Universal Studios because it's a little less crowded and doesn't have a surrounding theme park. It's all about the movies and TV, and Warner Brothers has a huge catalogue of hits - ***Casablanca, Rebel Without a Cause, The Big Bang Theory, Friends, Barbie*** and many more. After a short film on the studio's movie and TV hits, you hop on a large golf cart to tour the back lots and sound stages. The guides have lots of stories about the latest hit shows, and it's really fascinating to drive through block after block of exterior sets (yes, lots of fake streets and bricks!) that can be transformed into a Midwest town center, 1920s New York, or a jungle lagoon. You'll pass through a working sound stage and marvel at the tremendous infrastructure of lighting, booms and filters - all designed to produce magic on screen. During the last part of the tour, you'll have free time to explore all sorts of interactive exhibits, costume sets (***Game of Thrones, DC Superheroes***), film clips, and photo opportunities where you're part of your favorite movie or TV show (***Friends*** Central Perk set, ***Harry Potter***, ***The Big Bang Theory*** and more!) The visual quality of the exhibits is impressive and, of course, you'll end up in a gauntlet of shopping memorabilia. The staff is friendly and helpful, snacks are ever present, and the Warner Brothers Studio Tour does not disappoint!

Lunch - There are plenty of restaurants in surrounding Burbank, and nearby North Hollywood (NoHo) has a nice walkable atmosphere. **Glendale's Americana at Brand** is a great option - an attractive, outdoor lifestyle center with good restaurants. And, of course, you could pack a picnic for your next stop in Griffith Park.

You'll probably find your favorite Superhero here!

PM: Autry Museum of the American West - The mission statement of this museum is to "bring together the stories of all peoples of the American West, connecting the past with the present to inspire our shared future." Once you see the diverse collection of paintings, sculptures, film memorabilia, photographs, historic firearms and more, you'll probably agree that it succeeded. The bottom floor contains the museum's permanent exhibits, including the **Cowboy Gallery**, the **Ethnobotanical Garden**, a chuckwagon, and one of the largest and most significant collections of Native American materials in the United States. The first floor contains a diverse collection of **Art of the West** and special installations. The Autry challenges the visitor to compare their personal view of the West with that of popular culture and of the multiple cultures who have called it home. The museum's architecture (1988) is a great example of "postmodern" design, with contemporary materials representing the colors of the Southwest and rounded gables representing Mission Revival architecture. This is one great museum of the West - check for its current and often thought-provoking exhibits!

Other LA-Area Studio Tours: Living in Southern California, we often overlook the many great movie studio tours offered. Despite the stereotype that LA is all about "the new," studio tours show us how much history and "myth making" originated here. Here is a listing of some other great studio tours:

- **Disney Studios** - Great for Disney history and animation
- **Paramount Pictures** - Best for Hollywood nostalgia (see Outing #15)
- **Universal Studios** - Combines tram tour with great and sometimes frightening special effects
- **Sony Pictures (on former MGM lot)** - Best for TV game shows and a nod to *The Wizard of Oz*"

OUTING #15: EAST HOLLYWOOD ROCKS!

Paramount Studios, Larchmont Village and Hollywood Forever Cemetery

There's a lot to be said for this part of East Hollywood: the oldest remaining movie studio, one of LA's most charming neighborhoods, and a famous cemetery for the stars. This outing recommends the Paramount Pictures Studio Tour in the morning, lunch in nearby Larchmont Village, and then an afternoon visit to Hollywood Forever Cemetery.

Background: Along with Universal and Warner Brothers, Paramount Studios is one of the bucket-list tours for movie lovers and the only studio operating in Hollywood. The famous company began in 1912 when Adolf Zukor, owner of a New York nickelodeon, released the country's first full-length drama. After merging with Lasky Company in Hollywood, the current site opened in 1926. Today it consists of 65 acres with 40 sound stages. The history of the studio is a who's who of famous stars and classic movies series, from the **Golden Age of Hope and Crosby** to '60s and '70s classics such as ***Psycho*** and ***The Godfather*** series, and then more recent blockbusters such as ***Titanic***, *Saving Private Ryan, Star Trek*, and ***Mission Impossible***. The jump to television in the mid-1960s included scores of great shows including *The Odd Couple*, *Taxi*, and *The Brady Bunch*.

The Bronson Gate (1926) is one of Hollywood's most famous icons.

Itinerary:

AM: Paramount Studio Tour: You can book the standard two-hour tour or upgrade in time and price to the Premier or VIP Tour. Regardless, it's a wonderful experience to explore this historic and modern studio. After a brief orientation film on the studio's history, you'll hop on a modified golf cart with a Studio Page and cruise the lot to see the magic of movie- and TV-making. You'll even see the parking lot where the **Red Sea was parted in *The Ten Commandments***! You'll also explore sound stages and back lots, and even get the chance to walk through a prop warehouse with its multitude of cool stuff. The tour ends with some interactive displays, snacks and, of course, the Official Paramount Store. This tour is really a great experience, right in the heart of old Hollywood.

Lunch in Larchmont Village: This is one of LA's nicest neighborhood main streets, and it's only five minutes from the studio. There are copious restaurants, trendy stores, wide sidewalks and outdoor seating - together creating a relaxed vibe in a sometimes hectic city. In addition, the Village is located adjacent to two of LA's most beautiful historic districts - **Windsor Square** and **Hancock Park**. If you like attractive, century-old neighborhoods, just drive south from the Village and you'll see the results of historic preservation (see Outing #19 - Historic Districts of Los Angeles).

Wide sidewalks, outdoor seating, and three blocks of stores and restaurants make Larchmont Village just plain wonderful.

Johnny Ramone's tomb celebrates his guitar prowess. Notice the Greek temple in the back and LA's ubiquitous palm trees.

The discovery of King Tut's tomb increased popularity of Egyptian tombs and symbology.

PM: Hollywood Forever Cemetery: Visiting a cemetery doesn't sound like fun, but remember this is Hollywood. Along with **Glendale's Forest Lawn Memorial Park**, Hollywood Forever is the most interesting resting place in Los Angeles because here you will find the gravesites of many famous stars - **Rudolph Valentino**, **Cecil B. DeMille**, **Mickey Rooney**, **Johnny Ramone**, to name a few. Grab a cemetery map at the entrance and take some time to explore the interesting mausoleums and architecture. Unlike memorial parks that tend to have expansive grassy areas with flat grave markers, here you will find interesting temples to the deceased with classical, Gothic and even Egyptian forms. In true Hollywood style, Hollywood Forever screens movies during the summer and fall, projected on the back walls of Paramount Studios!

Nearby Attractions:

- Hollywood Boulevard
- Frank Lloyd Wright Hollyhock House
- Pantages Theatre
- < Griffith Observatory

OUTING #16: MODERNIST MASTERPIECE

The Getty Center

We're certainly fortunate that J. Paul Getty decided to locate both his Getty Center and Getty Villa in the LA area. Whereas the Getty Villa is a historical recreation of a Roman country home, the Getty Center is a monument to modernist architecture on a grand scale. This outing is at least a half a day, and you'll love the architecture and setting as much as the art. Sitting high above the 405 Freeway in Brentwood, the Getty Center is like a modern-day acropolis with expansive views of the city, mountains and the ocean. It is free of charge, but you'll pay for parking. Check for special exhibitions that complement the four pavilions of the permanent collection. The spectacular Central Garden, by artist Robert Irwin, culminates with a maze of 400 azalea plants. You can bring a picnic lunch, but the Restaurant, Garden Terrace Cafe and coffee carts provide great options.

The Museum Courtyard is an inviting public space embraced by surrounding buildings and their play of light.

Background: Not surprisingly, the Getty Center is consistently rated in the top three attractions in the Los Angeles area, with almost two million visitors per year. Called **"the commission of the century"** and opened in 1997 at a cost of $1.3 billion, the Center was the first building in the US to win LEED (Leadership in Energy and Environmental Design) Certification from the US Green Building Council. **Architect Richard Meier** chose white **Italian travertine marble** - over 300,000 pieces - as an enduring symbol of public buildings. Some critics think that modern architecture can be boring and sterile, but this dramatic, 100,000 square foot center is anything but. With its textured surfaces, varied building masses of linear and curved shapes, and beautiful public spaces, The Getty Center is modernism at its most dramatic. Oh, yes, and the art! The collections are comprehensive, including paintings, sculpture and decorative arts from the medieval period to the twentieth century.

The Entrance Hall is another example of Meier's brilliant use of natural light.

Itinerary:

Tram Ride - The driverless tram that takes you from the parking garage to the top of the hill is a dramatic and fun way to start your visit and take in the views. From the Arrival Plaza, just walk up the steps to the Museum Entrance Hall.

Book a free tour in the Entrance Hall - Daily tours are offered on the architecture and gardens, the Museum's collections, and special exhibitions. Also, you can download the excellent Getty App for more detailed explanations of the collections.

Explore the Art Pavilions - As you walk through and admire the beauty of the Museum Courtyard, pick your collections to visit. Starting from the North Pavilion to your left and working clockwise, each pavilion displays art in a roughly chronological order. The North Pavilion features art before 1700; the East and South Pavilions - art between 1600 and 1800; and the West Pavilion - art after 1800. At the plaza level in each pavilion, you'll find decorative arts and often sculpture.

Van Gogh's Irises *is one of the most popular paintings in the West Pavilion.*

View south over the LA Basin. People love the architectural spaces of the Getty.

Stroll the Central Garden - Artist Robert Irwin called his creation "a sculpture in the form of a garden aspiring to be art." Take the zigzag path downhill along the stream to the circular maze of azalea plants. The groupings of other plants are grouped by color and texture. The South Promontory is a recreation of a desert landscape in keeping with the Center's energy-efficient, "green" footprint.

Experience the Architecture - Architecture is a functional art, and, in this case, also a tactile one. You won't be able to resist touching the rough travertine stone from Italy. Blocks on the building facades were broken apart to create these delightfully rough surfaces. Check these rocks for fossils of shells and leaves.

Nearby Attractions:

- **Skirball Cultural Center** - Ten minutes north on the 405, this dynamic educational center has one of the world's largest collections of Jewish ceremonial art, ritual objects and material culture. Its museum's permanent exhibits include *Visions and Values - Jewish Life from Antiquity to America* and *Noah's Ark*, an award-winning child and family exploratory space. The Skirball sponsors rotating exhibitions, concerts, lectures and classes for all ages.

- **Hammer Museum, Westwood** - The Hammer opened in 1990 displaying the European and American paintings of the founder, Armand Hammer. It has since become one of the hippest contemporary art museums in the region after a renovation by LA architect Michael Maltzan. The redesigned interior courtyard, sculpture terrace and new gallery spaces enliven the original building with its distinctive horizontal bands of light and dark stone.

OUTING #17: HIDDEN GEMS, FREEWAY CLOSE

Glendale Forest Lawn and Museum of Neon Art

You can call this adventure "Hidden Gems of Glendale." It highlights LA's largest and most famous cemetery - a memorial park with century-old architecture and a first-class museum - along with two fun stops in downtown Glendale: the Museum of Neon Art and The Americana at Brand, an attractive mixed-use shopping and dining destination. The visit to Forest Lawn includes both a scenic drive as well as a visit to a historic mausoleum with dozens of sculptures and over 100 stained glass windows (including life-size reproductions of Michelangelo's Pieta *and Leonardo da Vinci's* The Last Supper*). Your visit to the Forest Lawn Museum can include a viewing of the largest religious painting in the Western Hemisphere, so large in fact that it required a new building to display it! Lunch in downtown Glendale's Americana at Brand, an attractive, mixed-use lifestyle center, can be easily followed by the unique and conveniently located Museum of Neon Art.*

Background: It may seem strange to visit a cemetery, but **Forest Lawn Glendale**, **founded in 1906**, speaks to LA's history and has exceptional art and architecture. It also represents the movement away from crowded cemeteries full of large tombs and monuments (from 1831 to 1900) to the more expansive memorial park designs. Construction of the Great Mausoleum began in 1917 and is based on the Campo Santo in Genoa, Italy. The Tudor-style Administration Building and Church of the Flowers (1918) are beautiful period pieces. The drive up the hill to the **Forest Lawn Museum** affords great views of Griffith Park, Glendale and the San Gabriel Mountains.

The Great Mausoleum has Gothic, Romanesque and Art Deco styling.

Itinerary:

AM: Forest Lawn Memorial Park, Glendale

- Because there is so much to see, make sure you stop at the park entrance information booth to get an Art Tour Map and Great Mausoleum brochure. The winding drives through the hilly park are beautiful, but the true highlights are the **Great Mausoleum and Museum**. Entering the Mausoleum is like going back in time to medieval Europe with its Gothic marble forms. Highlights include Elizabeth Taylor's crypt, reproductions of Michelangelo's and da Vinci's art, and Poet's Corridor. The Museum has an excellent permanent collection of statuary as well as excellent rotating exhibits. Don't fail to see the 195-foot-long, 1904 painting - ***The Crucifixion*** - and its later companion piece - ***The Resurrection*** - in the theater adjoining the museum.

The statuary in the Great Mausoleum are convincing reproductions of some of Europe's masters.

Lunch - Make the short drive to downtown Glendale's popular mixed-use center - **The Americana at Brand**. The developer, Rick Caruso, is famous for his beautiful shopping centers such as The Grove at Farmer's Market. His attention to detail is obvious, and The Americana is unique in that it is truly mixed use, with several stories of luxury apartments above the shops and stores. You'll find over 10 restaurants in the center where the pedestrian plan is that of a *U* with two entrances on Brand Avenue. This is a high-end center with well-appointed architecture, a fountain and plenty of opportunities to spend money.

Rick Caruso's Americana at Brand is a popular, mixed-use dining and shopping center. What attention to detail!

PM: Museum of Neon Art - Literally right across Brand Avenue from The Americana is this small and fascinating museum dedicated to the preservation and appreciation of **neon**, **electric** and **kinetic art**. It is the only museum in the world devoted exclusively to art in electric media and contains outstanding examples of historic neon signs. It's open Thursdays through Sundays. Here you'll find a workshop where you can see demonstrations in glass bending and neon gasses, a wonderful gallery of historic neon signs (the collection has over 333 pieces), and a special exhibition room. Neon art is romantic and fanciful, and this museum puts a major emphasis on education and appreciation. Try to call ahead and see if you can arrange a small group tour from the very passionate staff and directors.

Executive Director Corrie Siegel demonstrates glass bending in the Neon Museum workshop.

A note on Rick Caruso's wildly popular retail centers: Developer Caruso opened The Grove next to Farmers Market in 2002. It became an overnight sensation. This open-air retail and entertainment center - with a cineplex, Nordstrom's and upscale restaurants and shopping - is beautifully proportioned, semipublic space. Using Colonial, Italianate, and Art Deco themes, the architecture is nostalgic and beautiful. Caruso was inspired by the urban scale of Savannah and Charleston, designing wide streets and two-to-three-story buildings. Critics say that The Grove is artificial, isolated from the true LA streets, and a substitute for missing public places. But you can't deny that people love the safety, cleanliness, and variety of The Grove.

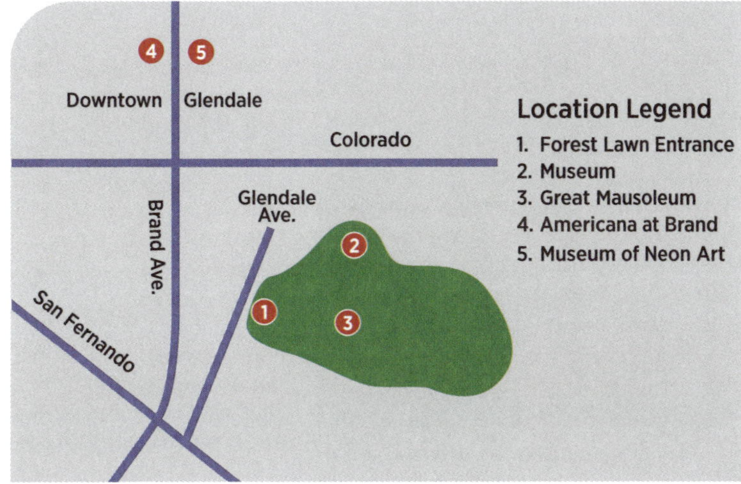

OUTING #18: DIVERSE FAITHS IN THE CITY OF ANGELS

Landmark Churches of LA

A great way to know multicultural Los Angeles is through its many churches. Whereas Los Angeles is known as a smorgasbord of architectural styles, churches may be even more varied. This outing chooses a few of LA's most famous places of worship, but there are many more to choose from. We will start just west of Downtown LA and work our way to the center. The first stop will be the First African Methodist Episcopal Church followed by the Greek Orthodox Saint Sophia Cathedral. The short drive downtown will take in the Koyasan Buddhist Temple in Little Tokyo and the Our Lady of the Angels Cathedral. You may want to contact the churches before your visit to make sure they are not closed for a special event.

Background: Southern California is one of the most religiously diverse places in the world. Although there has been a strong trend away from religion in the past two decades, approximately 65% of the population identifies as Christian - Evangelical, Mainline Protestant, and Catholic. The non-Christian faiths include Jewish (3%), Muslim (2%), Buddhist (2%), and Hindu (1%). Los Angeles has the second largest population of Jews in the US , with the majority living near the Hancock Park neighborhood and West LA. The greatest concentration of Buddhist temples is found in the San Gabriel Valley due to its large Chinese population. Orange County has a large population of Muslims (120,000) and almost equal numbers of Buddhists concentrated in the Little Saigon area of central Orange County. The Hindu population finds its greatest concentration in Artesia and Cerritos as well as the San Fernando Valley.

Exterior and interior murals grace the First AME church.

Itinerary:

AM: First African Methodist Episcopal (First AME) Church

- Founded in 1872, this is the oldest African American congregation in Los Angeles. Located in the **Adams-Normandie Historic District**, it has been a major center for political and social action for the African American community. Its architect is the trailblazing **Paul R. Williams**, the first African American member of the American Institute of Architecture. Williams designed over 2,000 buildings including the homes of many famous LA celebrities. The church's style is Late Modern with a zigzag roofline and decorative murals.

Saint Sophia Greek Orthodox Cathedral - Built in the area formerly known as "Greek Town" and now called the **Byzantine-Latino Quarter,** St. Sophia was built in 1952. The architecture is a combination of Romanesque/Byzantine, with its domed roof and mosaic murals. This active Orthodox Christian church serves a primarily Greek congregation from a 60-mile radius. The cathedral's gold-covered altar and stained glass windows are spectacular. It was declared a Los Angeles **Cultural-Heritage Landmark** in 1973.

Lunch - **Papa Cristo's**, right across the street from St. Sophia, is a Greek deli and restaurant. Opened in 1948, it is one of LA's cherished legacy businesses and a fun choice for lunch. You can also eat in **Little Tokyo** or **Grand Central Market** near the downtown churches.

PM: Koyasan Buddhist Temple - Located at the end of an alleyway in the heart of Little Tokyo, this is one of the oldest Buddhist temples (1912) in North America. It focuses on **"Shingon" Buddhism**, a major school of practice in Japan focusing on the **three mysteries - "mudra, mantra, and mandala."** Two blocks away on Third Street is the larger Hongashi Temple which focuses on Shin Buddhism, one of the largest denominations in Japan. The beautifully ornate interiors of these temples contain an altar with images of the Buddha, symbols of lotus flowers, and offerings of incense, candles and fruit.

Our Lady of the Angels Cathedral - Three blocks away on Temple St. at the base of Bunker Hill, you'll find this large, modern cathedral - the Mother Church of the Catholic Archdiocese of Los Angeles. Rather than select a more traditional Gothic or historicist design, the Church chose a very contemporary form by Pritzker Prize-winning **Spanish architect Rafael Moneo**. Completed in 2002, the exterior consists of large, colorized concrete blocks with earth tones reminiscent of adobe brick, arrayed with no right angles. Call the facade contemporary, postmodern, brutalist, or deconstructivist, but it is the massive interior that is truly stunning. The nave is 133 feet long and 132 feet high with diffused light from the many **alabaster windows** and skylights. A highlight is the life-like **tapestries** of famous Catholics and ordinary people by **artist John Nava**, which line the walls on both sides of the nave. The effect is one of awe.

The lifelike tapestries by John Nava are a highlight at Our Lady of the Angels.

Visit the downstairs mausoleum with its over 1200 crypts (including one for Gregory Peck) and check out the stained-glass window rescued from the **St. Vibiana Cathedral**, which was damaged by the 1994 Northridge earthquake. The former cathedral, built in 1876, is now an upscale event space, home to Redbird Restaurant.

As you leave the cathedral, check out the angels etched in the glass wall fronting the 101 Freeway. Across the street you'll see the fanciful steel design of the **Ramon Cortines Performing Arts High School**.

Further Exploration - There are many other important and architecturally significant religious sites in Southern California. **The Wilshire Boulevard Temple** is one of the largest Jewish congregations in Los Angeles in a Byzantine Revival (1928) style with **Hugo Ballin murals**. The temple is both on the National Register of Historic Places and an LA Cultural-Heritage Monument. The Sinai Temple on Wilshire Boulevard in Westwood has the oldest and largest Conservative congregation in LA.

OUTING #19: PRESERVING LOS ANGELES

Historic Districts of LA

Individual landmarks are fun, but entire historic districts really capture a larger sense of place. This outing will take you to some beautiful, century-old neighborhoods, and show you that LA celebrates its past as well as its future. The City has actually designated forty-one (and counting!) historic districts of diverse architecture using a process called "historic preservation overlay zones." This tour is a driving one, so go with friends who can help navigate and be careful at the wheel as you admire your favorite building. The itinerary below starts in the western part of the City near Farmers Market and moves east towards downtown along Wilshire Boulevard. If you love vintage architecture, this outing will rock!

This QR code will open the link to LA's historic districts and map.

Background: Los Angeles has become a national leader in historic district planning. In the 1970s, many residents grew worried that their city's historic neighborhoods were losing their character from overdevelopment. In response, the City passed a **Historic Preservation Overlay Zone (HPOZ) Ordinance** (1979), adding an important layer of protection (the term "overlay" means that the underlying zoning or land use doesn't change, but rather design review is added to the zone). Within a historic district, demolition is more difficult, and new development and alterations must be compatible with preservation standards. "HPOZs" have proven very popular as residents have enjoyed tax incentives, higher property values, and an enhanced sense of community. The period of the 1920s was particularly productive in LA and you will see lots of "Revival Styles," including Spanish, Mission, Colonial, Egyptian, Tudor, Norman/Châteauesque, Dutch, and Mayan (see **Appendix B** for a complete **list of architectural styles**). Sadly, most of these neighborhoods were off limits to minority groups - Blacks, Asians, Latinos, Jews - due to racial restrictive covenants, which were declared unconstitutional in 1948.

Pre-1900 Victorian homes did not shy away from color!

Itinerary:

Including lunch, this is a four-to-five-hour adventure starting near the Farmers Market in the Fairfax District of LA.

Lunch at Farmers' Market: This is an LA favorite, so arrive before 11:45 am to beat the crowd. A popular specialty is freshly ground peanut butter with raisins at Magee's House of Nuts!

Explore Four Historic Districts

1. Start with the South Carthay Historic Preservation Overlay Zone (1930s) in the Carthay District. Bordered by Pico, Crescent Heights, La Cienega and Olympic Boulevards, the area is typical of the beautiful neigh-bor-hoods found behind LA's large commercial streets. Traveling south on Fairfax Ave. from Farmers Market, turn right on Pico, go seven blocks and turn right into the district on La Jolla Ave. This is LA's second "HPOZ" and has an outstanding concentration of small Spanish Colonial homes with stained-glass windows, extensive tiles, and arched doors and windows. Almost half the single family homes were designed and built by Greek developer Spyros George Ponty. Check out the district's northern boundary at Olympic Boulevard for an impressive line of Châteauesque/French Normandy style apartments.

Spanish Colonial Revival homes are the most common style in South Carthay's historic district.

2. Hancock Park (1920s) - After admiring the cute homes of South Carthay, it's time to see some much bigger homes. Go east on Wilshire Boulevard, turn left on Highland, and right on Beverly to enter the district. This is LA's second largest historic district and is known for its huge, two-story **period revival homes**. You'll see a lot of **Tudor**, **Gothic**, **Spanish** and **Colonial Revivals**. Keep your eyes peeled for **Monterey**, **Georgian** and **French** styles as well. One of the best concentrations of gorgeous homes is between 3rd and Wilshire, McFadden and Rimpau Streets.

3. Windsor Square (1911 on) - Bordering Hancock Park to the east, this district has even older and larger homes! First subdivided in 1911 and designed to be LA's most exclusive neighborhood, here you will find many Classical Revival and Craftsman homes as well as later period revivals. Windsor, Lorraine and Irving Boulevards are the best to explore, lined with large Canary Island palms framing views of the Hollywood Sign. In all three of these historic districts, the number of "contributing structures" (homes that have retained their historic integrity) is over 90%, and it's interesting to note how alterations to older structures and newer homes are compatible with the character of the larger district.

Tudor Revival, with its steeply-pitched roofs, massive chimneys, and decorative half-timbering, was a very popular style in the 1920s.

4. Angelino Heights and Carroll Avenue - Go even further back in time to the first HPOZ and its charming Victorian street - Carroll Ave. It occupies a small hill only two miles northwest of downtown LA near the communities of Silver Lake and Echo Park. To get there, continue east on Wilshire Boulevard, make a left on Alvarado and then a right on Sunset Boulevard. Enter the district by making a right on Douglas. Go up the hill, make a left on the 1300 block of Carroll Avenue, park your car and take a stroll. You'll probably let out some "wows" as you view the intricate wood detailing of these Victorian beauties. The two major styles are **Queen Anne** with their **corner turrets**, fish-scale shingles, and latticed porches, and the more squarish **Eastlake** variant with their long, arched windows and **bracketed cornices**. The entire block is listed on the **National Register of Historic Places**. The surrounding HPOZ is of a more mixed character with large Craftsman and Mission Revival homes as well.

French eclectic styles feature tall, steeply pitched hipped roofs.

5. End your adventure in Downtown Los Angeles - You're only two miles from Downtown LA, so why not enjoy a nice evening before heading home? Check out one of the many rooftop bars for great views (Perch LA, Spire 73 at the Intercontinental Hotel, the Hoxton, or the Conrad) and grab a bite to eat in Little Tokyo, Chinatown, LA Live, or the Arts District. Take the stunning, illuminated 6th Street Viaduct (aka, bridge!) as you conclude this historic district adventure!

OUTING #20: MAN, THAT'S A COOL BUILDING!

Historic Cultural Landmarks

Saving historic buildings and places makes a city more fun to explore and gives residents a sense of perspective and a source of pride. So this outing is different. Rather than provide a specific itinerary, it gives you some tools to explore areas and topics of your choosing. There are some excellent online resources where you can search and find historic landmarks (see next page below) on a digital map. Wherever you live, you can find out if your city has a historic preservation program or a local historical society. Let's now explore what LA has done. Convenient links are underlined in text below.

Formerly a tire company, now an outlet mall, this Assyrian Revival beauty (1929) has Art Deco influences.

Background: Lucky for us, LA may have the most diverse architecture in the world. And despite its reputation as a "new-ish" city, Los Angeles actually passed their **Cultural Heritage Ordinance** (1962) earlier than most major cities. To date, the city has designated over 1200 Historic-Cultural Landmarks (**Historic Landmark Programs**). Since LA is so enormous, the city is divided into 35 Community Plan Areas to make your search easier. The City has also designated 41 **Historic Preservation Overlay Zones**. In 2017, it completed the amazing **Survey LA** - the largest historic resources survey in the nation - assessing all 880,000 separate properties within its 466-square-mile area to guide future planning. The Los Angeles Conservancy, the City's premier, nonprofit historic preservation advocacy group, also has wonderful resources to find in its **Historic Places in LA**.

Look for the sign or plaque! There are many types of historic designations, from local to national (see Appendix D for a list). National Historic Landmarks are the highest designation a place can have (there are about 2,600 in the US), but you'll see many more markers placed by cities, counties and states. Let's explore what the City of Los Angeles has done to preserve landmarks.

Criteria for Landmark Designation:

1) Architectural Style - By far the most common, these are buildings that embody "the distinctive characteristics of an architectural style" or a notable work of a famous designer, builder or architect. Here you can find 200-year-old adobes, Victorian mansions, Art Deco theaters, and modernist skyscrapers. The period of the 1920s was particularly exciting in LA and you will see lots of "Revival Styles " including Spanish, Mission, Colonial, Egyptian, Tudor, Norman/Châteauesque, Dutch, and Mayan **(see Appendix B for a complete list of styles).**

2) Association with Historic Events or Social/Cultural History - These landmarks are much less numerous, but tell important stories. For example, the site of Campo de Cahuenga (City Landmark #29) was the location of the signing of the treaty that ended the Mexican American War in California.

3) Association with "Historic Personages" - These are properties associated with famous people important to local, state or national interest. LA examples include the boyhood home of Nobel prize-winning diplomat Ralph Bunche and the house where Walt Disney created his first animation studio.

Itinerary: Now go out and explore! - Use the resources and links below and your own ingenuity to find local landmarks. Here are some fun landmarks in the LA area.

Canter's delicatessen has been an important "third place" for the Jewish community.

Frank Lloyd Wright's Hollyhock House (1921) represented his textile block period.

LAX Theme Building (1961) is futuristic architecture at its finest.

UCLA's Royce Hall is a dramatic example of Romanesque architecture, popular before 1930.

Broadway's most ornate movie palace, LA Theatre (1934), is baroque on the outside and rococo inside.

Julia Morgan's Herald Examiner Building (1914) is a great example of the Mission Revival style.

The Venice Canals were designated as a Cultural Heritage Landmark in 1983.

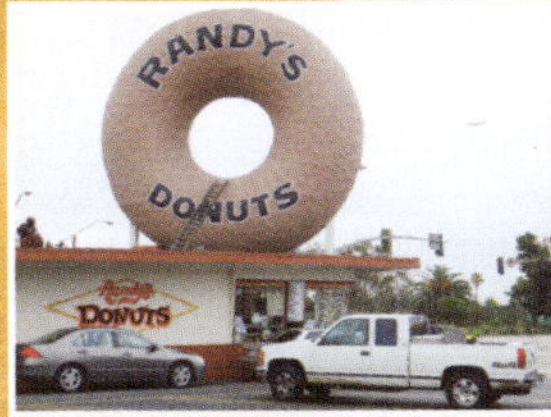

Randy's Donuts (1953) is LA's best example of programmatic architecture - where the building design equals product sold.

La Placita Church (1822) - LA's first church has an active Roman Catholic parish to this day.

Resources for the Urban Explorer:

1. **LA Conservancy: Historic Places in LA** - Great interactive map of over 800 historic places in LA County
2. **Survey LA: Historic Resources Survey** - Look up historic resources by LA's Community Plan Areas
3. **City of Los Angeles - Historic Places LA** - Online inventory with video guides to assist your search
4. **City of Los Angeles - Local City Landmarks** - Find more than 1200 landmarks on interactive map
5. **Wikipedia - Los Angeles Historic-Cultural Monuments** - Nice background, links and concise descriptions
6. **Preserve Orange County - OC Interactive Map** - Just click the circle of the historic place you want to explore
7. ***Preserving Los Angeles:*** *How Historic Places Can Transform America's Cities,* Bernstein; Schafer (2021) - Excellent book documenting LA's strong preservation program; lots of great photos as well

OUTING #21: BURRITOS, MURALS & MERCADOS

Boyle Heights and Eastside Los Angeles

This driving tour highlights Boyle Heights - an area known for its Chicano murals, Mexican food and multicultural past. Your starting point is Mariachi Plaza, followed by a drive down Cesar Chavez Boulevard to view some of the area's many murals. Before choosing your lunch or dinner spot, you may want to visit LA's oldest cemetery for a slice of cultural history. (Note: This is a crowded and somewhat gritty part of Los Angeles. Drive carefully!)

Background - This area played an important role as an "Ellis Island" for non-Anglo immigrants in the late 1800s, including European Jews, Eastern Europeans and Japanese. Over time, the area transitioned to a largely Latino population. In the 1960s, **Boyle Heights** became a leading center for the **Chicano civil rights** and **mural movement**. The Gold Line light rail and the Sixth Street Viaduct have finally connected the area to downtown. New construction has raised major concerns over gentrification.

Itinerary:

1. Mariachi Plaza (1831 1st St.) - This historic gathering place includes a subway portal in the shape of a colorful fan. There are often vendors and mariachi bands performing in the afternoon, and you can take the Gold Line here from Union Station.

2. Murals of Cesar Chavez Boulevard and Beyond - Head east on First Street, make a left on Cummings and then right on Cesar Chavez. Enjoy the murals and colorful storefronts for the next ten blocks to Evergreen St. Mural lovers should also consider visiting **Estrada Courts** (1942) - a garden apartment complex considered the birthplace of the Chicano mural art movement of the early 1970s.

3. Evergreen Cemetery (204 N. Evergreen) - LA's oldest, nondenominational cemetery (1877) is a portrait of the multiethnic past. Burial sites were segregated, with separate sections for African Americans and early residents of Chinese, Mexican, Japanese, Armenian and Jewish descent. Of particular interest are the **Chinese Shrine**, the **Japanese-American 442nd Infantry Regiment** and the **1903 Ivy Chapel**, a medieval stone structure with its four Gothic windows.

Lunch or Dinner - The area is replete with Mexican restaurants, but for a true lively atmosphere, try **El Mercadito** on 3425 1st St. This two-story food court is a representation of a traditional Mexican marketplace with lots of colorful merchandise and mariachi bands. You could also try **El Tepeyac Café** on 812 Evergreen for its massive burritos. Another favorite is **La Mascota Bakery** (2715 Whittier Blvd.) known for tamales, tortas and pan dulce.

Hidden Gem - Breed Street Shul (1923) - Last of Eastside synagogues - Byzantine Revival style (1923)

Farther Afield - The Great Wall of Los Angeles - half-mile-long mural depicting history of California; painted on west wall of Tujunga Flood Control Channel; artist Judy Baca.

Famous mural - The Wall that Speaks, Sings and Shouts - *in Ruben Salazar Park.*

Boyle Heights is now connected to downtown LA by subway, the Sixth Street Viaduct, and by bike during special events such as CicLAvia.

OUTING #22: SMALL CITY, BIG STYLE

West Hollywood

West Hollywood, known as "WeHo," is a small city with an outsized, stylish impact. Known for the classic Sunset Strip, Pacific Design Center, and a lively stretch of Santa Monica Boulevard, WeHo is 1.9 square miles of upscale shops, restaurants, hotels, music venues and distinctive architecture. Stop and walk at key places along the streets in this exciting, design-forward town.

The brilliant Pacific Design Center - Blue, Green & Red - spans four decades. *Santa Monica Blvd. is safe, walkable, and fun.*

Background: Before it was incorporated in 1984, the West Hollywood area had fewer regulations and a lighter police presence. This helped the town become a refuge for certain minority groups, such as the LGBTQ community, which today constitute a substantial portion of the 34,000 residents. Today, the City of West Hollywood is considered a model of city governance and has attracted a great number of high-end design firms, restaurants and hotels. Since incorporation, the City has adopted a strict historic preservation program with six historic districts and 80 designated landmarks. Since 2011, WeHo has consistently been voted one of the most walkable cities in California.

Itinerary: We'll take a scenic, counterclockwise driving loop through West Hollywood.

Sunset Strip - Start at the corner of Fairfax and Sunset and go west along the famous Sunset Strip. The lights and views are better at night, but during the day you can see the landmarks even better. Try to go slowly because you'll be assaulted by huge billboards and digital signs (somehow appropriate here). You'll soon see the celebrity hideaway **Chateau Marmont**, the gorgeous Art Deco **Sunset Plaza Tower**, the **"Googie-style" Mel's Drive-In**, swanky Sunset Plaza with its posh cafés, and the rock venues of **The Whiskey a Go Go** and **The Roxy**. Turn left on Doheny and head downhill from the Hollywood Hills.

Melrose and Pacific Design Center - Cross Santa Monica Boulevard and make a left on Melrose Ave. Make a left on San Vicente Boulevard and park your car by the enormous Pacific Design Center, built in the Late Modern style in three phases. The first was **"the Blue Whale"** (1975, by Cesar Pelli) followed by **Center Green** (1988) and **Center Blue** (2013). Critics say the buildings are out of scale with their surroundings, but there is no denying their bold, architectural statement.

Walk Santa Monica Boulevard - Continue along trendy Melrose and make a left on Crescent Heights and drive four blocks to Santa Monica Blvd. Park your car and walk to the west along the boulevard all the way to La Cienega Boulevard. You will notice wide sidewalks, a generous tree canopy, a median replete with lots of public art, and plenty of fun restaurants, bars and specialty retail. This attention to streetscape detail, sadly so lacking in many other cities, is why WeHo has been named one of California's most pedestrian-friendly cities. And you can see why Santa Monica Boulevard is the route of the annual LGBTQ+ Pride Celebration.

OUTING #23: STREETS OF GLAMOUR

Rodeo Drive and Beverly Hills Homes

Explore one of the nation's wealthiest communities and rub shoulders with the rich, famous and hopefuls! This outing includes a walk along Rodeo Drive, the nation's most expensive retail street, a stop at an elegant hotel, and a beautiful drive through some of the gorgeous neighborhoods. You'll find that the landscaping is as beautiful as the homes!

Background: Beverly Hills, totally surrounded by the City of Los Angeles, grew from the early-nineteenth-century Mexican "Rancho Rodeo de las Aguas," which means "gathering of waters." After oil exploration was abandoned in the early 1900s, landscape architects designed curved streets that hugged the hills, and the City was **incorporated in 1906**. The famous **business district**, now called the **"Golden Triangle"** (formed by Crescent Drive, Wilshire and Santa Monica Boulevards), was planned with grid streets running at a 45-degree angle northwest from Wilshire. The Beverly Hills Hotel, built in 1912, ushered in the glamour era of movie stars, and the City hasn't looked back since.

Itinerary:

AM: Stroll Rodeo Drive and the Golden Triangle

1. You will approach Rodeo Drive from two famous boulevards - Wilshire or Santa Monica (aka, Route 66). Park your car above Santa Monica Boulevard on Rodeo. Turn left and walk one block to the Beverly Hills Sign in the linear park on the north side of Santa Monica Boulevard. Take time for a photo op at the Beverly Hills Sign along the linear park. Notice the ornate Spanish Renaissance tower of the **Beverly Hills City Hall** (1932) across the street.

2. Walk one block west and cross the boulevard to enter Rodeo Drive. Enjoy this three-block, slightly downhill stroll by luxury storefronts of every boutique designer imaginable. You may find that the people watching is as fun as the shopping. As you approach Wilshire Boulevard, you'll see dramatic **Two Rodeo Drive** pedestrian street to your left. This gorgeous cobblestone walk of luxury is another LA imitation of classical European architecture in an intimate setting. Try to visit Rodeo during the holiday season. Decorative lighting on palm trees is so LA!

3. Cross the street and walk into the lobby of the Beverly Wilshire Hotel (1926) - a great example of the Italian Renaissance style (rounded windows, squarish massing with projecting cornice). This landmark has seen many celebrity guests and is called "the *Pretty Woman* Hotel" for the classic film starring Julia Roberts and Richard Gere.

A classic design for an early '30s city hall: broad base and dramatic tapering tower.

Lunch

There are literally dozens of restaurants on the two streets east of Rodeo - Beverly and Canon Drives - between Wilshire and Santa Monica Boulevards.

PM: Beverly Hills Residential Driving Tour

1. Anything north of Santa Monica Boulevard is eye-popping. Explore the calm streets west of Rodeo and find the **Spadena House** (aka, **Witches House**, 516 Walden) originally built as a movie set and office in Culver City. Notice how every north/south street in this area has a different street tree.

2. Drive a few blocks east to Beverly Boulevard and turn left. Go slowly and take in the iconic Mexican fan palms that frame the luxury homes. This might be the most filmed street in the LA area.

3. Cross Sunset Boulevard to the classic Beverly Hills Hotel (1912). Notice the rounded pink gables of the Mission style and the iconic script Beverly Hills signature. The landscaping is lush and you might want to have a drink at the famous Polo Lounge.

4. Continue east on Sunset Boulevard and make a left after a few blocks on Foothill. Here the homes become mansions, often blocked by huge hedges, and the streets become narrower. It might be hard to believe, but the homes in the Bel Air neighborhood of LA are even bigger. Regardless, you could get a celebrity homes map and explore for hours (make sure you have a navigator with you!). A popular stop is the **Doheny Greystone Manor and Gardens** (905 Loma Vista). This huge Tudor estate (1928) and gardens were built by oil tycoon Edward Doheny for his son, Ned, who died there in a tragic murder-suicide. The Estate and park grounds were purchased by the City of Beverly Hills and are open to the public except during special events or filming.

Beverly Boulevard is a favorite for filming. Tall palm trees indicate an older neighborhood.

Store front architecture on Rodeo Drive is as stylish as the clothing and jewelry!

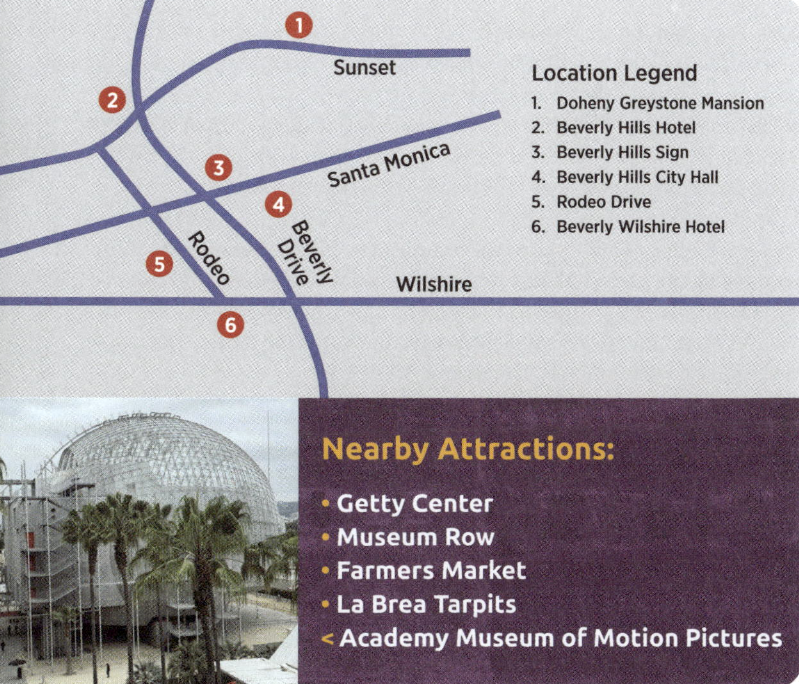

Nearby Attractions:

- Getty Center
- Museum Row
- Farmers Market
- La Brea Tarpits
- < Academy Museum of Motion Pictures

OUTING #24: INNOVATIVE ARCHITECTURE

Creative Culver City and the Cold War Museum

This outing takes you to one of LA County's most creative cities - Culver City. It's freeway close and there's lots to enjoy. You'll spend the morning exploring some of the most innovative architecture in the nation in an area called the Hayden Tract. There are plenty of lunch options in the comfortable downtown, and, in the afternoon, you'll visit a unique Cold War Museum. You could also tour Sony Picture Studios or visit one of several hip, mixed-use centers.

Background: Culver City, like Beverly Hills, is totally surrounded by the City of LA. Founded in 1913 by promoter Harry Culver, it maintained its own identity. The City has always been known for its movie studios, in particular MGM, which was purchased by **Sony Pictures** in 2004. The downtown saw a major revitalization around the famous **Culver Hotel** (1924) in the 1990s. Here you will find wide, tree-shaded sidewalks and plenty of restaurants. Many older buildings have been repurposed such as the Art Deco **Helms Bakery** (1931), which is now an interior design complex. The City is best known for its creative architecture and is well connected to the Expo light rail, which goes from downtown LA to Santa Monica.

Itinerary:

AM: Hayden Tract Walking Tour - Start your architectural adventure at the Hayden Tract - a four-block industrial neighborhood that has been transformed into an architectural petri dish! It's just one mile east of the downtown. From the 405 Freeway, take Venice Boulevard east to National Blvd. Turn right and go five blocks to Hayden Ave. Turn right again and park your car near the corner of Hayden and Steller.

The Umbrella Building (1999) is a dramatic example of "deconstructivism."

The architecture walk is a **counterclockwise**, **forty-five-minute loop starting at the corner of Hayden and National Boulevard**. The creative designs you will see are the work of architect Eric Owen Moss, who worked with developers Fred and Laurie Samitaur starting in the 1980s. The result of this long collaboration is truly unique in the US.

1. Samitaur Tower - This twisted, rusted tower marks the entrance to the Hayden Tract. The conical shapes project images at night.

2. Continue south on Hayden. On your left, after the long metallic **Samitaur Building** with its many impossible angles, walk into the private parking driveway. To the east inside the parking courtyard, you will see more of Moss' creations - **The Umbrella Building**, which explodes from its own wall and **Pterodactyl** built atop a parking garage. Both designs defy labels, but perhaps "deconstructivism" best describes their chaotic forms.

The Pterodactyl Building (2014). Post-modern architecture rejected modernism. Deconstructivism rejects both!

3. Continue walking up Hayden to the corner of Steller Ave. Look across the street to **The Vespertine** (2014 - pictured to the left) - a twisted, 3-story tower with horizontal and vertical metal plates framing the glass. This striking building houses a restaurant with a ground-floor garden.

4. Turn left on Steller and left on Eastman to National Boulevard. Look east to the dramatic, 16-story **Wrapper Tower**. The office tower's exterior is covered in curved bands that obviate the need for interior support columns. This is LA's most unique skyscraper.

5. Finish your walk west along National. See if you can spot **The Box** and **The Beehive** before you reach Hayden Ave. to complete the loop.

Architect Dolan Dagget believes that creative design attracts innovative clients. Wrapper Bldg. in background.

Lunch - Several options here. You could have lunch in the Hayden Tract at Destroyer Cafe (3578 Hayden) to continue the hip vibe or venture downtown to one of the many restaurants near the Culver Hotel. Another favorite is **Tito's Tacos** (11222 Washington Place), famous since 1959 for their crunchy-shell tacos with grated cheese. Not fancy - just delicious!

The Beehive on National Blvd. in the Hayden Tract.

PM: Visit the Wende Museum of the Cold War (10808 Culver Blvd.) This museum and art center was founded in 2002 and has over 100,000 unique artifacts and material culture from the former Soviet Union and East Bloc. In addition, it has an ongoing series of exhibitions and programs related to the Cold War and authoritarianism. It's fascinating to see objects produced behind the "Iron Curtain," but also to see the struggle between East and West portrayed through art and case studies.

Other options for the afternoon: You could also explore other venues downtown. Everything is close to the landmark **Culver Hotel**,a six-story, brick beauty that resembles the Flatiron Building in New York City. You could book the **Sony Pictures Studio Tour** (Amazon and Culver Studios are also close by); visit The **Culver Steps** - a mixed-use center with lots of dining; explore the **Helms Bakery District** - a 1931 Art Deco building converted to dining, art and design; check out the bizarre **Museum of Jurassic Technology**; or take in a play at the **Ivy Substation** - a 99-seat theater adapted from a 1907 railroad storage building. As you can see, Culver City uses the past to create a vibrant present.

Ivy Substation, a 99-seat live theater, was created from this 1907 Mission Revival building. Adaptive reuse at its best!

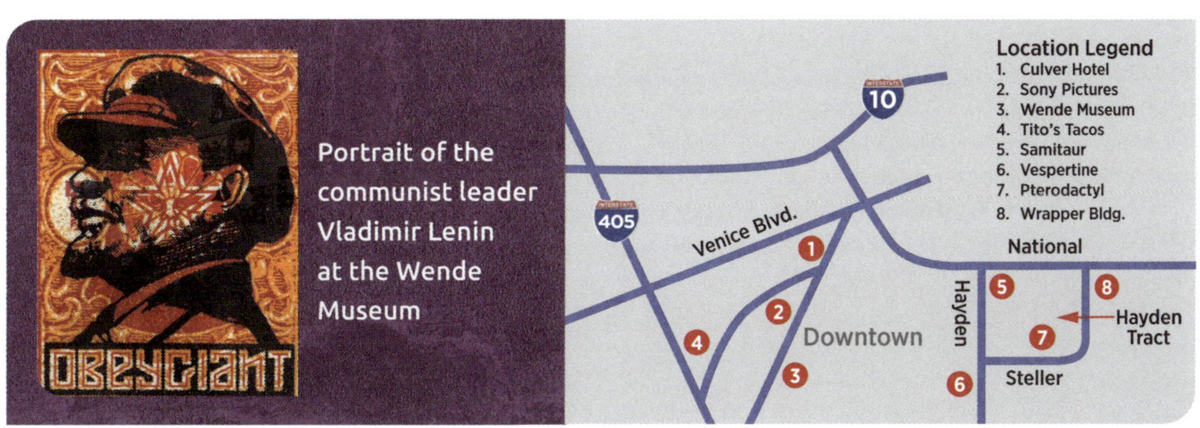

OUTING #25: SURF & TURF

SoFi Stadium and Manhattan Beach

Southern California is known for its famous sports venues and beautiful beaches. This outing shows you the best of both. SoFi Stadium, a $6 billion masterpiece, is considered the nation's most state-of-the-art football and entertainment venue. Of course, it's great to see a game or concert there, but a tour really opens your eyes to the architectural planning involved. Manhattan Beach Pier, built in 1920, contains a small aquarium and is connected to its stylish beach community by a popular boardwalk called The Strand. Morning tour, afternoon beach and sunset. Not a bad way to spend a day!

Background: In many societies, stadiums represent some of the most dramatic building forms. That is certainly true in the sports-loving US. In SoCal, we have the classic **Rose Bowl (1922)**, designed to emulate Greek and Roman stadia. The **Los Angeles Coliseum (1923)** was built for 77,000 people and hosted two Olympic Games. **Dodger Stadium (1962)** is the nation's third-oldest ballpark and is considered a classic in mid-century modern design. Starting in the 1990s, we've experienced an explosion of high tech new arenas and stadiums - Crypto.com in downtown LA, BMO Soccer Stadium for the LA Football Club, SoFi Stadium for the Rams and Chargers and the Intuit Dome for the LA Clippers.

For seismic safety, the massive roof, supported by 37 columns, is structurally independent from the rest of the stadium.

Itinerary:

SoFi Stadium, Inglewood - Several behind-the-scenes tours are available, but make sure you call ahead. This is a perfect indoor-outdoor venue for Southern California, and the tour will take you behind the scenes and onto the field. One of the big design challenges was the requirement to place the seating 100 feet below grade to accommodate the flight path into LAX. To compensate, the architects created a low-lying, sweeping roofline that evokes a Pacific Coast wave. The landscape plan reflects the diversity of Southern California's Mediterranean biomes with terraced gardens of sycamores, mountain evergreens, palms and even Joshua trees. A six-acre lake in front combines reclaimed and on-site captured stormwater.

A series of gradual walkways rather than elevators and escalators leads fans inside the stadium. Here, the **translucent roof** - composed of a lightweight alternative to glass - filters natural light and contains thousands of independently operated panels for ventilation control. The real showstopper is the **360-degree, dual-sided video screen** symmetrically placed above the field. Fans can't miss the action since the images appear on both sides of the amazing video oval. At SoFi, the stadium is truly part of the experience.

Called the Infinity Screen, this dual-sided 4,000 LED display is 122 feet above the playing field.

Built in 2018 for the Los Angeles Football Club (LAFC) in Exposition Park, **BMO Stadium** (originally called Banc of California) was an instant success. Soccer fans loved the fact that the 34-degree seating meant that the farthest seat was only 135 feet from the pitch. The sweeping steel overhangs add protection and beauty, and afford views of the downtown LA skyline. Energy efficient design and natural Bermuda grass won the stadium designers a LEED (Leadership in Energy and Environmental Design) Award. Could it be that both a good team and beautiful design contribute to the fact that almost every game in the 22,000 seat stadium has been a sellout?

At BMO Stadium, the closest seats are only 12 feet from the touchline! This could be the best ticket in town.

Intuit Dome - The new home of the LA Clippers, near SoFi Stadium, is another dramatic architectural statement. The sleek, oval-shaped arena is covered with a seismically-independent structural grid with diamond-shaped panels and plenty of solar panels. Let's call it "armadillo modern." Inside the 18,000 seat arena is **"The Halo"**, an awesome ellipse-shaped, double-sided video board with over 200 million LEDs. This is roundball in its most technology-rich environ. Go Clippers!

The famous LAFC "standing" section of 3,252 supporters. No seats - just railing, flags and spirited chants! They love LA!

Lunch and Pier Walk in Manhattan Beach - After your sports adventure, it's time to head to the coast, and Manhattan Beach is a great option for a pier walk and a bite to eat. From the 405 Freeway, take Rosecrans Blvd. west to Pacific Coast Highway (Sepulveda Blvd.). Turn left and then right on **Manhattan Beach Blvd**. In a mile you'll leave the residential area and arrive at Manhattan's beachfront commercial downtown starting at Valley Dr. Park your car in one of the adjacent garages and enjoy a leisurely beach stroll. The boulevard slopes gently downhill for four blocks of fun restaurants and stores and ends at the Manhattan Beach Pier.

Cross the pedestrian-only Strand and continue on to the pier, the oldest concrete pier on the West Coast. See if you can find the State Landmark plaque! Walk to the end of the pier to the **Roundhouse Aquarium Teaching Center** inside the 1922 Art Deco/ Spanish Colonial octagonal building. After checking out the exhibits, enjoy the views from the end of the pier. To the north, you may be able to see the Santa Monica Mountains and Malibu and to the south, the Palos Verdes Peninsula.

Looking north all the way to the Santa Monica Mountains.

Just one mile north of the pier is a coastal park - **Bruce's Beach** - with an important story to tell. Once a thriving African American beach resort built by the Bruce family, it was condemned by the city in 1924. The Bruces were forced out and their resort was leveled. Almost 80 years later, the City acknowledged its unfair action, and the county returned the land to the descendants of the Bruce family. In 2023, the Bruce family sold the land back to the County for $20 million. It's never too late to do the right thing.

The concrete Manhattan Beach Pier leads directly to four blocks of restaurants and shops.

OUTING #26: COMMUNITY SPACE & GARDEN APARTMENTS

Baldwin Hills, Village Green and Leimert Park

These two areas of Los Angeles tell different but important stories. Village Green in Baldwin Hills is a famous example of the postwar "Garden City" idea of a central greenbelt with homes facing away from streets. Leimert Park Village became a significant African American cultural center beginning in the 1960s. Start your adventure at Village Green and then plan on lunch and exploring in nearby Leimert Village.

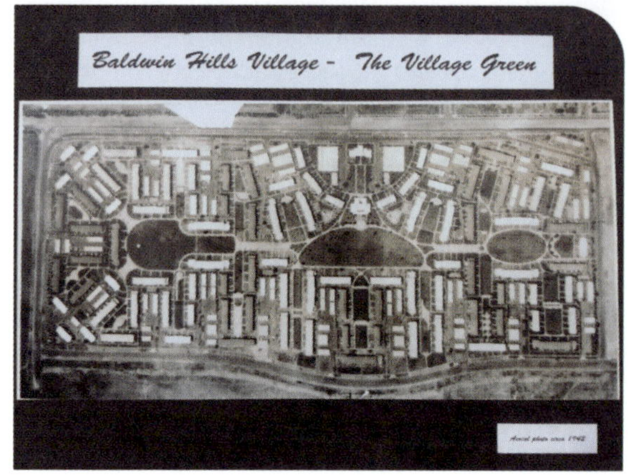

The original "superblock" plan for Baldwin Hills Village featured three central parks and no through traffic.

Background: Garden Apartments and the **Green Commons** - After World War II, demand for housing boomed, but not everyone could afford to buy a single-family home. Influenced by the **"Greenbelt Towns"** in Europe and Radburn, New Jersey, planners envisioned families living in low-rise modern buildings with shared green spaces, not unlike the amenities of modern planned communities (see Outing #55 - Planned Community Mecca). In total, fifteen garden apartment developments were built in the LA area between 1937 to 1955. Most of them survive to this day and are an interesting case study in urban design.

Itinerary:

Village Green: From the 10 Freeway, take the La Cienega Exit going south. Make a left on Obama Boulevard and enter the complex by making a right at Cloverdale Ave. Follow the path south past the office and clubhouse to the Village Green. Take a leisurely stroll along the three oval green parks with their mature landscaping. The design goal was to create a tranquil setting in the midst of the city.

Mature sycamore trees in the central green. This shared space is used for picnics, film screenings and passive enjoyment.

Village Green contains 97 two-story buildings and 629 townhouses or flats over 67 acres. **Opened in 1942**, cars and roads were confined to the perimeter of the **superblock**. Residents and visitors would leave their cars in motor courts and then access the idyllic central green. In 1973, the complex became a condominium development and owners established strict control over the exterior appearance of the buildings. The architecture is mid-century modern with an approved historic palette of greens, blues, tans and grays.

The Village is such a beautifully maintained example of the "Garden City" concept that it was declared a **National Historic Landmark** in 2001, the highest level of designation by the National Park Service. Garden apartments come in many site plans. **Laguna Woods Village** in Orange County is a gated community with communally owned green space and private patios, while **Park La Brea** in the Fairfax District of Los Angeles features high rises amid townhomes.

This garden apartment features distinctive window designs.

Pastels seem to be the colors of choice for many garden apartments.

The People's Street in Leimert Park Plaza stamped the concrete with "Adinkra" symbols from Ghana and the Ivory Coast.

The Vision Theatre is the artistic anchor of the Leimert Park community.

Itinerary:

Leimert Park Village: Leaving the Village Green, go east on Obama Boulevard and make a right on Crenshaw. Continue south to 43rd Street and start your visit. Leimert Park neighborhood was developed in the 1920s as an early planned community, designed by the famous landscape architect Olmsted brothers (of Central Park fame!). The **Leimert Park Historic District** contains over 1000 homes in a variety of styles, including Spanish Colonial Revival and Streamline Moderne. The neighborhood successfully broke through restrictive racial covenants to become home to African American and Japanese residents. The core of the neighborhood is Leimert Park Village, which was declared a Cultural-Heritage Monument.

The Village has become a mecca for Black art and culture. Explore the colorful shops between 43rd St., Leimert and Crenshaw. The community's hub is the **Vision Theater** (Art Deco, 1931) that fronts Leimert Plaza Park. There is an African Marketplace and drum circle on Sundays, and many of the stores and vendors display their wares along the sidewalk. Restaurants include those offering Ethiopian, Jamaican and soul food cuisine, and African-inspired clothing and designs abound. This vibrant community is another example of multicultural LA.

You can also explore the small ethnic enclave of Little Ethiopia on Fairfax Avenue in the Mid-Wilshire district of central Los Angeles.

< Ethiopian food at Azla Restaurant

OUTING #27: FROM DOWNTOWN TO THE SEA

Driving Wilshire Boulevard

LA is a city of grand boulevards, and there's no better way to experience it than to cruise Wilshire Boulevard from downtown to the coast! This outing will suggest various sights and stops along the way, so follow your interests and drive carefully. You'll see the wonderful diversity of LA neighborhoods with landmark architecture, museums and parks. You'll pass through Koreatown and then experience the palatial, 1920s homes of Hancock Park. From there you'll cruise the Art Deco Miracle Mile and motor past Museum Row and the La Brea Tar Pits to glamorous Beverly Hills. Your final leg will be through the apartment towers of Westwood ending at Ocean Boulevard and the Pacific Ocean in Santa Monica. Now, eyes on the road!

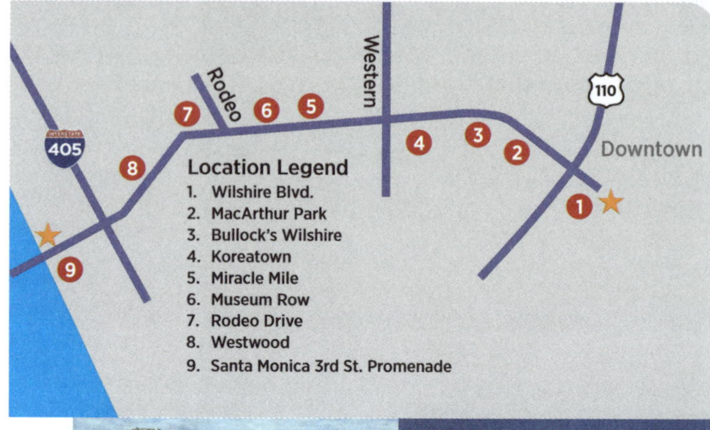

Background: Wilshire Boulevard was LA's first glamorous street, named after Henry Gaylord Wilshire, who in 1895 donated land to the city to provide access to his subdivision. As the City grew, Wilshire Boulevard continued to move westward and became home to luxury department stores such as **Bullocks Wilshire** (1929). Today, bus and subway lines make Wilshire Boulevard the most important east/west corridor in the City. Wilshire Boulevard is 16 miles of fascinating real estate!

Before 2014, all LA skyscrapers were required to have a flat roof to accommodate helipads.

This dramatic gold cylinder of the 1939 May Co. was meant to attract motorists.

Itinerary:

Start downtown at the Wilshire Grand Center - Wilshire Boulevard starts in the financial district downtown at Grand Avenue. Begin your adventure at the Wilshire Grand Center - the tallest skyscraper on the West Coast (1,110 feet. tall!) with the highest rooftop bar (Spire 73) in the Western Hemisphere. Valet your car and hop on one of the high-speed elevators to the 70th-floor Sky Lobby. The 360-degree views are thrilling. **The Wilshire Grand**, which contains the 889-room Intercontinental Hotel, is the **first skyscraper since the 1928 City Hall not to have a flat roof**. In 2014, the City dropped the requirement due to improvements in building technology. Architects will now have a freer rein to create a more interesting skyline.

Continue west through **MacArthur Park** in the Westlake neighborhood. This high-density, largely immigrant neighborhood is bustling with street vendors by day, but can be dangerous at night. Angelinos love nearby Langer's Delicatessen and Restaurant known for its hot pastrami sandwiches since 1947. Just beyond Hoover St., find the Art Deco **Bullocks Wilshire Building** (now Southwestern Law School) on the left. Turn left on Wilshire Place and drive to the port cochere in back. This luxurious department store's entrance was here, not on busy Wilshire. Under the porte cochere, notice the beautiful **Art Deco mural** depicting the love of transportation!

Koreatown - As you drive west, the boundaries of Koreatown are somewhat blurry, but as you approach Vermont Avenue you will begin to notice more and more signs in Korean. This three-square-mile neighborhood of 110,000 residents is one of the most densely populated in the nation. "K-Town" is famous for Korean BBQ, great shopping and nightlife, but is a bit hard to navigate. Don't miss two cultural landmarks - the **Wilshire Blvd. Temple** (home to the oldest Jewish congregation in a 1923 Byzantine Revival building) and the **Wiltern Theatre** (a turquoise, terra-cotta Art Deco beauty at Western Ave). Continuing west we encounter **Windsor Square** and **Hancock Park**, two of the most beautiful historic districts in the city. Turn right at the signal at Irving to see some well-preserved, century-old residential architecture.

Check out the wonderful Art Deco mural (1929) on the ceiling of the porte cochere of the Bullocks Wilshire Building.

Miracle Mile Art Deco and Museum Row - At La Brea Avenue begins the Miracle Mile, a historic district known for its Art Deco and Streamline Moderne architecture. You'll notice the famous zigzag ornamentation and rounded corners on buildings short and tall. Just past Curson Avenue is a multitude of great sights! You'll see the oily pools of the **La Brea Tar Pits** and its trapped elephants on the right. You'll pass under the sleek new **LA County Museum of Art** and quickly, on your right, see the forest of streetlamps which is Chris Burden's popular art piece **Urban Light**. As you approach Fairfax Avenue, on your left you'll see the curvy metal stripes of the **Petersen Automotive Museum** and, on your right, the famous gold mosaic cylinder preserved by the **Academy Museum of Motion Pictures**. Wow, maybe you should just circle the block to take it all in again!

Two Rodeo Drive is a crowd favorite.

Beverly Hills - As you approach San Vicente Boulevard, you'll spot the famous "Beverly Hills" sign on your right. Now it seems that all the commercial buildings are white! In a little over a mile, you'll see the flags of the landmark, Renaissance Revival **Beverly Wilshire Hotel** (on your left) and Rodeo Drive (on your right). Turn right on Rodeo and slowly enjoy the three blocks of the nation's most expensive commercial real estate. If you have time, park your car and stroll the street with its glamorous designer stores and people watching. Maybe even have a virgin margarita at the Beverly Wilshire. After all, you are driving!

Westwood - Leaving Beverly Hills, you'll drive through a canyon of luxurious, high-rise apartments. For art lovers, a great stop is the **Hammer Museum**, a contemporary art museum one block north of Wilshire. If you have time, turn right on Westwood Boulevard into the Village. It has some architectural gems and the gorgeous **Romanesque Revival buildings of UCLA**. Just past Veteran Ave. on your right is the **Los Angeles National Cemetery**.

Santa Monica - The last leg of your journey is through Santa Monica. Explore the **Third Street Promenade** that stretches three blocks to Broadway and the entrance to the **Santa Monica Place** shopping mall. What is your opinion of the Promenade as a pedestrian experience and a break from the car? Walk the last three blocks of Wilshire to its terminus at the **statue of Saint Monica** (1939) in **Palisades Park**. This Art Deco sculpture is another example of artwork funded by the New Deal's Public Works of Art Project. Enjoy the views of the ocean at the end of your Wilshire Boulevard adventure!

Another Notable City Drive:

- **Sunset Boulevard to the Sea** - Start in downtown; pass through Echo Park, Silver Lake, Hollywood, the Sunset Strip, Beverly Hills, Bel Air and Pacific Palisades.

OUTING #28: ROMANS & SURFERS

Getty Villa with Malibu's Surfrider Beach

This outing takes you along the coast near Malibu to the Getty Villa - a recreation of a grand Roman country residence buried by the volcanic eruption of Mt. Vesuvius in AD 79. It's a perfect Mediterranean setting in Pacific Palisades where you'll get a fascinating peak at the life of wealthy Romans in the first century AD. The architecture is vibrant; the galleries of Greek, Roman and Etruscan antiquities are intimate and well organized, and the gardens are stunning. You could spend 1/2 a day here, have lunch at the on-site Villa Cafe, and then head a few miles north to Malibu to check out the famous Surfrider Beach. Make sure to make a timed reservation before you visit.

Background: There are actually two Getty locations in the greater LA area: the **Getty Villa** and the **Getty Center**. J. Paul Getty, who died in 1976, left four million shares of stock to the Getty Foundation, transforming it into one of the wealthiest art institutes in the world. After he moved to England, he opened rooms in his Malibu home as a public museum. When the home proved too small for his collection, the Getty Villa was born in 1974. Most of the original Villa on the Bay of Naples is still underground, but Getty's architects adapted a plan of the exposed part and incorporated details of other nearby ancient homes in Pompeii and Herculaneum. Ironically, Getty never lived to see either the Villa or the Getty Center, although he is buried on the Villa grounds. One of Getty's wishes was that admission to all Getty facilities be free, a policy still in effect today.

The view from the Outer Peristyle back toward the central villa.

Itinerary:

AM: Getty Villa - Have fun exploring this beautiful Roman house. You won't need a toga, but, when you first arrive, sign up for one or more of the free guided tours on the Villa's architecture, gardens, and collections. The sign-ups are only available on-site and provide a great introduction to your visit. All of the galleries are oriented around the **Atrium** and **Inner Peristyle**, located in the large building just south of the amphitheater at the main entrance.

1. Enter the Atrium off the amphitheater - This was the main public room in a Roman home with an open ceiling and sunken "impluvium" to capture rainwater. The surrounding galleries display Greek antiquities and background exhibits on the Villa dei Papiri and the Classical World.

2. Continue into the Inner Peristyle - This beautiful, two-story Classical space features Corinthian columns, around which you will find the bulk of the galleries. To the left is the Temple of Hercules with its imported marbles and special exhibits. To the right is Roman art including sculpture, glass, sarcophagi, and ceramics.

The Adamson House (1929) has Spanish and Moorish influences.

Athenian vases are a collection highlight.

1st century AD Roman statue of Zeus.

Reproduction of ancient bronze statue from Villa dei Papiri.

The rugged Santa Monica Mountains are a hiker's and mountain biker's dream.

3. Stroll the Outer Peristyle and East Garden - This formal garden with its long pool, arcaded walkways and bronze statues might be the most photogenic spot at the Villa. The surrounding walls are painted with garlands and floral patterns, and the smooth marble floors have intricate geometric patterns. The East Garden has a colorful mosaic fountain with shells and theater masks, and the Herb Garden has a variety of Mediterranean trees and shrubs. How these Romans lived!

Lunch: You can enjoy the Villa Café, bring a picnic, or head up the coast to nearby Malibu. I recommend the relaxing views at the Getty Villa.

PM: Explore the Malibu area Just up the coast from the villa are some great options. You can stroll the **Malibu Pier** with views of the famous **Surfrider Beach**. This point break is the best in LA County and the site of many surfing movies from the 1950s and '60s. For architecture lovers, you could book a tour at the famous **Adamson House**. This 1929 Spanish Colonial home has art deco flourishes and lots of famous Malibu tile. It's located right on Malibu Lagoon State Beach and its extensive wetlands. For shopping or food , try the trendy and comfortable **Malibu Country Mart** across the street. Lots of options. Finally, for hikers, the adjoining and rugged **Santa Monica Mountains National Recreation Area** offers over 500 miles of trails. Nature survives next to one of the world's largest metropolitan areas. Park scientists are monitoring over 100 mountain lions in the area.

Malibu
PCH
Pacific Palisades
Santa Monica
405
10

Location Legend
1. Santa Monica Pier
2. Getty Villa
3. Malibu Pier
4. Surfrider Beach
5. Adamson House

The Malibu Pier offers great views of the South Bay and Surfrider Beach.

Nearby Attractions:

The Santa Monica Pier is an LA favorite. It's tacky, crowded and affords great views of the coast - north and south. Ride the Carousel and make sure to take a picture of the Route 66 sign. This is where the famous roadway ends, traveling all the way from Chicago! The Looff Hippodrome (1916), which surrounds the Carousel, is a National Historic Landmark. See if you can find the plaque!

OUTING #29: BEAUTY & THE BEACH

Santa Monica Pier & Third Street Promenade

Santa Monica has embraced its tradition of the pleasure pier. It's fun, historic, and tacky, with great views of the coastline. You can ride the Ferris Wheel, carousel, or roller coaster, or simply take in the ocean breezes and people watch. Nearby is bustling Santa Monica with its 3rd Street Promenade, the area's longest-running pedestrian street. For this outing, you might want to visit the pier in the midmorning to beat the crowds and then head to the Promenade area for lunch and shopping.

Background: Built in 1909, the Santa Monica Pier was the first concrete pier on the West Coast. To compete with nearby Venice and Ocean Park's amusement piers, the **Looff Pleasure Pier** was opened in 1916 with its famous carousel. The original Moorish-style building with its octagonal windows is still standing. The pier went through many iterations and storms, and, in 1996, was remodeled as Pacific Park with its current rides and attractions.

The history of the Third Street Promenade is an interesting case study. Like many large cities in the '60s and '70s, Santa Monica decided to open its main commercial street to pedestrians only. Although successful for a time, business activity began to decline in the late '70s. However, whereas many cities reopened their pedestrian streets to cars, Santa Monica decided to double down and redesign the mall as a promenade in 1987. With more attractive street furniture and better retail options, the Promenade became a huge regional draw. However, with retail challenges after the pandemic and with increased issues with the homeless, the Third Street Promenade has lost some of its earlier luster. The success of this three-block pedestrian experiment could be a "canary in the coal mine!"

Santa Monica preserved its historic carousel. Below, the Third Street Promenade.

Itinerary:

AM: Enjoy the Santa Monica Pier: Park your car in the large lot just north of the pier. The best access is on the south side by crossing under the pier and then taking the stairs. You'll immediately see the **Looff Hippodrome Building** and its marvelous carousel inside. You may notice the National Historic Landmark plaque on the inside before you take a ride. As you walk out on the pier, you can't miss the **Route 66 End of the Trail Sign**. Here's where the famous "Mother Road" ends its 2,448-mile journey from Chicago.

Lunch and PM: **Exploring Third Street Promenade** and downtown Santa Monica: You could certainly retrieve your car and park in one of the several parking structures near the Promenade, but it's only four blocks to downtown by foot.

1. From the pier, walk to the top of the street to the famous Santa Monica Yacht Harbor Sign (1941). Notice **Tongva Park** (named for the area's original inhabitants) across the street with its interesting art sculptures and native plantings.

2. Turn left on Ocean Avenue and walk north through **Palisades Park**. In two blocks, you'll encounter the art deco Saint Monica statue marking the terminus of Wilshire Boulevard (see Outing #27).

3. Enter Wilshire Boulevard and walk two blocks to the entrance of the Third Street Promenade. You will find plenty of restaurants the rest of the way. Enjoy your stroll down the three-block promenade. **The Santa Monica Art Museum** is on your left, and the Promenade ends at the two-story, semiopen shopping center - Santa Monica Place. How was your pedestrian experience?

The Third Street Promenade is the region's longest-lasting pedestrian street.

PEDESTRIAN STREETS WORTH EXPLORING

- **State Street, Santa Barbara**
- **Main Street, Ventura**
- **Olvera Street, Los Angeles**
- **Forest Avenue, Laguna Beach**
- **Piazza della Famiglia, San Diego**

Nearby Attractions:

Getty Villa - Restored Roman villa in Pacific Palisades (see Outing #2)

Venice - Lively boardwalk, historic canals, hip shopping (see Outing #30)

Malibu - Surfrider Beach and 22 miles of coastline

OUTING #30: LA'S "OUT-THERE" COMMUNITY

Venice Boardwalk & Canals

This is LA's quirky, colorful, street carnival by the beach, and there's plenty of history here too. The outing will start at the historic Venice canals - a calming stroll before the hustle and bustle of the Boardwalk. After the canals, you'll visit the stylish and überhip Abbot Kinney Boulevard for lunch and browsing. Then get ready for the festive energy of the Venice Boardwalk.

Background: Venice was born from the dreams of developer **Albert Kinney**, who created a replica of that northern Italian town complete with canals, gondolas and Venetian-style architecture. It opened in 1905 and even included an amusement pier jutting over the water. Venice was annexed to LA in 1925 and slowly the Venetian dream faded. The piers burned down and many of the canals were filled in. In the 1960s and '70s, Venice was infamous for hippies, drugs and the counterculture. Some of the canals remain and the **boardwalk** (aka, **Ocean Front Walk**) is one of LA's biggest tourist draws. The urban ills of crime, homelessness and lack of parking affect the area, but the lure of quirky Venice is very strong. There is much to explore.

Itinerary:

AM: Explore the Venice Canals Historic District: You can access the canals from Washington or Venice Boulevards near Pacific Ave. The pedestrian paths are narrow, but the lush landscaping, colorful and varied homes, and occasional bridges make this a peaceful and memorable stroll.

Lunch and Stroll Along Abbot Kinney Boulevard: Take Venice Boulevard from the canals, turn left on Abbot Kinney and try to find parking. This mile-long stretch of restaurants, shops and galleries has been called **"the coolest block in America."** The street is unique for its specialty retail and creative, single-story architecture. And, of course, it's lined with palm trees.

Afternoon: Cruise the Venice Boardwalk: Park your car near Pacific and Windward Avenues. You'll immediately notice the street-spanning "Venice" sign. Here you'll find the best historic architecture on the north side of Windward as you approach the Boardwalk. The arcaded commercial buildings were named "Venice Renaissance" by developer Kinney in 1904. On the right side, notice the famous black-and-white mural - *Touch of Venice* by Jonas Never. Once you reach the Boardwalk, you can go in either direction for fun in the sun, street performers and merchandise galore.

Rent a bicycle and ride along the curvy Strand bike trail (it's between the Boardwalk and the shore).

Check out the acrobatics at the Skate Park - a little north of Windward on the ocean side of the Boardwalk. The skateboarders are among the best around and a crowd gets them going.

Find the hulking bodies at Muscle Beach (1800 Ocean Front Walk) and admire the many **murals** and street art, including ***Venus on the Half-Shell***, ***Jim Morrison*** and ***Green Goddess***. The word "unique" seems like an understatement for Venice!

Urban Side Trip: **Playa Vista** - Just two miles south of Venice is the innovative mixed-use neighborhood of Playa Vista, sometimes called "Silicon Beach." Built on the site where aerospace entrepreneur **Howard Hughes** built his famous "Spruce Goose" (319-foot wingspan!), this connected community of homes, creative offices, specialty retail and open space is the largest infill development in Los Angeles. With 29 parks and connected to nearby trails and **Ballona Creek**, it has won several environmental sustainability awards. If you like creative design and modern place-making, consider exploring Playa Vista. Entrance is at the corner of Lincoln and Jefferson Boulevards.

Playa Vista creates comfortable pedestrian space with colorful graphics and car-blocking bollards.

A Touch of Venice *by Jonas Never captures Venice in an earlier time.*

Renting a bike is a great way to see Venice.

OUTING #31: FISH, ART DECO & THE *QUEEN MARY*

Aquarium of the Pacific and the *Queen Mary*

This Long Beach outing combines sea life with one of the most famous passenger ships in the world - the Queen Mary. *The Long Beach Aquarium is the perfect size, and a two-to-three-hour visit will allow you to see all the major exhibits. Just around the corner is the* Queen Mary, *where you can dine while enjoying great views of the harbor. Choose from several tour options, including Glory Days, Art Deco, Steam and Steel, and even Haunted Encounters. A good option is to book the 70-minute Glory Days tour, which gives you time to explore the ship on your own.*

The leafy Sea Dragon from Australia is all about camouflage!

Background: Built in Scotland in 1931 by the Cunard Lines, this famous ocean liner is **one of the world's best Art Deco landmarks**. Its luxurious ballrooms, bars and meeting rooms were adorned with etched glass, bas-relief sculpture and paintings. During World War II, the *Queen Mary* was camouflaged as "the Grey Ghost," serving as a troop ship. At one crossing, it ferried over 16,000 soldiers - a record. As air travel became more convenient, ocean liner travel became less popular. The *Queen Mary*'s last great voyage was in 1967 when she was purchased by the City of Long Beach. She is now a floating hotel, museum and event space.

Itinerary:

AM: Visit the Aquarium of the Pacific - Located right on the Long Beach Harbor across from the *Queen Mary*, the Aquarium was opened in 1998. It contains over **500 aquatic species** with 100 exhibits and **19 habitats**. As you enter the Great Hall of the Pacific, you'll be greeted by a life-size blue whale suspended above. On your right, follow the Southern California/Baja Gallery and then continue outdoors to visit the Shark Lagoon, Touch Labs and Seals and Sea Lions enclosure. Upstairs you'll find the penguin and sea otter habitats. Don't miss the Northern Pacific and Tropical Pacific Galleries as you head back towards the entrance. The displays are great, and the staff is committed to teaching the public about conserving our precious ocean life.

Lunch Options: You have several options here. The aquarium has a café and snack carts, but you could venture into downtown Long Beach for a greater selection. Finally, you could have lunch on board the *Queen Mary* at the Promenade Café with views north over the harbor. If you go downtown, the best concentration of restaurants is around Pine St. and Broadway.

PM: Touring the *Queen Mary*: It's a short drive along Queen's Way to the RMS *Queen Mary*. Tours begin on the fourth floor. Use the website to book your tour in advance, but definitely leave some free time to explore the ship on your own. Both the Glory Days and Art Deco Tours will take you into several ballrooms and lounges. Here are some fun areas you won't want to miss.

At over 1,000 feet in length, the Queen Mary *was longer than the* Titanic. *By the way, she did not have stabilizers!*

1. Main Hall - As you enter the ship's Main Hall, you'll immediately notice the workmanship that made the *Queen* the most elegant ship of its time. You'll see the etched glass, art deco lamps and bas-relief sculpture. Check out the displays on both sides of the staircase. You'll see why the *Queen Mary* was called the **"Ship of Woods"** with over 50 different varieties found throughout.

2. Observation Bar, an Art Deco Lounge - At the bow of the ship on the Promenade Deck, this was reserved for first-class passengers. The room is adorned with its original 1930s decor including torchiere lamps and a festive painting over the bar. Check out the fashions!

3. First Class Main Lounge - This stunning room has a huge gold- and silver-leaf bas-relief mural, etched glass and onyx floor lamps. Not a bad place for dinner and dancing.

4. Keep exploring: You can take the stairs up one flight to the sun deck to the Captain's Deck and Quarters. You can also go to the stern of the ship to level two and explore the fascinating **Engine and Boiler Rooms**. This technology allowed the ship to travel at over 30 knots, faster than any submarine at the time. There are other lounges (second and third Class) and bars to explore, but maybe you'll just book one of the 347 hotel rooms on board!

Nearby Attractions:

Take the Long Beach or San Pedro Harbor Tour - A 45-minute, narrated cruise with the company Harbor Breeze Cruises.

Cross the new Gerald Desmond Bridge to San Pedro - From Long Beach, follow **Highway 47** across this new, stayed cable bridge to Terminal Island. Continue across the older **Vincent Thomas Bridge** (a suspension bridge) into San Pedro. It's fun to see all those containers below!

The Cunard Line commissioned prominent Art Deco artists to decorate the Queen Mary.

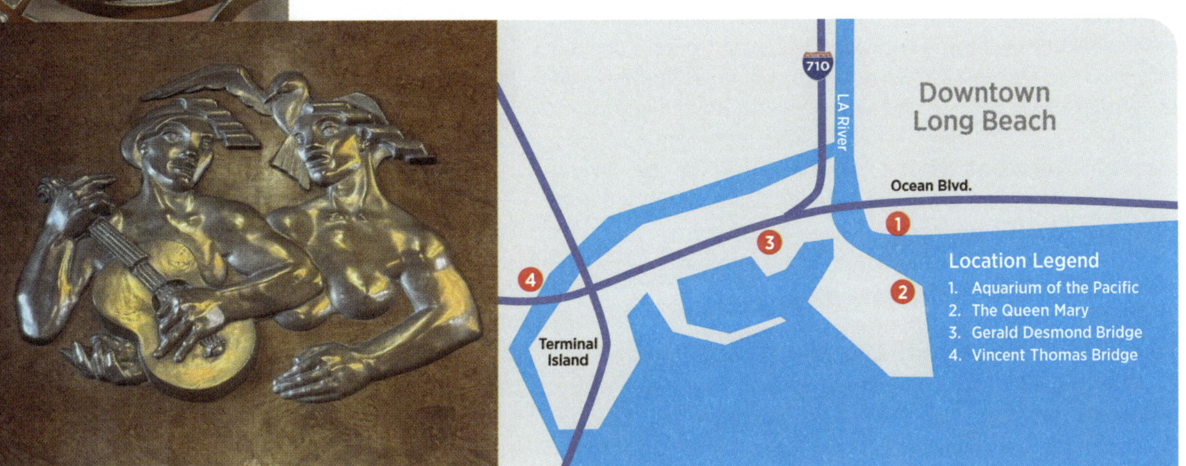

OUTING #32: DIVERSE NEIGHBORHOODS, HISTORIC RANCHOS

Eclectic Long Beach

Although best known for its shoreline attractions - the Queen Mary, *Aquarium of the Pacific, the Harbor and beaches - Long Beach offers the urban explorer diverse cultures and neighborhoods, varied architecture, fun restaurants, unique parks, great vistas, and historic ranchos. This driving tour starts in the southeast portion of the city by the Naples canals, moves into the downtown's East Village, visits a Latin American Art Museum, and ends at one of Southern California's most famous early ranchos. Check out the attractions below and plan a great day.*

Villa Riviera, a châteauesque tower from 1929, represents the City's glamour period.

Background: Long Beach is huge - both in land area (77 square miles) and population (449,000), making it LA County's second-largest city. Built on two huge Spanish land grants - **Rancho Los Cerritos** and **Rancho Los Alamitos** - the town incorporated in 1897 and grew rapidly with the discovery of oil in 1921. This boom helped establish the town as a seaside resort with its popular entertainment area known as **"The Pike."** Sadly, a 6.4-magnitude earthquake in 1933 flattened much of the downtown, and many of the new buildings were built in the Art Deco style. The City has since designated 18 historic districts. The historic preservation advocacy group - **Long Beach Heritage** - provides docent-led walking tours. The City has also officially recognized over 50 distinct neighborhoods, although residents claim there are even more.

Itinerary: Start this adventure at the corner of Pacific Coast Highway and 2nd Street as you cross over Los Alamitos Bay onto the island of Naples.

Explore the Naples Canals on foot, by kayak, or by gondola.

AM: Stroll the Naples Canals - Make a left on N. Ravenna Drive, cross the canal and park your car along the **La Bella Fontana Park**. You can walk in any direction to access the canal's foot path under any of the five bridges. The circular route is about a mile. You can also rent a kayak or tour by gondola. The area was built in the 1920s, and, yes, the name "Venice" was already taken!

Bustlin' Belmont Shore - Continue west on 2nd Street, cross the bridge and enter the Belmont Shore neighborhood. These short, twelve blocks of retail might have more restaurants and shops per linear foot than anywhere in Southern California. If you have time, make a right or left into the residential area and admire the concentration of Spanish Colonial style architecture built in the 1920s and '30s.

Beautiful Coastal Bluff Cruise - Leaving Belmont Shore (if you can!), make a left on Livingston to connect to Ocean Boulevard - Long Beach's beautiful coastal route. On the left, you'll enjoy great views of the Harbor, the **four man-made oil islands**, the *Queen Mary*, the huge cranes of the Long Beach/LA Harbor, and one of the longest breakwaters on the West Coast. On your right, you'll see excellent examples of the City's vintage architecture - Tudor, Craftsman, and more.

Visit the Museum of Latin American Art (MOLA) - As you approach the skyline of downtown, make a right on Los Alamitos and go six blocks to 628. Founded in 1996, it is the only museum in the US dedicated to Latin American and Latino art. Don't miss the outstanding sculpture garden with its permanent display of over 30 abstract and figurative pieces representing artists from many Latin American countries. The majority of the indoor space is dedicated to special exhibitions.

Lunch - There is an excellent concentration of restaurants in the downtown area bordered by **Pine**, **Long Beach Boulevard**, **3rd** and **1st Streets**. This is where you'll find the highly rated Ammatolí, specializing in Eastern Mediterranean cuisine.

PM: Explore 4th Street Retro Row - If you like vintage clothing, unusual merchandise and unique restaurants, this three-block area between Cherry and Junipero Avenues is a good bet. The stores are small, creative and varied, ranging from street-style to high end. Coffee abounds and the window shopping is great!

Visit Rancho Los Alamitos (6400 Bixby Hill Road) - Located at the top of a hill in a gated subdivision, you'll find this 7.5-acre historic gem. (Just let the security guard know you're visiting the rancho!) It was originally part of a 200,000-acre Spanish land grant in 1804. The **Bixby family** eventually purchased the property in the late 1800s, raising cattle, sheep and wheat. The property contains the Ranch House, Dairy Barn, Blacksmith's Shop, and **historic gardens**, truly representing the atmosphere of rural California. Meet one of the wonderful docents and **tour the Ranch House** with its beautiful period furnishings. The gardens, designed in the 1920s and '30s by the Olmsted Brothers (of Central Park fame) and Florence Bixby herself, include both formal and informal patterns. Don't miss the Cactus Garden and Old Garden, which includes two huge Moreton Bay Fig trees planted in 1890.

The MOLA sculpture garden has received international recognition.

More Long Beach Fun!

1. **Rancho Los Cerritos** - Long Beach's other famous rancho from 1844, this is the largest adobe residence built during the Mexican period. Located in the Bixby Knolls neighborhood, this property was designated a National Historic Landmark in 1970.

2. **Earl Burns Miller Japanese Garden** and the Walter Pyramid on the Cal State Long Beach campus.

3. **Cambodia Town** (Anaheim St. between Atlantic and Junipero Avenues) - Long Beach has the greatest concentration of Cambodians outside of that country. Try the famous beef jerky at Sophy's: Cambodian Town Food Restaurant.

Art Deco beauty in East Village Arts District.

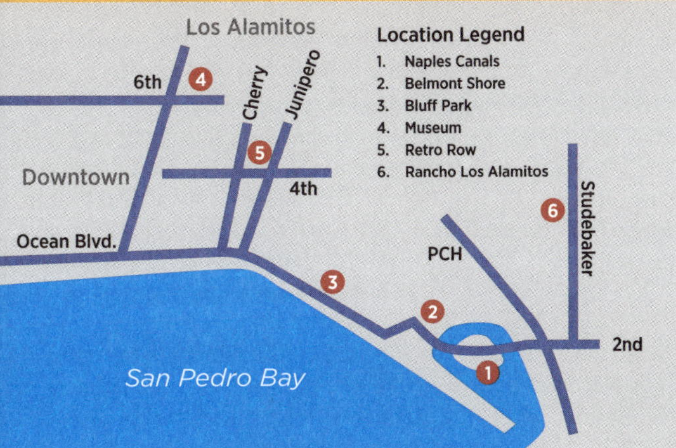

OUTING #33: LA'S HIDDEN GEM ON THE COAST

San Pedro and LA Harbor

San Pedro is just plain interesting. It doesn't seem like part of LA, but it is. Bordering the bustling LA Harbor and sharing some dramatic Palos Verdes Peninsula coastline, this neighborhood is drawing more and more attention. This outing shows you the fascinating variety of this area - part commerce, part nature, and part history. You'll take a short boat tour of the massive LA Harbor, enjoy a picnic by an 1874 lighthouse, and do a nature walk to some World War II bunkers. If you add the small and charming Maritime Museum and Cabrillo Aquarium, you'll have more than a full day.

This beautiful Art Deco mural portrays the tuna that spawned an LA industry.

Background: Located at the southern end of the Palos Verdes Peninsula at the southern end of Los Angeles, the harbor at San Pedro attracted Spanish explorers like Juan Cabrillo and Yankee traders such as Richard Henry Dana. It became the traditional fishing village of Los Angeles and **birthplace of the West Coast tuna industry** in the early 1900s. San Pedro grew rapidly with European immigrants and a large Japanese community on nearby Terminal Island. The City of Los Angeles saw the growth potential of the Harbor area and **annexed San Pedro in 1909**. Today, San Pedro is the largest cargo gateway in North America.

Itinerary:

AM: If you enter San Pedro from the south from Long Beach, you'll have the thrill of crossing two landmark bridges: the new **Gerald Desmond Bridge** – a 550 ft. stayed-cable bridge – and the older, but beautiful **Vincent Thomas Bridge** – a dark turquoise suspension bridge that drops you into San Pedro. Colorful shipping containers, towering cranes, trucks and container ships – feel the energy of one of the biggest transportation hubs in the world!

It's awesome to see the huge container ships enter LA Harbor in San Pedro.

For your morning activity, book a tour of the LA Harbor aboard the **Harbor Breeze Cruises**. This 45-minute narrated cruise is not fancy, but it gets you close to several container ships and takes you around Terminal Island with its federal prison and military housing. Along the dock, take some time to enjoy the **West Harbor** entertainment and shopping complex, which replaced the old Ports O' Call Village. Military buffs will want to tour the **USS *Iowa*** - the largest and final class of Naval battleships – which fought in WWII, the Korean War, and Gulf War of 1991. Docked near the Vincent Thomas Bridge with great views of the Harbor, this is a very interesting look at an engineering marvel of its time.

After your harbor tour, stop at the delightful **Maritime Museum of Los Angeles**. This Streamline Modern building, placed on the National Register of Historic Places (1996), used to serve as the Municipal Ferry Building from 1943 to 1992. The small museum, open from noon to 5:00 pm Thursdays through Sundays, is free, but make sure to leave a donation! As you enter, notice the beautiful Art Deco mosaic depicting the five types of tuna that sustained the fishing industry.

Lunch: You certainly could enjoy the new West Harbor complex, but I recommend one of the most beautiful parks in LA – the **Point Fermin Lighthouse Park**, situated cliffside in western San Pedro and shaded by the huge canopies of the centuries-old Moreton Bay Fig trees. Locals love the sandwiches at Busy Bee if you need a picnic lunch. Make time to take in the Point Fermin Lighthouse, an example of the unusual Victorian Stick Style architecture. Walk or drive to the **Korean Bell of Friendship** in Angel's Gate Park for views of the Pacific, the Palos Verdes Peninsula and Santa Catalina Island.

These massive sea coast batteries were built from 1943 to1945 to protect the LA Harbor during WW II.

PM: For the afternoon, you have two choices – one, a hike through the **White Point Nature Preserve** and to the **World War II bunkers**; the other, a visit to Cabrillo Beach and its delightful aquarium. For the former, park along Paseo del Mar at White Beach State Park and take the loop trail, which winds uphill to the massive World War II bunkers – built to protect the coast from a possible Japanese attack from the sea. The ocean views are expansive, and during spring the native plants are in full bloom. If you love tide pools, White Beach has some of the best in LA County – just make sure it's low tide.

The **Cabrillo Beach** option is only half a mile from Point Fermin Park. Park by the Cabrillo Bathhouse and take a stroll along the beach with access to the San Pedro Breakwater. In the distance, you'll see the iconic **Angel's Gate** – the 1913 lighthouse at breakwater's end. Stroll over to the small and wonderful Cabrillo Aquarium, another donation-based museum dedicated to education and preserving marine life. You'll love the small exhibits and the nursery where the staff is raising baby white abalone to repopulate the coast. San Pedro packs a full submarine sandwich of tastes for the urban explorer!

Pt. Fermin Lighthouse is one of the oldest on the West Coast.

Terminal Island

San Pedro

Location Legend

1. Vincent Thomas Bridge
2. LA Harbor
3. USS Iowa
4. Maritime Museum
5. West Harbor
6. Cabrillo Aquarium
7. Pt. Fermin Lighthouse / Park
8. White Pt. Nature Preserve

Nearby Attractions:

Aquarium of the Pacific – Long Beach – Located at the waterfront in Long Beach Harbor, this extensive aquarium displays marine life in 19 major habitats. You'll want to spend two-to-three-hours here.

HMS *Queen Mary* – It's awesome to board this historic 1,091-foot-long ocean liner and learn about its storied history. The *Queen* is famous for her Art Deco styling from grand ballrooms to etched glass, and her use of 56 types of wood!

Lloyd Wright's Wayfarer's Chapel – A small chapel designed by Lloyd Wright (son of the famous Frank Lloyd Wright) in 1951 for Swedenborgian Church. Made of glass and wood and surrounded by redwoods, the chapel was designated a National Historic Landmark in 2023. Sadly, unstable ground in the area caused the Chapel to be dismantled. Its future was uncertain when this book was written.

OUTING #34: 26 MILES ACROSS THE SEA

Catalina Island Adventure

Catalina is Southern California's island getaway. It's a short, usually smooth (!) boat ride from numerous coastal towns (the Catalina Express *is the shortest ride from Long Beach at one hour). Whether you go for a long day or an extended stay, there's a special feeling to being "Twenty-Six Miles Across the Sea," to quote the Four Preps' classic song. Your main stop is the small and colorful city of Avalon - both beautiful and tourist tacky - nestled in a valley on the southern leeward side of the island. This outing lists a few recommended activities: exploring Avalon and its beautiful casino; taking an eco tour by jeep to the rugged interior; hiking, swimming and snorkeling in the clear waters; and lounging on Descanso Beach with a nice refreshing drink!*

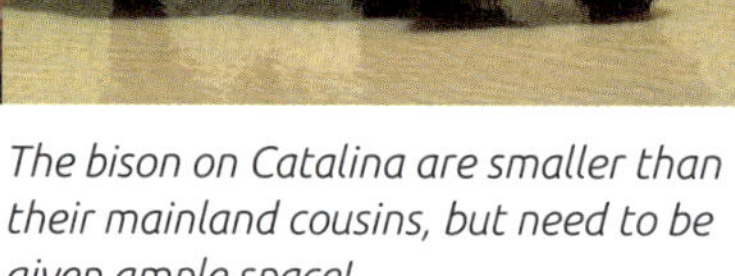

The Avalon Theater's murals are Art Deco on steroids!

The bison on Catalina are smaller than their mainland cousins, but need to be given ample space!

The iconic 1929 Casino building never had gambling. The word means "gathering place" in Italian! Multo bene!

Background: Catalina is one of California's Channel Islands, although not part of **Channel Islands National Park**. It's a rugged, 22-mile long island, with an elevation high of 2,000 feet. 88% of the island is owned by the **Catalina Conservancy** that works to restore the island to its native flora and fauna. Of the 60 endemic species, the most notable is the Catalina Island Fox. This cute predator is much smaller than its mainland cousins due to "insular dwarfism" - the process where animal species become smaller with the reduced food supplies found on islands. The same process can be seen in the island's bison population. They were brought to Catalina in 1924 for a silent film version of the **Zane Grey novel** - *The Vanishing American.* The herd eventually grew to almost 600, but is currently limited to just over 100 to preserve the island's ecosystems.

In 1919, **William Wrigley** purchased development rights to Catalina as well as bringing his team - the Chicago Cubs - to the island for spring training until 1951. The cozy town of **Avalon**, with a population of 3,500, boasts a fun, bayside promenade and numerous landmarks, the most famous being the dramatic 1929 **Mediterranean Revival/Art Deco Casino** where couples danced to Big Band music on one of the country's biggest dance floors. Also of note is Mt. Ada, former Wrigley home and now a bed and breakfast, and the Zane Grey Pueblo Hotel, the former home of the famous Western fiction writer. The island was popular with the Hollywood elite from the 1930s to '50s, and more than 500 films, documentaries and TV programs have been shot here. Expect huge crowds in the summer with all the stops by Catalina ferries and cruise ships. But the water is delightful!

Itinerary:

Here's a list of some of the most popular activities on this wonderful island. Your happy task is to fit them into your schedule.

1. Swimming and Snorkeling - The waters are clear and generally warm on this leeward side of the island. There's great snorkeling at **Casino Point** (follow the wide path to the north of the Casino) where you'll swim around giant kelp forests and copious fish including the goldfish-like garibaldi, sheepshead and bass. Careful! It gets deep quickly. A less crowded snorkel spot is to enter the water at Descanso Beach and follow the coast north.

2. Rent a Golf Cart - Cars are tough to come by here, so renting a golf cart is the hot ticket. Not surprisingly, the main rental shop is right after you get off the ferry! Maps are provided as there are scenic roads climbing the hills on both sides of the valley affording excellent views.

3. Explore Avalon - This is a very walkable town due to its narrow valley setting and small lot sizes, which developed from earlier tent homes. Most of the action centers on Crescent Avenue - the promenade that hugs the bay. Notice the iconic Catalina tiles as you walk around the city. Whether you sign up for a walking tour or take the self-guided approach, make sure you walk a few blocks inland away from the hubbub and toward the golf course - one of the oldest in Southern California. Make sure you visit the **Catalina Island Museum** for beautiful displays on the storied history of the island. Also, visit the **Green Pleasure Pier** where you will find a tourist center and the official weigh station for sports fisherman.

4. Tour the Casino Building - an Art Deco Wonder - William Wrigley wanted to give Catalina a monument from the world's best artisans, and that he did. The circular Mediterranean/Moorish landmark is graced with stunning Art Deco detailing in the exterior ticket lobby, the first floor of the **Avalon Theater**, and its second-floor ballroom. As you approach the exterior ticket lobby, look up to behold the massive, fanciful oceanscape murals designed by John Beckman, an artist who worked on Graumann's Chinese Theatre and numerous Hollywood set designs. These murals transport you to an underwater tropical fantasy, but there's more.

Enter the Avalon Theater and behold the "Art Deco confection" that greets you on all sides. These auditorium murals are a fantasy combination of Greek mythology, early California life, sailing ships and nature, all in reddish and soft purple hues. Go to the second floor to the Ballroom and behold the massive circular dance floor with its ridiculously ornate central light fixture. Wow!

5. Explore the Island - Take a Jeep Eco Tour - To explore nature and the interior of the island, this is an exciting way to go. Run by the **Catalina Island Conservancy**, you'll hop in an open-air Jeep with a trained naturalist and learn how the Conservancy is working to restore the island to its natural state. The island's hills are steep and you'll get some breathtaking views. Nature lovers will love the information about native and invasive species, and you're likely to get up close and personal with a Catalina bison. You can take a two- or three- hour tour. A first-rate experience!

6. Take a Hike - Catalina has over 165 miles of hiking trails, the most dramatic of which is the 38.5-mile **Trans Catalina Trail**. For a shorter experience, take the half-hour hike to the **Wrigley Memorial** and **Botanic Garden**. The Memorial is constructed of local stone and decorated with the famed Catalina Tile.

7. Chill Out at Descanso Beach - Just north of the Casino, this picturesque beach offers food, drink, beach chairs and cabanas for rent. You can rent a kayak here or just soak in the views.

8. Ride the Zip Line Eco Tour - Just up the canyon from Descano Beach, you'll find this thrilling attraction. You'll go from 600 feet to sea level on five separate zip lines, attaining speeds of 35 miles per hour. No wonder this is the island's highest rated activity.

OUTING # 35: MANSIONS, MANUSCRIPTS & LANDSCAPES

Huntington Library and Gardens

This day trip will take you to one of the most beautiful destinations in Southern California. No venue in the region contains such a wide variety of world class art, historic manuscripts and stunning gardens. Of course, it's best to visit in spring with the Rose and Shakespeare Gardens in bloom. Don't worry about leaving the grounds for lunch – you have four great options here. To round out the day and to take advantage of Pasadena's legacy architecture, add a brief car tour of Bungalow Heaven Landmark District with its beautiful concentration of early-twentieth-century craftsman bungalows. These are the cutest and coziest craftsman homes you've ever seen!

The Huntingtons purchased The Blue Boy *for $728,000 in 1921 - $9.3 million in today's dollars!*

Background: **Henry Huntington** was a railroad magnate, real estate promoter, and collector of rare books and manuscripts who married the widow of his famous uncle, Collis Huntington - one of the "Big Four" of western railroading. Henry formed the Southland's famous **Pacific Electric streetcars** (the "Red Cars") - the largest interurban rail system in the world at the time. **Arabella Huntington**, one of the richest women in the world in the early 1900s, was an ardent collector of decorative arts and European art. The couple amassed their collections on the San Marino Ranch and mansion that opened in 1919. The 120-acre property contains three art galleries, a library of historic manuscripts and 16 themed botanical gardens.

Itinerary:

AM: The Huntington can be a bit overwhelming, so don't plan on seeing everything in one day. Nevertheless, here's a good plan:

1) As you first walk in, turn left and take an outdoor stroll through the amazing **Desert Garden**, the best collection of cacti and succulents on the West Coast.

2) As you loop back through the Jungle Garden, visit the **Huntington Art Gallery** (just to the right as you enter) – the beautiful, 1911 Beaux Arts home (by noted architect Myron Hunt) of Henry and Arabella. Here you will find one of the best collections of **British Art** in the nation along with countless objects of decorative arts from the 15th century on. Highlights include Gainsborough's *The Blue Boy*, Lawrences' *Pinkie*, furniture from the Louis XIV & XV period, and **Arts & Crafts designs from William Morris and Company**.

Lunch - You can decide on lunch at either **Café 1919** (near the entrance) or make your way to the **Chinese Garden** for the Freshwater Pavilion or **Jade Court Café** for Asian fare. Of course, you could also make the coveted reservations at the Rose Garden Tea Room!

PM: For your afternoon exploration, visit the western portion of the Huntington - combining the Japanese and Chinese Gardens with the **Scott Galleries of American Art**. Don't miss the restored **Japanese Heritage House** from the Edo Period of the 18th century. On your way, walk through the beautiful Rose and Shakespeare Gardens. The Scott Galleries include such notables as Frank Lloyd Wright, Edward Hopper, Andy Warhol and Charles and Henry Greene, along with exhibits on American folk art.

For your last stop, visit the Library with its rare manuscripts, archival collections of American history, and research facility. Highlights include the **Gutenberg Bible** (1455), **Audubon's *Birds of America***, and poetry holdings from Chaucer and Shakespeare. Finally, you may want to shop at the amazing **Huntington Store**. Its huge variety of items is almost as beautiful as the Huntington itself. Why are museum stores so tasteful? Oh, well, a very good thing!

Over a century old, the Japanese Garden has been a place of beauty and contemplation.

Hidden Gem – Well, there are many, but here's a favorite: Visit the stunning **Mausoleum** of Henry and Arabella. This marble, Roman-Revival monument was designed by John Russell Pope. This architect also designed the Thomas Jefferson Memorial in Washington, DC. You'll immediately see the similarities with the rounded dome supported by classical columns. Jefferson admired Roman architecture as is evident in his design for his Monticello home and the University of Virginia. The style is even called **Jeffersonian Classicism**.

Afternoon Visit - **Bungalow Heaven Landmark District** - Graceful Pasadena has over 15 historic districts, and Bungalow Heaven Landmark District is its most famous. Here you will find 800 modest craftsman bungalows built in the early 1900s, many in the Arts and Crafts style and built from mail-order kits. The neighborhood became Pasadena's first Landmark Historic District in 1989, was placed on the National Register of Historic Places and was named one of **"the 10 great places in America"** by the American Planning Association. As you cruise the leafy neighborhood, notice the wood detailing, prominent porches and gable roofs. Bungalow Heaven has Annual Home Tours every spring and it's fun to see the craftsman detailing inside these wonderful homes. Bungalow Heaven is located above the 210 Freeway between Orange Grove Blvd., Lake, Hill and Washington Streets. The best concentration of homes is found on Mar Vista and Michigan Streets.

The single room on the second story makes this an "Airplane Bungalow," popular in the early 1900s.

Nearby Attractions:

- **Norton Simon Art Museum**
- **Gamble House**
- **Old Town Pasadena**

OUTING #36: CRAFTSMAN CLASSIC

Gamble House and Norton Simon Museum

Not only is Pasadena a major cultural destination, it has some of the most beautiful historic neighborhoods in Southern California. This outing combines two of its finest venues: the Gamble House, a masterwork of the Craftsman Bungalow style, and the Norton Simon Art Museum, one of the nation's finest private collections of European masterworks. Book a morning guided tour of the Gamble House, have lunch in nearby Old Town Pasadena, then spend a delightful afternoon enjoying Impressionist and European art in a very manageable museum. All three of these venues are only one mile apart. The Norton Simon is closed on Tuesdays and Wednesdays, so plan accordingly. If you have time to explore some of Pasadena's 15 historic districts, see Outing # 37 - Pasadena Architectural Highlights.

Notice the exposed rafters, sleeping porch, "clinker" brick and craftsman lamp at the Gamble House's back veranda.

Background: Pasadena was born in 1875, founded by winter-weary folks from Indiana who loved the temperate climate. At the same time, the **Arts and Crafts movement**, which rejected the machine-age designs of the Industrial Revolution in favor of natural, hand-made materials, was reaching its peak. When the architecture team of brothers **Charles** and **Henry Greene** opened up shop in Pasadena, the Craftsman Bungalow style took off. Featuring gabled roofs, exposed joints, decorative roof beams, and large porches with river rock pillars, the craftsman bungalow was perfect for the Southern California climate. The homes could be modest - built from a Sears and Roebuck bungalow kit for $675 - or more high style, featuring **Batchelder tiles** and **Stickley furniture**. Regardless, craftsman-style homes proliferated until 1920 when the style fell out of favor. Today, Pasadena is a leader in historic preservation, having designated 15 historic districts. Nowhere else in the US will you see more and varied Craftsman bungalows. For aficionados of the style, visit Bungalow Heaven Landmark District (see previous outing).

Adaptive reuse in action - an Art Deco building from the 1920s converted to retail spaces in Old Town.

Itinerary:

AM: Visit The Gamble House. Built in 1908 by Henry and Charles Greene for David and Mary Gamble of Procter & Gamble fame, this magnificent home is **"architecture as art."** The Greenes designed every feature of the home - from the light fixtures, rugs, furniture, landscaping and leaded glass entry door. Even the bedroom furniture featured inlaid mother of pearl. Although the interior lighting is dim, the sleeping porches and backyard veranda embrace the outdoors. Look for Japanese design details, as the Greene brothers were influenced by visiting two World Fairs (Chicago and St. Louis). No wonder the Gamble House was designated a National Historic Landmark in 1978. If you want a quick walking tour, visit adjacent **Arroyo Terrace Historic District**, home to nine Greene & Greene homes.

Lunch - Old Town Pasadena. Pasadena also set the standard for how to build an Old Town. Instead of tearing down their early 20th century architecture, they used it to create a distinct sense of place. The City hired an urban design firm to create design guidelines as well as building peripheral parking structures to avoid having to build surface parking lots. The center of Old Town is **Colorado Boulevard** and **Fair Oaks Avenue**. Excellent restaurants and stores abound, and make sure to explore the alleyways of Old Town with their public art and outdoor seating. Comfortable public space, attractive architecture, convenient access, and specialty retail are a formula for happy pedestrians!

This 1633 still life by Spanish master Zurbarán is considered a masterpiece of the genre.

PM: Norton Simon Museum. At the corner of Colorado Boulevard and Orange Grove, you'll find one of California's best art museums. Industrialist Norton Simon (1907—1933) amassed a stellar collection of European art from the Renaissance to the 20th century, featuring artists such as **Zurbarán**, **Rembrandt**, **Goya**, **Gauguin**, **van Gogh**, **Degas**, **Renoir**, **Picasso** and **Ruscha**. Downstairs you'll find a large collection of South and Southeast Asian painting and sculpture that spans a 2,000-year period. This is a perfectly sized museum, and the outdoor sculpture garden and café provide a scenic place to relax.

The leaded glass front door features a Japanese Black Pine.

The Gamble House was designated a National Historic Landmark in 1978.

Nearby Attractions:

- **Bungalow Heaven Landmark District**- Just north of the 210 Freeway in east Pasadena, you'll find a charming, 16-block, turn-of-the-century neighborhood with one of the highest concentrations of small craftsman bungalows in the US. The district was named one of American's 10 Great Places by the American Planning Association.

- **Huntington Library and Gardens** - In nearby San Marino, the Huntington combines spectacular gardens, art museums, and a world renown library of rare manuscripts and books (see Outing #35). There are twelve themed gardens, including the stunning Desert, Chinese and Japanese Gardens. The art includes British, American and Asian pieces housed in Henry and Arabella's 1912 Beaux Arts mansion.

- **LA County Arboretum and Botanic Garden** - Located on 127 acres in nearby Santa Anita, the Arboretum is a great stop for garden and history lovers with extensive themed gardens and historic structures. Created on land from the original Mexican Rancho Santa Anita, it has several historic structures, including the very picturesque "Lucky" Baldwin Queen Anne Cottage and Coach Barn. Sited next to a small lake surrounded by palm trees, it's no wonder this ornate home was featured in many movies and television programs, most notably *Fantasy Island*.

OUTING #37: DRIVE-BY BEAUTIES

Pasadena Architectural Highlights

Pasadena is much more than the Rose Parade on New Year's Day. This proud city actually has some of the best-preserved historic buildings in California and has designated fifteen historic districts. If you love architecture and want to see some of the most beautiful, period-revival residential neighborhoods anywhere, try this outing. Remember that Pasadena also has some impressive municipal structures and world-class educational institutions. Make sure you have a navigator and don't worry if you don't see everything. You can always come back.

Background: With its balmy climate and lush gardens, Pasadena was a popular winter destination in the late 1800s for snowbirds from the Midwest. The wealthy built large mansions here designed by famous architects such as brothers **Charles** and **Henry Greene**, **Myron Hunt**, **Wallace Neff**, **Frank Lloyd Wright** and **Sylvanus Marston**. The Depression took its toll on many buildings, but, over time, the citizenry and the nonprofit group Pasadena Heritage fought to save many of its architectural treasures.

Itinerary: Start downtown at . . .

#1 Pasadena City Hall (100 N. Garfield) - This 1927 Beaux Arts style building with its Spanish Baroque detailing and 200-foot dome is one of the most beautiful city halls in Southern California. Walk through the courtyard and fountain and, across the street, check out the large bronze sculptures of local heroes Jackie and Mack Robinson. If you walk east through the courtyard, you'll come to the cool **Postmodern Plaza Las Fuentes** with its fountains and decorative tiles.

#2 Cahill Center for Astronomy (1216 E. California Blvd.) - A fittingly modern design from 2009. By the way, the campus of **California Institute of Technology (Cal Tech)** is an architectural treasure. Early Mission, Spanish and Art Deco designs from 1910 gave way to some great modern buildings.

#3 Broad Center for Biological Sciences (360 S. Wilson) - Clad in travertine and steel, this building's varied massing makes for a lively design in the NW corner of Cal Tech.

#4 Beckman Auditorium (center of Cal Tech campus) - An Islamic-influenced design by **Edward Durell** Stone; resembles some of late work of Frank Lloyd Wright.

#5 Prairie Style Home - Madison Avenue Historic District (1011 S. Madison) - Prairie-style home by famous Pasadena architect Sylvanus Marston. The district contains three blocks of immaculate, period revival homes (Colonial, Dutch and Spanish) mixed in with some craftsman bungalows. Not far away is the landmark **Blacker House** (1177 Hillcrest Ave.) - the most lavish craftsman bungalow by the Greene & Greene architects. The neighborhood is an architectural treasure.

#6 Bubble House (1097 S. Los Robles) - Architect Wallace Neff inflated a balloon, covered it with chicken wire and sprayed it with gunite. The idea was to promote affordability, but the idea never got off the ground!

#7 Wrigley Mansion (391 S. Orange Grove Ave.) This 1914 Italian Renaissance-style mansion was the home of chewing-gum baron William Wrigley Jr. It has 21 rooms and is home to the **Tournament of Roses Association**.

#8 Gamble House (4 Westmoreland Place) - Designed for David and Mary Gamble of Procter & Gamble in 1908, this is the premier example of the high-style craftsman bungalow. The Greene brothers designed everything - from furniture, light fixtures and carpets. Described as "architecture as art," it was designated a **National Historic Landmark** in 1978.

#9 Millard House (645 Prospect Crescent) - This 1923 home, Frank Lloyd Wright's only Pasadena commission, is an example of the experimental **"textile block" technique**.

#10 Art Center College of Design (1700 Lida St.) Hidden in the hills to the west of the Arroyo Seco and Rose Bowl, this is a beautiful example of modernism by **Craig Ellwood** that doesn't ruin the natural landscape.

#11 Castle Green (99 S. Raymond Ave.) - This 1898 annex to Hotel Green combines Moorish, Victorian and Spanish styles. It has been converted to condos, with public rooms for special events.

Further Exploration

- Explore West Pasadena along Orange Grove, Grand Ave. and S. Arroyo Boulevard
- Learn more about historic preservation through the Pasadena Heritage website

Beckman Auditorium (1963).

Cahill Center (2009).

Castle Green (1898).

Bubble House (1946).

Broad Center for Biological Sciences (2002).

Art Center College of Design (1977).

OUTING #38: PLANETS & PLANTS

Jet Propulsion Laboratory and Descanso Gardens

A visit to Jet Propulsion Laboratory (JPL) - the world's leading facility for planetary exploration - is both inspiring and humbling. It's fascinating to see where the spacecraft are built and what they have discovered. You will have to book the three-hour tour in advance on the "jpl.nasa.gov" website, and the competition for reservations is intense. Combine this celestial experience with a visit to nearby Descanso Gardens, a 150-acre botanical garden in La Cañada Flintridge, famous for its camellia gardens and coast live oak forest. Since most JPL group tours are in the afternoon, visit the Gardens in the morning, have lunch in La Cañada Flintridge, and then visit JPL.

Voyager's famous 1977 Golden Record meant to represent Earth to extraterrestrial life who might encounter it.

Background: JPL has explored our solar system and beyond for more than 80 years. It was founded in 1938 by Caltech rocket scientists and was originally funded by the US Army. It evolved to concentrate on unmanned space exploration and is currently **managed by Caltech** and federally **funded by NASA**. JPL's spacecraft have explored every planet, the sun, and even interstellar space, searching for conditions that support life. It was a JPL-engineered mission - Voyager 1 - that turned its camera on the infamous pale blue dot of Earth from 3.7 billion miles away. Closer to home, JPL spacecraft, science instruments, and airborne missions help humanity study and track climate change, manage natural resources, monitor water resources and respond to disasters. This wonderful facility has been lovingly called ***"Disneyland for Nerds!"***

Itinerary:

Jet Propulsion Laboratory - All public, educational tours are conducted by JPL's Public Service Office - very knowledgeable guides who are also Caltech employees. The tour includes the following highlights:

- a multi-media film entitled *Journey to the Planets and Beyond* with amazing photos of the latest research about our solar system;
- the **Von Karman Visitor Center** with displays of the spacecraft that have conducted so many famous missions;
- the **Spacecraft Assembly Facility** - the "Clean Room" - where the Mars Rovers and other spacecraft are assembled;
- the **Spaceflight Operations Facility** where spacecraft are monitored as they transmit data to Earth. This "mission control" facility has monitored all interplanetary and deep space exploration for NASA since 1964. With such famous missions as Voyager and Cassini Saturn orbiter, it was declared a National Historic Landmark in 1985.

JPL optics for the Hubble Space and James Webb telescopes have brought deep space into greater focus.

The JPL Campus is quite interesting in itself, with over 60 buildings - many of mid-century design - sitting at the base of the steep San Gabriel Mountains. On the JPL website, you'll find awesome images from current and past missions, including views of deep space from the **James Webb Telescope**. If you can't book a public tour and are interested in space exploration, definitely check out JPL's excellent virtual tour at: **jpl.nasa.gov/virtual-tour**.

JPL's Cassini probe was the first spacecraft to orbit Saturn where it discovered scores of new moons.

Top right: The Juno spacecraft, the farthest traveling solar-powered vehicle, relays information about Jupiter.

Descanso Gardens, La Cañada / Flintridge: This beautiful botanic garden is only ten minutes from JPL. Here you will find winding paths through cultivated and semiwild groves, most notably the massive 100-foot-tall Coast Live Oaks. As you enter the garden, the **Japanese Garden and Ancient Forest** will be on your left. Straight ahead and slightly to the right are the extensive **Camellia Gardens**. Take the forest walk up the hill to the Boddy Mansion, a 22-room estate design by "architect to the stars" James Dolena in the Hollywood Regency style. To the right is the **Rose Garden**, **Promenade**, **Oak Woodland**, and **California Garden** with native plantings. Check the website for what's in bloom and special events. Peak season for the camellia bloom is December through February. A popular holiday event is the **Enchanted Forest of Light** when special light installations make the gardens come alive after dark.

Descanso is home, in fact, to North America's largest camellia collection whose backstory is particularly sad. The original property owner - E. Manchester Boddy - was able to buy the nursery stock of camellias at a very low price because three prominent Japanese growers were forced to sell prior to their internment by the US government during World War II. Research by the Garden's staff is attempting to give credit to the original Japanese America growers with specialized markers. There are over **700 species of camellias** at Descanso that do well in the shade of the huge evergreen Live Oaks.

OUTING #39: MIDWEST CHARM CITY

Graceful South Pasadena

Little South Pasadena is like a Midwest town located within the sprawl of LA County. Many of its neighborhoods are so charming, in fact, that it is often the choice of movie and TV film crews. The relative lack of palm trees and Spanish Colonial architecture belies the fact that it is indeed in Southern California. Yes, it is the smaller sister of impressive Pasadena, but if you like a slower pace, tree-lined streets, early 1900s architecture, and a fun transit village, this is a great place to explore for half a day.

Background: Incorporated in 1888 during the **"Grand Resort Era"** of the Pasadena area, South Pasadena was able to attract tourists with its opulent Raymond Hotel, Cawston Ostrich Farm, and Pacific Electric "Red Car" Trolley. Much of the town was built before the widespread use of cars and modern zoning, creating pedestrian-friendly streetscapes not dominated by front-facing garages. Amazingly, about 40% of the town consists of pre-1930s development - first with Victorian and Craftsman homes and then Period Revivals (Colonial and Tudor styles). New residential construction was limited for over 40 years while the city successfully **fought the extension of the 710 (Long Beach Freeway)** through its center. For a town of only 25,000, South Pasadena has an impressive number of local historic landmarks (50 designated; 1,975 potential) and historic districts (5 designed; 39 potential!).

Exposed roof rafters, overhanging eaves and large porches are typical of the Craftsman style.

Irving Gill's 1911 Miltimore Home uses simplified forms to embrace outdoor living.

Itinerary:

Almost anywhere you drive in "South Pas," you will find century-old, well-maintained architecture. But here are the best spots to explore.

1. Explore southeastern So. Pas: Start your architectural car tour in front of South Pasadena High School on 1401 Fremont Ave. The high school was built in 1939 during the New Deal in the **Art Deco/Streamline Moderne style** with Public Works Administration funding. Go south on Fremont, turn left on Oak and go four blocks to make a left on Milan Ave. You'll love the Colonial Revival, Craftsman, Tudor and Spanish Colonial on this street. One block east on Chelten Way is a real gem - the 1911 Miltimore residence by **Irving Gill** (1301 Chelten Way). Gill was one of California's first modernists, simplifying Mission and Spanish Colonial styles by using flat roofs, rectangular forms and ground-level arches. Much of his early work is found in San Diego, a city that holds him in very high esteem! Next, cruise **Bushnell St.** between Oak and Huntington Drive. Here you will see an almost continuous street of Craftsman bungalows and a gorgeous overhead tree canopy. Not surprisingly, this is where scenes from *Back to the Future* were filmed.

Notice the horizontal emphasis of this Prairie Style beauty in the Oaklawn Historic District.

2. Walk the block of mansions on historic Oaklawn Avenue: Find Oaklawn Avenue between Fremont and Fair Oaks. Enter from Columbia St., park your car and take a delightful stroll. Admire the arroyo-stone entrance portals designed by the illustrious Charles and Henry Greene of craftsman architecture fame. They also designed the bridge at the end of the street. Almost every home is an architectural gem. Of particular note is the 1908 Craftsman bungalow at 217 purchased by Theodore Roosevelt's Vice President, Charles Fairbanks. On the other side of the street, find the beautiful Prairie-style (thank you Frank Lloyd Wright!) home with its horizontally projecting eaves. Another masterpiece is the massive English Tudor residence at 423 Oaklawn, which served as the Pasadena Showcase Home for 2022.

3. Visit SP's transit village and vintage pharmacy: **Fair Oaks Pharmacy** at the corner of Mission and Fair Oaks is home to a beautifully restored 1915 Soda Fountain. Across the street is **Gus's BBQ**, a South Pasadena institution with great food. Continue west on Mission St. to SP's original downtown. Park your car near Meridian Street and check out a true "transit village" - **Mission West**.

LA Metro's Gold Line stops here and here you'll find cafés, specialty retail shops, and original, two-story brick, commercial buildings. The whole idea of this type of "transit-oriented development" is to locate mixed uses near train or bus stops, creating a vibrant neighborhood. As you explore the district, is Mission West a success?

4. Cruise El Centro Street from Fremont to Pasadena Ave.: To get your last flavor of this quaint town, drive along El Centro Avenue west from Fremont. You'll start with the classic, New Deal, Spanish-style Post Office (1935) and Mediterranean-Revival Public Library (1930). Enjoy the tree-lined residential streets with their small craftsman and Victorian cottages. It's remarkable that this town has preserved the character of so many historic neighborhoods with so few modern intrusions.

Camphor trees create a beautiful canopy on Bushnell St.

Mission West, with its light rail Gold Line stop, is a great example of "transit-oriented development" or TOD.

Nearby Attractions:

- **Gamble House - Tour this Craftsman home and National Historic Landmark**
- **Norton Simon Art Museum - Region's best collection of Impressionist art**
- **Huntington Library and Gardens - Art, botanical gardens and historic manuscripts**

Craftsman architects Greene and Greene created this arroyo stone entrance portal on Oaklawn Ave.

OUTING # 40: FIRST IN CLASS!

Claremont Village and Colleges

This outing highlights the Southland's most delightful college town - Claremont - along with its famous colleges. Dubbed the "City of Trees and PhDs," Claremont hosts a comfortable, walkable downtown village next to five renowned colleges containing world-class art and architecture. This adventure recommends a morning walking tour through the colleges, lunch in the Village, and an afternoon visit to the nearby California Botanical Garden. You will find a great map online at "transitinglosangeles/claremont," and you can access this delightful town by train using the Metrolink San Bernardino Line. You can also explore the town online at "discoverclaremont.com."

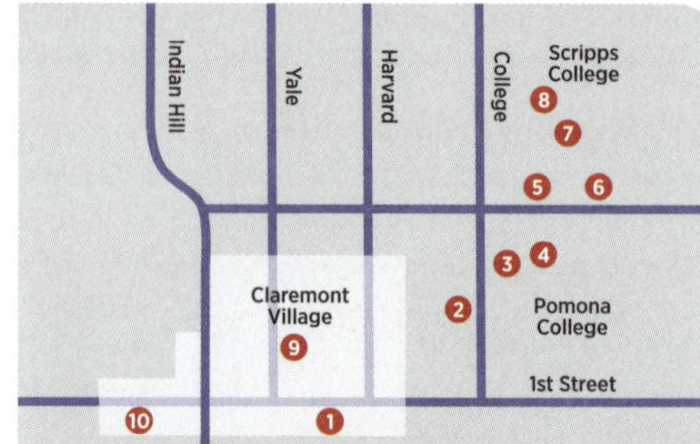

Location Legend

1. Train Depot
2. Benton Museum
3. Bridges Music Hall
4. Bridges Auditorium
5. Turrell Skyspace
6. Prometheus
7. Kravis Center
8. Margaret Fowler Garden
9. Folk Music Center
10. Packing House

Background: Claremont was founded in the late 1800s with the introduction of the Southern Pacific Railroad. The early 1900s saw the growth of **Pomona** and **Scripps College**, attracting prominent architects and artists. The additions of **Harvey Mudd**, **Claremont McKenna** and **Pitzer Colleges** transformed Claremont into one of the most notable college towns in the country. City leaders managed to grow and maintain a gracious, small-scale downtown with wide sidewalks, sittable space and great stores and restaurants. People who live, visit and work here love this town, and you'll notice the pride of place everywhere you turn.

Itinerary:

AM: Claremont / Pomona College Walking Tour - This is a beautiful, 1.5-mile walk through some of the most beautiful campuses in the US. The distinctive architecture is no surprise as college campuses usually do not have to follow local zoning regulations and often have the space and money to attract great urban designers and architects. The walk through these leafy campuses is gorgeous, but you may want to call ahead to access the museums and murals mentioned below.

1) Start your tour at the ornate 1920s Spanish Colonial Revival **Claremont Metrolink Station** on First Street. Here you will find the small Claremont Lewis Art Museum open Friday through Sunday.

2) Walk one block east on First Street; turn left on College Avenue. In 1.5 blocks on the left, you'll find **Pomona College's Benton Museum of Art**. The museum is free and has some wonderful exhibitions.

3) Continue north on College Ave. where Victorian and neoclassical buildings have been converted to college offices. Two blocks up from the museum, you'll notice the striking neoclassical **Carnegie Hall**. To your right is the parklike **Marston Quad** flanked by redwood trees. Enter the Quad on the right side and view **Bridges Hall of Music** (1915) by renowned architect Myron Hunt. It resembles a triumphal arch with classical and Spanish detailing. At the end of the quad is the **Bridges Auditorium** (1931) with Romanesque detailing on the outside and Art Deco detailing and frescoes inside.

Pomona College boasts the best free light show at dawn and dusk.

4) Turn left in front of the auditorium, cross Sixth Street and enter the courtyard of the buildings on your left. Here you will find light and perception **artist James Turrell's** stunning ***Skyspace***. Turrell's metal canopy frames a window to the sky visible from the benches below. It's worth seeing any time of day but especially at dawn and dusk when the canopy is bathed in a series of vivid colors, contrasting with the changing sky beyond. Turrell's *Skyspaces* are world-famous, and this is the only one in Southern California. If you visit later in the day, enjoy this **free light show at sunset** and then dinner in the Village.

5) If you're a fan of Mexican muralists, make arrangements to see ***Prometheus*** (1931) by **José Clemente Orozco**. It's the first Mexican mural painted in the US and is located in the Frary Dining Hall of Pomona College off of Sixth Street. If classes are in session, you may have to make an appointment, but the dramatic mural is well worth the effort. Orozco was one of **"los Tres Grandes"** ("the Three Great Ones") along with artists **Diego Rivera** and **David Siqueiros**.

The Kravis Center, with its glass "Kube" floating on a black granite reflecting pool, is the best in contemporary design.

6) Continue north to the contemporary **Kravis Center** of Claremont/McKenna College on Columbia Avenue. This beautiful piece of contemporary architecture, with its "floating" cube study area and sustainable design, won awards for the best collegiate design in 2011.

7) Walk north on Columbia Avenue and enter the Scripps College quad on your right. Designed by architect Gordon Kaufman, the gorgeous Spanish Colonial architecture dates from the 1920s. This graceful campus has many beautiful courtyards, but the crown jewel is the "agrarian deco" mural – ***The Flower Vendors*** (1947) - in the **Margaret Fowler Garden**, by **Andres Ramos Martinez**. This muralist was one of Mexico's finest and another example of how the Claremont Colleges became an art mecca.

The 100-foot-long mural by Ramos Martinez is a Scripps College hidden gem.

8) By now you're hungry. Walk back to the Village by going west on10th Street and south on Yale. Enjoy the tree-lined streets and craftsman homes.

Lunch in the Village – Stroll delightful Claremont Village along Yale Avenue for unique shopping and dining. It has over 150 unique shops and restaurants and the Inland Empire's largest Farmers and Artisans Market on Sundays. Make sure to visit the wonderful **Claremont Folk Music Center and Museum** – owned by the Harper Family (of Grammy fame) for over 50 years. The Center sells guitars, gives lessons, hosts folk music concerts and is a regional treasure. A visit to Some Crust Bakery is a must, and The Cheese Cave is a town favorite. Two blocks east on First Street is the popular **Claremont Packing House** with Eureka Burgers and Gus's BBQ.

Afternoon – You can certainly enjoy the afternoon in the Village, but a nice add-on is a visit to the **California Botanical Garden** - located just north of Claremont Village at 1500 N. College Ave. This is the largest botanic garden in the state dedicated to native plants and exhibits over 2,000 plant species found from the Oregon border to Baja, California.

A visit to the Folk Music Center and its talented staff is a Claremont Village highlight.

Nearby Attractions:

- **Sam Maloof Foundation** - Unique home of master woodworker
- **American Museum of Ceramic Art** - Pomona

OUTING # 41: MASTERS OF WOOD & CLAY

Sam Maloof Foundation and the American Museum of Ceramic Art

This outing is great for those who admire woodworking, ceramics or art in general. These two venues near the border of LA and San Bernardino Counties are truly hidden gems. The Sam Maloof Foundation, located in Alta Loma at the base of the San Gabriel Mountains, is the beautiful home and workshop of the most famous furniture craftsman of the 20th Century. AMOCA (American Museum of Ceramic Art) in downtown Pomona is the largest institution in the US devoted to ceramic arts. Both museums are open Fridays and Saturdays, and you'll need to book a docent-led tour for Maloof. Lunch in Claremont Village is a great way to break up the day.

Itinerary:

AM: Sam Maloof Foundation: You'll love the beautiful location of the home, workshop, gardens and galleries. Book a morning tour and give yourself at least two hours for a tour and free time to explore the special exhibition gallery and gardens. Sam Maloof began designing and creating furniture in the 1950s, and his flowing, organic shapes won him international fame and the MacArthur Foundation Genius Grant. The tour takes you through his home and workshop where his design creativity is on display.

The Jacobs Education Gallery has unique pieces of woodworking art.

Lunch: It's only a 15-minute drive to **Claremont Village** for great restaurant options. From there, it's another 15 minutes to the ceramic museum in Pomona.

PM: American Museum of Ceramic Art (AMOCA) - This highly-regarded museum has over 7,000 pieces of ceramic art. Among its permanent collection is work from Mettlach, Germany, of the 1800s, along with exquisite Art Nouveau pieces and a beer stein library. There are extensive contemporary pieces on display and make sure to check the website for the current and future exhibitions. Some of the nation's most famous ceramic artists display their work here, and visitors are amazed at what can be created from clay. Interestingly, the museum has an added artistic bonus - a **77-foot mural** commissioned by the former tenant of the building - Pomona First Federal Bank. One of the artists - **Milliard Sheets** - is famous for his over-100 glass mosaics that graced Home Savings (now Chase Banks) throughout the Southland.

Art Nouveau piece from AMOCA's permanent collection.

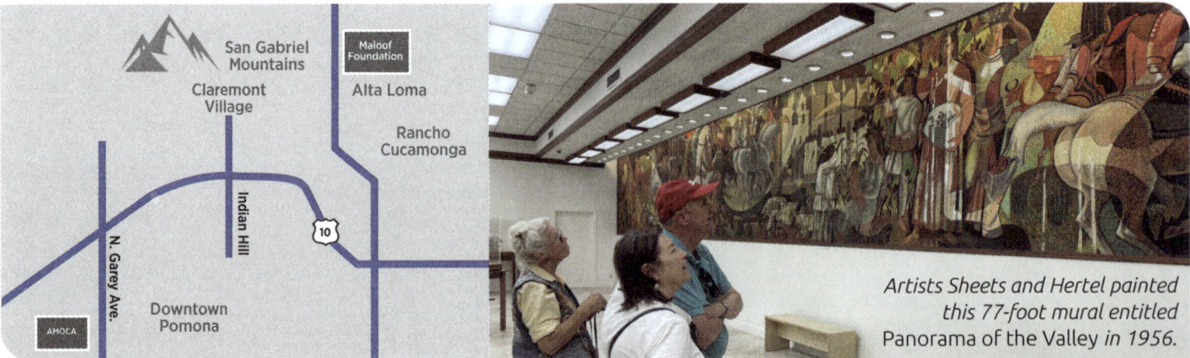

Artists Sheets and Hertel painted this 77-foot mural entitled Panorama of the Valley *in 1956.*

OUTING #42: OF TEMPLES & MAIN STREETS

Hindu Mandir and Glendora Village

This outing combines the exotic with a delightful slice of Americana. A morning visit to the BAPS Mandir, a Hindu place of worship in Chino Hills, is both educational and awe inspiring. You'll marvel at the intricately carved temple and have a chance to observe a ritual showing of sacred images. Then a 20-minute drive will take you to one of Southern California's best main streets in the Glendora Village. During lunch, you can stroll the specialty shops and restaurants of Glendora Avenue with its distinctive "gum drop" trees. For your afternoon activity, you can visit the unique Rubel Castle or take a downtown walking tour.

Background: A mandir is a Hindu place of worship. The **BAPS Mandir** in Chino Hills was inaugurated in 2012, part of a worldwide organization promoting spirituality, humanitarian services and family unity. It is one of only six hand-carved stone mandirs in the US and embodies the strong tradition of Hindu art and architecture. Hindus comprise just over 1% of the US population, with the largest concentrations found in New York, New Jersey, Northern California and Houston.

With its distinctive "gum drop" trees and great retail, Glendora Avenue is one cool main street!

Glendora's motto - "Pride of the Foothills" - describes the town's strong identity. Incorporated in 1911, it has grown from a small community of citrus farmers to an urban population of over 50,000. With a distinctive downtown Village, a nearby historic district, and over 16,000 City-maintained trees, Glendora is a great town to visit.

Itinerary:

AM: BAPS Mandir - As you enter the Visitor's Center, you will immediately notice the two-story, intricately carved teak atrium. Look closely and you will see images of peacocks - the national bird of India - along with elephants, revered as sacred symbols. Walk outside and up the steps into the Mandir. Your first view inside will take your breath away! Thousands of minutely carved, **white Italian Carrara marble** figures and symbols decorate the ceilings, walls and columns. Try to time your entry for 11:15 AM to view the short daily ritual as the sacred images of Hindu deities are revealed. As you leave the Mandir, check out the Souvenir Shop and cafeteria at the Visitor's Center.

Lunch and PM: Glendora Village - (use 224 N. Glendora Ave. for directions) Locals call it **"The Avenue"** - three blocks of specialty restaurants and stores on Glendora Ave., just north of Foothill Boulevard. With parallel parking, shade trees, and a continuous line of shops, this is a classic, comfortable main street. You can take a historic walking tour that starts from Glendora Avenue and moves east. You won't even have to move your car! Type in **"Glendora Walking Tour"** on your device and you'll find the map and descriptions of a wide variety of historic buildings from Victorian to Craftsman to Italianate styles. Another option is to visit the unusual **Rubel Castle** - an amazing piece of folk architecture built by Michael Rubel from 1956 to 1986. Using river rock, recycled materials and relics from Glendora's agricultural past, he achieved his dream of creating a truly unique landmark. Glendora is proud to have created such a beautiful and charming city. Why not top off your visit with a stop at the iconic **Donut Man** on Route 66?

San Gabriel Mtns.
Foothill Blvd.
Route 66
210
57
Glendora Ave.
10
71
Chino Hills

Location Legend
1. Baps Hindu Temple
2. Glendora Village

OUTING # 43: LANDMARKS ALONG THE MOTHER ROAD

ROUTE 66

Famous Route 66 travels 2,448 miles from Chicago to the Pacific Coast, entering California at the Mojave Desert Preserve and ending at the Santa Monica Pier. This outing focuses on fun landmarks along the route from San Bernardino to points west. Choose any stretch of interest or go all the way to the terminus. A good option is to download the app "Ultimate Route 66 Guide" or use the excellent guide at www.roadtrip.com/route66/california. *Navigate with caution, and get your kicks on Route 66!*

Background: Route 66 was completed in 1926 and completely paved by 1938. First immortalized in Steinbeck's novel *The Grapes of Wrath* in 1939, the **"Mother Road"** soared in popularity in the 1950s with more leisure travelers, auto camps, motels, and roadside diners.

Itinerary: Route 66 follows several major boulevards as you travel west: Foothill, Huntington, Colorado, Sunset, and Santa Monica. It's a veritable "Who's Who" of classic roadways!

1. McDonald's Museum (1398 N. E St, San Bernardino) - Site of the first McDonald's restaurant opened in 1940. Largest collection of pre Roy Kroc memorabilia anywhere. The first mascot was **Speedee, not Ronald!** Check out the nearby 1928 **California Theatre of the Performing Arts** (562 W. 4th), with Art Deco and Churrigueresque detailing and the original Wurlitzer organ.

2. Wigwam Motel (2728 E. Foothill Blvd.) Built in 1949, its 19 iconic rooms actually resemble teepees, not wigwams. Regardless, this famous example of roadside architecture was placed on the National Register of Historic Places.

3. The Donut Man (915 E. Route 66, Glendora) - Opened in 1972 and famous for its famous Fresh Strawberry Donut. Glendora's Big Tree Park is nearby.

4. Aztec Hotel (311 W. Foothill Boulevard Monrovia) - One of few SoCal examples of **Mayan/Aztec Revival (1924)**. Check out the fun bar.

5. Pasadena City Hall (100 Garfield Ave., Pasadena) - A 1927 Italian Renaissance beauty just off Colorado Boulevard. You'll also find **Vroman's Bookstore** at 695 E. Colorado - open since 1894!

6. Fair Oaks Pharmacy (1526 Mission Ave., South Pasadena) - Classic soda fountain since 1915. Across the street is Gus's BBQ, a great lunch stop.

7. Arroyo Seco Parkway (aka, Pasadena Freeway 110) - California's first freeway will drop you in downtown LA. Narrow, curvy lanes and stop signs at on-ramps make this a picturesque nail biter! Route 66 moves west from downtown's Olvera Street through the hip Echo Park and Silver Lake neighborhoods.

8. Hollywood Forever Cemetery (6000 Santa Monica Blvd.) - Resting place for many Hollywood stars including Rudolph Valentino and Judy Garland. **Paramount Studios** sits just south of the property.

9. Beverly Hills Sign - Route 66 follows Santa Monica Boulevard west through West Hollywood and Beverly Hills. Rodeo Drive shopping is on your left!

10. Santa Monica Pier - You made it! Park your car near the pier and take a selfie at the **"End of the Trail"** sign. Malibu is to the north, Venice to the south, and more adventures await.

Fun Fact: Route 66's shortest state route is its 13.2 mile slice through southeastern Kansas. Don't blink! You may be in Oklahoma!

Location Legend

1. McDonald's Museum
2. Wigwam Motel
3. Donut Man
4. Aztec Hotel
5. Pasadena City Hall
6. Fair Oaks Pharmacy
7. Arroyo Seco Fwy. (110)
8. Hollywood Forever
9. Beverly Hills Sign
10. Santa Monica Pier

4 3

Glendora

2 1

San Bernardino

OUTING #44: ART, HISTORY & NATURE ON THE COAST

Laguna Beach

Laguna Beach is a beach town with unique topography and immense pride. This visit will show you the best spots in this gorgeous art colony on the coast. You'll stroll the town's oldest park on a beautiful coastal path, visit a nature center in the prized Laguna Greenbelt, enjoy expansive views of the Pacific from 1000 feet up, and visit some great art galleries in the scenic, walkable downtown. You will need a car to get you to each fun place.

Background: The beauty of Laguna Beach, with its many sheltered coves, steep hills and beautiful greenbelt, attracted artists as early as the 1880s. These artists developed a California **"plein air" style**, and by 1918, the town opened one the state's first art museums. Laguna Beach incorporated in 1927 and soon developed its famous **"living pictures" Pageant of the Masters**. The high school mascots were even called "The Artists"! During the 1960s, Laguna had its brush with "hippie mafia" - The Brotherhood of Eternal Love - and established a strong environmental movement. Laguna's passionate citizens voted for a 36-foot building height limit and design review of new buildings to maintain their quaint village identity. During the '80s, the town established its beloved **"Laguna Greenbelt"** - thousands of acres of open space surrounding the city. Today, Laguna Beach is more popular than ever, with millions of visitors per year enjoying the beautiful beaches and summer art festivals - **Pageant of the Masters**, **Festival of Arts**, **Sawdust Festival** and **Art-A-Fair.**

Itinerary: AM

1. Nix Nature Center - Want to experience the natural beauty of the Laguna Greenbelt? Stop at this sustainably-designed nature center on **Highway 133 (Laguna Canyon Road)** just north of the 73 Toll Road. The exhibits on the geology, flora and fauna are excellent, and there's even a small room devoted to Laguna's famous "plein air" artists. Talk to the ranger and check out the wildlife log on the whiteboard as you enter. Take the hiking trail, which leaves the patio and winds through the coastal sage scrub. You can also take a walk back under Laguna Canyon Road to **Barbara's Lake - the only natural lake in Orange County**. Note: If you visit in the spring, you'll love the wildflower blooms.

Art is everywhere you turn in Laguna Beach.

2. Pacific Marine Mammal Center - If you like seals and sea lions, this is a nice stop before entering town. Here you'll find dedicated volunteers rehabilitating these pinnipeds before releasing them back into the ocean. By the way, sea lions have visible ear flaps and large flippers; seals do not! Consider a donation to this wonderful organization. Now head north to 455 Cliff Dr. and park by the Laguna Beach Lawn Bowling Club.

3. Heisler Park - The beautiful park before you is Laguna's number one attraction. Walk down the path to the right of the Lawn Bowling greens and you'll see the grassy area of Picnic Beach. Turn left on the trail and walk to Monument Point and the flagpole. From this vantage point, you can see why Laguna is called **"City of Coves."** Sandy beaches are nestled between rocky points, and the water is unpolluted by run off. To the north, you can see **Picnic Beach** and **Divers**, **Fisherman's** and **Shaw's Coves**. Here are great tide pools and snorkeling during low tides and surf, and great public art to admire along the way. Continue walking south and find the *Lunar Tides* art piece on the small, raised platform by the metal "breaching Whale." Keep walking past Rock Pile Beach all the way to the Gazebo. Here you can enjoy great views of Main Beach and points south all the way to the Dana Point Headlands. If you love art, consider a visit to the **Laguna Beach Museum of Art** on the corner of Cliff Drive and PCH.

Lunch and Galleries in Downtown Laguna - Laguna's compact downtown is a jewel. Lots of restaurants can be found along the car-free Forest Avenue Promenade between Coast Highway and Glenneyre St. The most popular galleries are Marc Whitney, Dawson Cole (don't miss its stunning sculpture garden), and Wyland (with its huge gray whale mural). The most iconic shop is the **Hobie Surf Shop** - named after the famous hometown surfing and sailing inventor and entrepreneur, Hobie Alter.

Itinerary: PM

4. Montage Resort and Treasure Island Park - Head south on PCH to the Montage Resort at 30801 Coast Highway. Walk to the turnaround at Montage Resort Drive and stop at the top of the steps above the park. Here is a wonderful story where everyone benefited. The site used to be a trailer park closed to the public. When resort developers bought the property, the City and the **California Coastal Commission** required public access and a dedicated public park. The result was the 2003 dedication of Treasure Island Park. Walk down the steps, make a right and enjoy the views of the protected cove. Great snorkeling here, and you'll often see harbor seals resting on the rocks. Continue south along the bluff trail to views of the luxury hotel and the scenic beaches - open to hotel guests and the public. The park's gorgeous Mediterranean landscaping is managed in a partnership between the City and the Montage Resort. Bravo!

Laguna Beach is a city of secluded coves.

5. Alta Laguna Park - For your final stop, we're going 1000 feet in elevation to Alta Laguna Park (3300 Alta Laguna Blvd.). Park your car either at the end of road or in the park's lot. Walk through the wooden gate at the end of the road and behold the 22,000 acre Laguna Greenbelt - the City's greatest achievement! To the north and east, you'll see **Santiago Peak** (the tallest mountain in Orange County at a mile high). The communities of South Orange County lie before you - Mission Viejo, Rancho Santa Margarita, Laguna Niguel and more. You may see **Mt. Baldy** (Mt. San Antonio - 10,060 feet) in the distance to the left. To the south, you can see Laguna Canyon Road and the Village. Beyond is **Catalina Island** - 26 miles out and the southernmost of the Channel Islands. Mountain bikers love the challenging trails and are very nice to the many hikers (they don't want to be banned from the trails!). Wildlife abounds in this **coastal sage scrub habitat** and the park closes at dusk - right around the time to view a great sunset. In 1993, a terrible fire raced down the canyon, aided by Santa Ana winds, and destroyed 441 homes. Since then, the City has hired a shepherd whose goats are eating a future fire's fuel. The small hill to the west at the end of the trail is actually a reservoir.

Long live the Greenbelt!

Laguna Canyon bloomage.

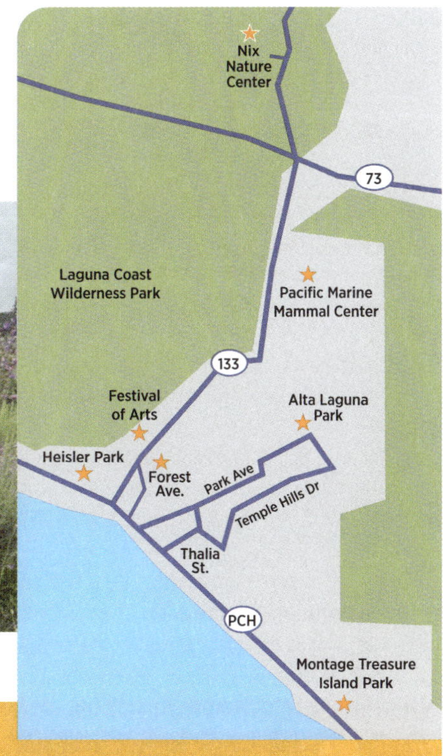

Fun activities:

- **Take a surf lesson at Thalia St.**
- **Snorkel at Shaw's Cove or Treasure Island Beach**
- **Enjoy first Thursday's Art Walk - 6 to 9 PM**

OUTING # 45: SAIL, SURF & CHOCOLATE-COVERED BANANAS

Newport Beach

Sparkling Newport Beach gives you a great view of the Orange County lifestyle: great beaches, a scenic boat harbor, and some excellent shopping. This outing includes a visit to a beautiful botanic garden, a famous shopping center, and a stroll in and around quaint Balboa Island. You can even rent an electric boat or take a harbor tour to gawk at multi-million-dollar mansions and yachts.

Background: Like many Orange County cities, Newport was originally built from Spanish and Mexican land grants. The entrepreneurs who helped create Newport -James Irvine, James McFadden, and Henry Huntington - specialized in ranching, shipping and land development, respectively. Fortunately, Newport had a small harbor, and, in 1906, **William Collins** began dredging to create **Balboa Island**. Today, there are seven islands nestled in one of the busiest small-boat harbors in the world. The tourist-friendly, affluent community of Newport Beach has grown to over 80,000 residents.

Itinerary:

AM: 1) Visit The Sherman Library and Gardens in Newport Beach's Corona Del Mar neighborhood. After admiring the beautiful botanic gardens, make sure to visit the Library - devoted to the history of the Southwest. It includes historic maps and exhibits as well as examples of the "plein air" style of landscape painting, which began in the early 1900s.

2) Explore Corona Del Mar. The relatively small lots were developed in 1920, and the streets were named after flowers - from Acacia to Poinsettia (Pansy was dropped). Notice the colorful **flower street signs**, and the lushly landscaped median along Pacific Coast Highway. If you want a beautiful view of the harbor and peninsula, turn beachward on Marguerite Parkway to **Ocean Boulevard's Lookout Point**.

3) Make the short drive to **Fashion Island** - one of California's most popular shopping and commercial centers. **Architect and planner William Pereira** (Transamerica Building; LAX Theme Building) used a circular circulation plan as he did for nearby UC Irvine. Opened in 1967, Fashion Island began as a more traditional shopping mall but was later remodeled to its current "Mediterranean style" retail village. The gleaming white towers of Fashion Island, including the headquarters of the Irvine Company, can be seen for miles.

The best experience on Balboa Island!

PM: It's time to hit the water. Take the short drive north on PCH, make a left on Jamboree, and **cross the bridge onto Balboa Island at Marine Ave**. (Note: Parking can be difficult and if you take the ferry across to Newport Peninsula and back, the walk is about 2 miles. With gorgeous views!)

4) Explore Balboa Island - Marine Ave. is Newport's best shopping street with three blocks of colorful, specialty retail and huge eucalyptus trees. Fuel up with an iconic **chocolate-covered banana** at **Sugar 'n Spice** (310 Marine Ave.) - the original since 1945! There is debate as to the exact origin of this delicacy, but most people just love the dipped chocolate with almonds or sprinkles. This store even inspired the hilarious sitcom *Arrested Development* and its dysfunctional Bluth family. If shopping's not your thing, definitely visit the excellent Balboa Museum (210 Marine).

5) Walk to the Balboa Ferry - Walk south on Marine Ave. to S. Bay Front - the pedestrian promenade that encircles the island. The views along the water are wonderful, and the residential architecture is varied and beautiful, even if the homes seem over scaled for the small lots. Look for the **oval historic plaques** placed on any original home built before 1960.

6) Take the Balboa Ferry to the Peninsula - You will soon see the Balboa Ferry - an island institution - at Agate Street. It's a short ride to the **Peninsula's Fun Zone**. Turn left and walk to the **Balboa Pavilion** - Newport's oldest landmark (1905). This is where Henry Huntington's Pacific Electric Trolley connected Balboa to points inland. Check out the fun historic photos in the foyer. Wow, the fishing was good and the bathing suits were ample in those days! Here's where you can catch the *Catalina Flyer* to Catalina Island.

You can take the ferry back to the island and your car or continue your walk across the street to the **Balboa Pier**, constructed in 1906. If you walk to the end, you'll see Laguna Beach and Dana Point to the south and Long Beach and San Pedro to the north. You'll walk through Balboa Village and cross the East Ocean Front Bike Path on your way back. Maybe you'll be hungry enough for another chocolate-covered banana!

The Victorian-style Balboa Pavilion continues to be center stage on the harbor.

Aerial view of Balboa Island.

Optional Activities:

1. Rent a "Duffy Electric Boat" - There's nothing like being on the water to experience Newport Beach. You can rent one for 2 - 4 hours with up to 12 people. The four companies on the harbor provide a map and a suggested route around the islands. The boats only go about 5 miles per hour but you can get close to the big yachts (like John Wayne's *Wild Goose*) and beautiful homes.

2. Book a narrated Harbor **Celebrity Home and Yacht Tour** - Fun Zone Boat Companies run daily, 45-minute tours with great stories about the celebrities, their boats and homes.

Narrated harbor tours give you a different perspective on island living.

Nearby Attractions:

- Laguna Beach
- Crystal Cove State Park
- Orange County Museum of Art, Costa Mesa

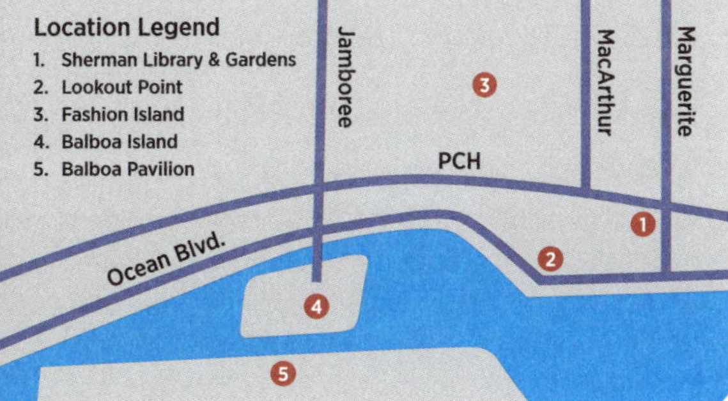

OUTING # 46: MISSION BELLS & CALIFORNIA HISTORY

San Juan Capistrano

Orange County's birthplace is the charming town of San Juan Capistrano. It has a famous mission, the oldest continuously-lived-in street in California, a train depot, and a beautiful, compact downtown with plenty of great shopping and restaurants. Whether you're a history buff, foodie, shopper, or stroller, San Juan Capistrano won't disappoint! Plan to spend at least a half a day on this adventure.

Background: Mission San Juan Capistrano, founded in 1776 as the 7th of the 21 Franciscan missions, is the town's major attraction. During the Mexican Rancho period (1831—1848), the mission fell into ruin but was gradually restored in the early 1900s. The popularity of the Mission was also enhanced by the arrival of thousands of cliff swallows from Argentina. The swallows no longer build nests at the Mission, but the town still celebrates them around St. Joseph's Day (March 19) with its jubilant **Swallows Day Parade**. With California statehood in 1850, SJC was a dusty, cowboy town with nearby ranching and agriculture. The town incorporated in 1926 and fought off massive growth in the 1970s. Strict architectural control – favoring Mission, Spanish Colonial and Western Ranch styles – makes SJC's downtown among the nicest of the county's 34 cities. Nearby **Los Rios Historic District** is a delightful stroll back in time, and you won't be able to resist a drink at OC's best cowboy bar – **The Swallow's Inn**. The new **River Street Market** is an upscale destination with farm-inspired architecture and a village green.

The Secret Garden is a favorite spot for wedding photos.

Itinerary:

AM: Tour Mission San Juan Capistrano – "the Jewel of the Missions." Plan on a 90-or-so minute visit and consider using audio headsets for your tour. As you enter the Mission grounds, walk in a clockwise circle to visit all the major exhibits:

1. Acjachemen Room - This exhibit documents the native tribe whose labor built the Mission. Originally hunters and gatherers, many of them converted to Catholicism, but sadly, deadly epidemics drastically reduced their population. The Acjachemen Nation, also called the Juaneño Band of Indians, is still active today and recently built a demonstration village, called **Putuidem**, north of town.

The original inhabitants - the Acjachemen Nation - built conical structures called kichas.

2. Mission Treasures Room - documents the three stages of Mission growth - 1) Spanish period, 2) Mexican secularization and decline, and 3) Mission restoration. Here you'll find interesting displays of vestments, chalices, paintings and rancho period saddles. Walk across the quadrangle where the hard work done by the natives took place – cooking, tanning hides, and making adobe bricks.

3. Serra Chapel - one of California's oldest buildings – (1779) – features an ornate gold-leaf altar and decorated adobe walls. It's the only chapel standing where St. Junipero Serra celebrated Mass. Serra founded nine missions and is buried at the Carmel Mission. As you leave the Serra Chapel, to the right of the altar, you will pass through the "Campo Santo" or cemetery where over 3,400 Native Americans, along with Spanish soldiers and padres, were buried in unmarked graves.

California poppies with Old Stone Church.

Contains California's oldest street.

Preparing for Swallows Day Parade.

4. Secret Garden - Continue through this sacred site to the picturesque, enclosed courtyard with a fountain and bell wall, built in the 1920s to attract more tourists to the Mission.

5. Great Stone Church - Finally, walk to your right around the tall ruins of the original church – once one of the largest structures of all 21 missions – felled by an **earthquake in 1812** and killing 40 Native Americans during Mass. Walk through the nave to the altar area and check out the massive stone walls, now reinforced with steel bars. Such a tragedy and now a memorial.

6. Mission Store - As you leave the Mission, you might want to enjoy the tasteful collection of religious articles, pottery, books and keepsakes.

7. Check out the Downtown - Walking out of the Mission Store, take a look down Camino Capistrano at a town with pride in its history. Here historic preservation, design guidelines and architectural review make for a unique, distinctive street. Even the IN-N-OUT looks like a Spanish Mission!

Lunch – You will find over a dozen restaurants around the Mission. Camino Capistrano has **El Adobe**, **Heritage BBQ**, and the famous and wonderful cowboy bar - **The Swallow's Inn**! If you go there, check out the ceiling and practice the Electric Slide! Nearby Verdugo Street has two restaurants with wine tasting. Another lunch option is to explore the new **River Street Market**.

PM: Stroll Los Rios Historic District – After lunch, walk down the short and lovely Verdugo Street which dead-ends at the railroad tracks and the **historic Depot** (Mission Revival – 1886). Here you can catch the train for San Diego or Los Angeles. Cross the tracks and stop at the metal historic marker/map describing the Los Rios Historic District. This street once had forty adobes during the Mission Period, and several survive today.

Los Rios Street runs in both directions. Take a right and stroll the tree-lined street with its shops and restaurants. On your left is Los Rios Park with its history wall, **Montanez Adobe**, and **Butterfly Garden**. Explore the garden with its native plants - also the work of the volunteer Gardening Angels.

Walk south along Los Rios Street past the Rios Adobe and the Olivares Coffee Shop. Take the small road to the right to the **River Street Market**. This upscale shopping and dining development with its agrarian-modern architecture is a testament to the increasing popularity of the town. It's an outdoor, rustic food hall and shopping venue with a central green, evoking San Juan's rural roots. Your last stop might be the **O'Neil Museum** – a cute, restored folk Victorian home at 31831 Los Rios Street. It's named for the O'Neil Family, one of Orange County's ranching families that developed several planned communities. San Juan Capistrano is certainly a gem… a beautiful combination of history and sensitive modern development.

OUTING #47: FARM TO TABLE

Ecology Center and Tanaka Farms

This outing provides a breath of fresh air in the nation's 6th most populous county. In the midst of suburban development, it's wonderful to visit a colorful organic farm to see people getting in touch with nature. There are two great choices - The Ecology Center in San Juan Capistrano and Tanaka Farms in Irvine. The former is free to visit and has an on-site café; the latter provides daily wagon rides with stops to pick seasonal produce for a small fee. Both farms are examples of "Community Supported Agriculture" where members receive boxes of seasonal produce, and both provide a wealth of special events and educational programs. This outing also recommends choosing a hike from OC Parks - the government agency that maintains and oversees the public parks in Orange County. Any time of year is great to visit, but it's great to catch spring native blooms.

Make your own salsa with ingredients fresh from the farm!

Itinerary:

AM: The Ecology Center (32701 Alipaz St., SJC) - Start your midmorning at this 28-acre, Regenerative Organic Certified farm and community center in San Juan Capistrano. Built from a plot with the original 1898 homestead **Congdon House**, the nonprofit Ecology Center officially opened in 2008 and recently celebrated a new 40-year lease with the City. You can visit any day of the week and there's a farm tour every Saturday at 10:00 AM.

Explore this creative village at you own pace, but you can do a nice counterclockwise loop to see everything. As you enter the Center, you'll notice the historic house on the right. Take the path on the right to the courtyard. From here you will see the **Market Garden** and **Fruit Forest**. Slightly to the left is the **Community Table** where guest chefs discuss seasonal palettes during farm-to-table dinners. Continue to the left past the Eco Tots Lot where small children learn to nurture plants and get their hands delightfully dirty. Continue to the left to the **Campesino Café** where you can relax with farm fresh dishes and drinks. Finally, on your way out, visit the **Farm Stand** where you can buy local organic fruits and vegetables. The Ecology Center grows over 100 varieties of fruits, vegetables, herbs and flowers.

Lunch - Consider lunch at the Ecology Center's Campesino Café. Enjoy a fresh pizza or salad made with ingredients right from the farm. Popular sides include heirloom beans, San Juan blue tortillas and pickles/ferments from the lab.

Tanaka Farms (5380 3/4 University Drive, Irvine) - The Tanaka family had to be very creative to continue farming in Orange County. They transitioned from wholesale farming to **agritourism** in 1998, becoming the only family-run farm in Irvine that hosts educational and U-pick tours.

Kids and their parents love Tanaka Farms. A reasonable entry fee includes a guided wagon ride around the farm, a stop to pick whatever is in season (lettuce, strawberries, melons, pumpkins), and a visit to the Barnyard to enjoy the furry animal friends. The farm's **Pumpkin Patch** (September - October) is extremely popular as is the Japanese **Hikari Festival of Lights** during December, with over a million twinkling lights. There is a produce market stand, gift shop and arts and craft booths in spring and summer. The farm boasts over 300,000 strawberry plants grown hydroponically! A friendly staff and lots to do make this a very special place to get your fingernails dirty!

PM: Hiking in Nature with OC Parks!: Choose your trail! In such a populous county, it's great that the government and the private sector have set aside natural open space for us to enjoy and preserve. You can go on the **OCparks.com** website to choose additional hikes and to download trail maps:

1. Casper's Wilderness Park (33401 Ortega Highway, SJC) - Only 7.5 miles east of San Juan Capistrano along the scenic Ortega Highway, this is the largest county park at 8,000 acres. It has more than 35 miles of trails and campsites and picnic areas located among large sycamore and oak trees. The Nature Center has displays on natural history and wildlife, and there are ranger-led hikes and campfire programs during peak season. During the spring there's the added scenic bonus of seasonal water in San Juan Creek.

2. Thomas F. Riley Wilderness Park (50952 Oso Parkway, Mission Viejo) - This is a good choice if your time is short. The 540-acre park has five miles of multiuse trails, a self-guided nature trail, and a butterfly garden. For a comparatively small park, it has quite a diversity of native plant communities with Riparian, Southern Oak Woodland, Coastal Sage scrub and Grassland represented.

3. Aliso and Woods Canyon Wilderness Park (28373 Alicia Parkway, Laguna Niguel) - This 3,330-acre jewel of a park is nestled between the communities of Aliso Viejo, Laguna Niguel and Laguna Beach. The best access is at the Alicia Parkway entrance where you'll find an excellent Visitor Center with displays of natural history and fossils along with interactive exhibits for children. The canyon trails are generally well shaded as you pass through oak and sycamore groves while the ridge trails provide more aerobic exercise and big thrills for mountain bikers. Two fun offshoot trails are to **Dripping Cave** and **Cave Rock**. Access to the Park from Laguna Beach is at scenic **Alta Laguna Park** which, at 1,036 feet elevation, provides 360-degree ocean and canyon views.

NOTE: If you prefer to get your hiking out of the way earlier in the day, then just reverse the tour and end up the day at the Ecology Center or Tanaka Farms.

The Red Diamond rattlesnake is the largest venomous snake in OC.

Tanaka Farms, U-pick tour gets you out in the fields.

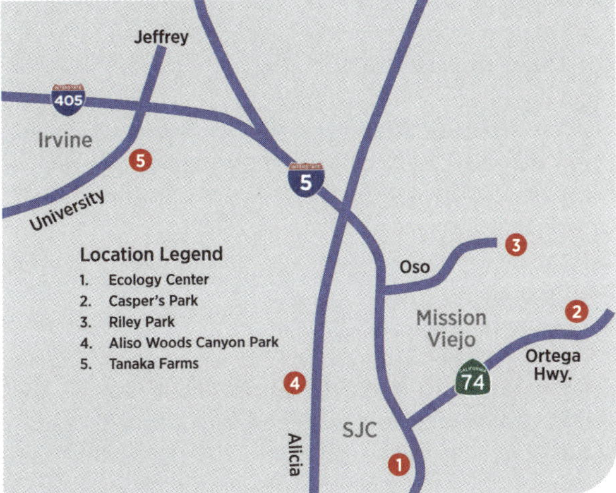

OUTING #48: OC'S CHARMING DOWNTOWN

Old Towne Orange

Delightful Downtown Orange is part of the largest National Register Historic District in California, and one of the County's most popular places. This outing is a 2-hour stroll combining vintage architecture, fun shops and restaurants, and a stop at a newly expanded museum of California Scene Painting. Optional side trips will take you to some unique mid-century neighborhoods and the Huell Howser California's Gold exhibit.

Background: Like many cities in the County, Orange was born from land subdivided from local Mexican ranchos. A **grid plan** was laid out with a **public plaza** in the middle. The town was **incorporated in 1888**, coinciding with a major boom in the citrus industry. Most of the downtown, built between 1905 and 1930, is a product of this agricultural legacy. Today, Orange has that small town feel because its citizens took the initiative to preserve it. The surrounding neighborhoods contain over 1,400 historic homes of diverse architectural styles.

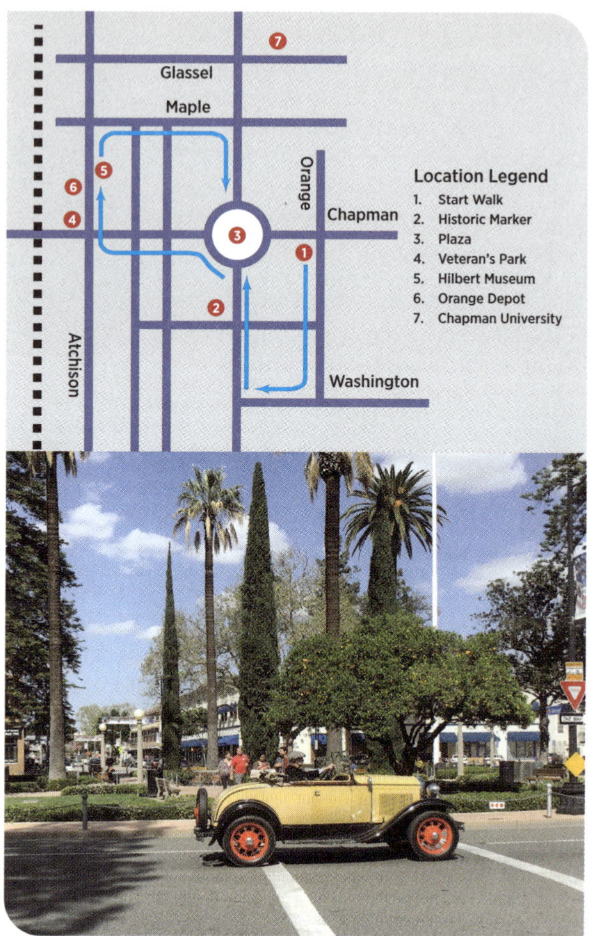

Orange started out with a plaza and built out. It's the pride and focal point of Old Towne.

Itinerary:

This walking tour begins one block east of **"The Circle"** at the corner of Chapman and Orange Avenues. Park your car in the large lot on the west side of Orange Avenue just below Chapman Ave.

1. Explore vintage architecture in the residential district - Walk one block south on Orange Ave. to the corner of Almond Ave. At the corner you will find a 1886, Gothic-Queen Anne church converted to a Mexican restaurant. This is how Orange rolls! Continue south one more block into the residential area. This one block gives you a good glimpse of the diversity of vintage architecture in the **Old Towne Historic District**.

Walk down the east side of Orange Ave. Next to the corner, you'll see a Folk Victorian cottage with its decorative woodwork below the eaves. Notice the large Craftsman Bungalows across the street with their large front porches. Farther down the street, you will notice a cool Mission Revival/Spanish Colonial bungalow court. The historic homes are well maintained, in part, because many owners apply for a Mills Act Contract with the City. This agreement (authorized by state law) gives the property owner a reduction in property taxes in return for maintaining the home to historic standards. The **Mills Act Program** is the single biggest economic incentive to restore and preserve historic homes in California. Turn right at Washington and again at Glassell.

2. Explore the historic commercial zone - **Old Towne Plaza Historic District**. As you walk north into the commercial downtown, stop at the large monument sign announcing "Plaza Historic District." Look up the street and notice how all the commercial buildings sit right on the sidewalk, creating excellent urban space. This is because downtown Orange was built before modern zoning and the widespread use of cars. Walk north on to the plaza.

Downtown Orange was built before parking requirements, creating a more walkable environment.

3. Enter Plaza Square Park - Walk past the antique stores and restaurants and enter the Orange Plaza, aka "The Circle." (Be careful to use the crosswalk and watch for traffic!) Town squares are very rare in Southern California, and this one is a delight. No wonder it was named one of **"America's Great Places"** by the American Planning Association. The first central fountain was built in 1887 and replaced in 1937. From here you can see the city's original grid pattern. Cross back over to the SW corner of Chapman and Glassell.

4. Peruse the shops and restaurants heading west on Chapman Ave. - As you round the Circle heading west on Chapman, you'll pass numerous restaurants converted from historic buildings - adaptive reuse at its best. You'll pass a great gallery - Country Roads Antiques - with over 30 creative vendors and antique dealers. Across from the Post Office you'll find the small exhibit and remaining tracks of the Pacific Electric Red Car. Continue one more block to Atchison and turn right into Veteran's Memorial Park with its huge camphor trees.

5. Visit the Hilbert Museum of California Art - As you walk through the park, you'll see the Hilbert Museum of California Art with its huge mosaic on your right. This is a delightful and free museum, owned by **Chapman University** and specializing in California Scene Painting from the 1920s to the present.

The Hilberts rescued this famous glass tile mosaic by Millard Sheets - Pleasures Along the Beach - *from storage in Santa Monica.*

6. Glassell Ave. stores, restaurants and lunch - Finish your Old Towne walk by turning right on Maple and walking two blocks to Glassell Ave. Here you will find a wonderful array of restaurants and shops as you head south back to the Plaza and your car. The historic buildings of Orange indeed have new life.

Many of the museum's pieces are iconic scenes of 20th century California.

Fun Side Trips

- **California's Gold Exhibit and Huell Howser Archives:** Nearby Chapman University has a permanent exhibit of the legacy of TV personality and California adventurer - Huell Howser. He explored California for over 30 years, produced over 500 TV programs and helped us appreciate our state with his delightful sense of wonder. Open Monday through Friday.

- **Mid-Century Modern Homes of Joseph Eichler: Fairhills, Fairhaven, Fairmeadows** - If you like mid-century modern residential architecture, you may want to visit these three neighborhoods in east Orange. Eichler built over 10,000 homes in the postwar era, the majority in the Bay Area, and these three tracts are his only Orange County work (1960—1964). It's interesting to compare the Eichler homes to traditional suburban ranch styles. His homes have a clean, modern look with low broad roofs, post-and-beam construction, atriums, and floor-to-ceiling glass for an "indoor outdoor flow." The City of Orange designated **the three Eichler tracts** as **local historic districts** in 2018.

Clean lines, floor-to-ceiling glass and low, broad roofs are common Eichler home features.

OUTING # 49: OC CULTURAL MOSAIC

Little Saigon, Islamic Institute and Little Arabia

This adventure highlights the diversity of Orange County including some great food options. You'll explore the heart of Little Saigon in Westminster with suggestions for shopping, tea and dim sum, followed by a visit to a Buddhist Temple. Then you'll visit one of two large mosques and afterwords enjoy some tasty dishes in Anaheim's Little Arabia.

Background: Once called "the Orange Curtain" for its lack of diversity, Orange County has become one of the most diverse counties in Southern California with large Latino (33%) and Asian (22%) populations.

1. Little Saigon – This roughly three-square-mile area between Brookhurst, Magnolia, Euclid and Westminster Boulevards contains the largest concentration of Vietnamese – almost 200,000 - outside of that country. Immigration to the area grew dramatically after the end of the Vietnam War in 1975, and the diaspora was officially named "Little Saigon" in 1989. As you explore the area, you'll find no franchises (hooray for specialty retail!), but rather **over 4,000 family-owned businesses**, mostly arrayed along wide boulevards of strip malls. With the OC's typically wide boulevards, the area is not pedestrian-friendly, but the strip malls are often hopping with shoppers.

2. Islam in Orange County - Orange County has a large Muslim population of over 120,000. There are nine mosques located mostly in the northern and central part of the county, the largest being the **Islamic Institute of Orange County** (Anaheim) and the **Islamic Society of Orange County** (Garden Grove). In addition, the Arab food scene was given a major boost in 2022 when the City of Anaheim officially designated the **Little Arabia District** - a concentration of Arab restaurants, dessert shops, markets and hookah lounges along Brookhurst St. between Broadway and Ball Roads. In 2023, Anaheim's City Council voted to put four freeway signs up designating "Little Arabia."

Dim Sum at Seafood Cove 2 is a communal culinary experience!

Itinerary:

AM: Explore Little Saigon - This outing takes you to the heart of Little Saigon - Bolsa Avenue between Brookhurst and Magnolia. As you approach the area, you will notice more signs in Vietnamese, decorative streetlamps, queen palms and even flags of the former country of South Vietnam.

1. Explore Asian Village, 9211 Bolsa Ave., Westminster - This is Little Saigon's oldest shopping center with lots to see and more interesting than the huge Asian Garden Mall across the street. Enter the **A Dong Supermarket** – a wonderland of Vietnamese staples whose exotic produce section transports you right to Southeast Asia. You can't beat the prices, and you may never see so many types of bok choy! Then visit one of the oldest family-run businesses in Little Saigon – **Dat Shun Tea & Ginseng Shop** (9211 Bolsa Ave., #118) - and sample some of their classic teas.

2. Savor Dim-Sum at the Seafood Cove 2 (9211 Bolsa Ave.; second floor) - In the same shopping center, you'll find this popular restaurant. Although you can find numerous restaurants with the Vietnamese specialties of pho and banh mi sandwiches, try this Chinese-style restaurant's dim sum offerings. Get a group table with a lazy Susan (rotating tray) and order to your heart's content - steamed buns, shrimp balls, Chinese broccoli, dumplings, and, yes, chicken feet!

3. Visit a Buddhist Temple - There are a number of Buddhist temples in the eastern part of Little Saigon. One of the most ornate is the **Bao Quang Temple** (713 N. Newhope, Santa Ana). The founding monk amassed a treasure trove of Buddhist artifacts within the 2-acre campus. The gardens, statuary and altar are beautiful, and visitors are welcome.

PM: Visit an Islamic Mosque and Little Arabia

- Driving north on Brookhurst, you can visit one of OC's largest mosques - the Islamic Society of Orange County (1 Al-Rahman Plaza, Garden Grove) or, later in the afternoon, visit the Islamic Institute of Orange County (220 N. State College Blvd.) in northern Anaheim. The former serves over 10,000 followers, contains a K-12 school, runs a food pantry, and contains a bookstore and small café; the latter has an education outreach program that offers educational tours for those who want to learn more about Islam. In both cases, contact the Mosque ahead of time for a guided visit and the opportunity to watch the daily prayers at midday or midafternoon.

Little Arabia - This cultural district - described as "Arab culture and cuisine in the heart of Orange County" - is located along the 300 to1200 blocks of Brookhurst Ave., north of Ball Road in Anaheim. Prior to your tour, use the website - **www.littlearabiadistrict.com** - to pick your stops. One of the best concentrations of options is at 512 N. Brookhurst. Here you will find an excellent Lebanese bakery - **Forn Al Hara** (delicious flatbreads and pastries), a Yemeni restaurant, House of Nuts and a hookah lounge. A great choice for groceries and meat is the **Altayebat** ("tasty and fresh" in Arabic) Market at 1217 S. Brookhurst. The market has operated for 40 years and specializes in Middle Eastern specialties, international produce and halal (meaning "permissible") meats.

The Islamic Institute of Orange County in Anaheim serves over 7,000 congregants.

Upturned or flying eaves in traditional Buddhist architecture allow more light into temples and symbolize movement toward enlightenment.

OUTING #50: ART & HIGH STYLE IN THE OC

Orange County Museum of Art and Bowers Museum

Sanford Biggers Of Many Waters *is a sixteen-foot tall sequined sculpture at OCMA.*

OCMA's galleries have natural and artificial light.

While LA has many world-class art museums, Orange County has its own burgeoning art scene,. This outing features one of the county's newest - the OCMA (Orange County Museum of Art) - along with one of its oldest - the Bowers Museum. It also includes a brief architectural walk highlighting the county's most outstanding grouping of contemporary architecture in the Segerstrom Center for the Arts - right next to the OCMA! Nearby is a nationally famous sculpture garden, and lunch is right across the street in South Coast Plaza.

Background: Orange County's art scene started in Laguna Beach over 100 years ago. Attracted to the natural beauty, these early **"plein air"** (outdoors) **artists** painted the ocean, hillsides and canyons. This tradition of painting "in the open" is still a strong part of the OC art scene, but modern art here really began in 1962 with thirteen women who rented space in the second floor of the Newport Pavilion to exhibit contemporary art. The latest incarnation of this original museum was the 2022 opening of the Orange County Museum of Art in the **Segerstrom Center for the Arts**. Providing a balancing contrast to the OCMA is the "grand dame" of the county's art - the Bowers Museum in Santa Ana. Founded in 1936, the museum has a large permanent collection and has hosted excellent special exhibits such as *Terracotta Warriors; Mummies: Death and the Afterlife in Ancient Egypt, Treasures of the British Museum;* and *Guo Pei: Art of Couture.* And its museum store is quite popular!

Itinerary:

AM: 1) Orange County Museum of Art (3333 Avenue of the Arts, Costa Mesa) - OCMA is committed to displaying innovative art from living artists in their prime. Make sure to check the website - www.ocma.art - to find out the current exhibitions. The two-story museum has three major pavilions - Special Exhibitions, Permanent Collection and Avenue of the Arts. Thanks to a grant from Lugano Diamonds, general admission to the museum is free for ten years.

The OCMA's "deconstructivist" architecture, designed by **Pritzker prize-winning architect Thom Mayne** of the firm ***Morphosis***, is half the experience. (Morphosis is a US-based architectural firm with projects all over the world. Check out its bold designs at morphosis.com.) Its radical geometry, curvy white terra cotta, numerous skylights, and steel-and-glass interior bridges make exploring the museum's spaces an adventure. Make sure to enjoy the second-story terrace with its excellent views of the center and surrounding buildings.

2) Architecture Walk at Segerstrom Center for the Arts: Stand at the fountain in **Argyros Plaza** and look north. Straight ahead is the signature Segerstrom Center (#4) - a 1986, Postmodern design with polished red granite from Malmo, Sweden. The massive arch surrounds the red, gold and silver steel *Fire Bird* sculpture. Just to the left is the Center Tower (#8) - 21 stories of polished red granite. Turn around and face the 2006 **Renee and Henry Segerstrom Concert Hall** (#3), by Cesar Pelli. The undulating white glass of the north wall literally glows in Southern California light. The multibalconied interior is simply spectacular, so try to attend a concert or book a tour.

Radical shapes of glass, steel and terra cotta describe Orange County's most interesting building to date.

Take the narrow walkway between the Concert Hall and OCMA to the 21-story, slightly tapered **Plaza Tower** (#1), commissioned by IBM in 1990. This is Orange County's most beautiful skyscraper, whose stainless steel skin subtly reflects light, especially at dusk.

3) Visit Isamu Noguchi's California Scenario Sculpture Garden - One block south of Segerstrom Center is one of the nation's most famous sculpture gardens (611 Anton St.). Partially hidden by trees and buildings, California Scenario is an "abstract metaphor of California's diverse natural environment" with elements symbolizing forests, deserts, water sources and land use. It's a peaceful, contemplative space, whose center-piece is ***The Spirit of the Lima Bean*** - fifteen, rust-colored granite rocks fit together perfectly.

Lunch - There are lots of great restaurants and a food court in **South Coast Plaza** - just across Bristol St. The Segerstrom family first opened the mall in 1967. It is now one of the highest grossing retail centers in the nation with over 300 stores. Not bad for this Swedish immigrant family who first raised lima beans on this land in 1898!

The Bowers has a diverse collection and very popular special exhibitions.

PM: 1) Bowers Museum (2002 N. Main St., Santa Ana) - The Bowers is Orange County's most popular and long-standing museum. Its permanent collection of over 91,000 pieces includes Art of the Pacific, Africa and Asia; pre-Colombian and Native American Art; and Southern California plein air paintings. **The California Legacies** and **Bounty Exhibits** are excellent. The museum has ongoing and special exhibits, a highly regarded restaurant - Tangata, and a very popular Museum Store. Use the website - www.bowers.org - to check the special exhibit schedule.

2) Art Merger in the Works - **OCMA may partner with collections acquired by UC Irvine.** This includes art from the Irvine Museum (featuring California landscapes of the late 19th and early 20th centuries) and the Gerald E. Buck collection (including works from David Hockney and Ed Ruscha). Dynamic art in a new OC home!

Plein air paintings from the early 20th century reflect Southern California's natural beauty.

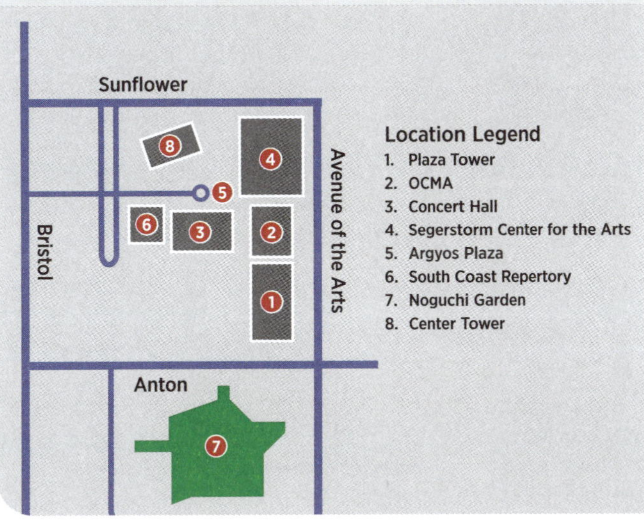

OUTING #51: BEACH BEAUTIES!

From Surf City to San Clemente

The stretch of coastline between San Clemente and Huntington Beach is the most beautiful and varied in Southern California. There are rocky coves, broad sand beaches, coastal parks, lively piers, state parks, and boat harbors. This outing lays out the coastal highlights from north to south. Start wherever you want and find the activities that you enjoy most. And, yes, apply sunscreen!

Huntington Beach - aka, **Surf City**, this town is all about riding waves and the surf culture. The hot spot is at the corner of Pacific Coast Highway and Main Street which empties into one of the longest piers in California.

• **Walking down Main Street** - This is Orange County's most crowded beachside street with bars, restaurants and more surf shops than you knew existed. Check out the **International Surf Museum** (411 Olive) with its famous Big Board, the **Surfer's Walk of Fame** embedded in the sidewalk and the statue of the legendary **Duke Kahanamoku** who surfed here in the 1920s.

Miles of secluded beaches await you at Crystal Cove State Park.

• **Cruise the pier** - At 1,850 feet, this pier is one of the longest on the West Coast. On a clear day, you'll look up the coast to Long Beach, Palos Verdes and the LA Harbor. On your walk back, you might want to stop for ice cream at Handel's or explore the trendy **Pacific City** beachfront mall.

• **Bolsa Chica Ecological Preserve** - If you're a bird watcher or want a nice nature stroll, this is prime estuary habitat only three miles north at 18000 Pacific Coast Highway.

Newport Beach - This affluent coastal town has two piers, a long, sandy shore for swimming, a charming island of shopping and strolling, and one of the biggest small boat harbors on the West Coast.

• **"Piering" down the peninsula** - Entering the Balboa Peninsula from PCH, follow the signs to **Newport Pier**. Here you'll find a small village of shops surrounding the pier. The beach just north of the pier - **Blackie's** - is known for its gentle waves - a fun place to learn to surf. Continue south to Balboa Village (you'll see a street-spanning arch) where you can stroll the **Balboa Pier**, rent a bike and ride the Newport Balboa Bike Trail, or walk over to the **Balboa Pavilion** and **Fun Zone.**

• **Balboa Island** - Drive your car onto the **Balboa Ferry**. It's a three-minute ride to the charming island and its popular Marine Ave. shops, chocolate-covered bananas, and beautiful homes. It's a classic, scenic walk (1.8 miles) around the perimeter of the island on the **Bayfront Promenade**.

Crystal Cove State Park - Where else can you find a state park with historic cottages right on the sand? Drive south on PCH through attractive Corona del Mar and park your car at the Los Trancos Parking Lot. Walk through the tunnel under PCH and you'll find yourself back in time at **Crystal Cove Historic District**.

• **Explore the Historic District** - Nestled on the sand you'll find the 46 rustic cottages that represent vernacular beach architecture from the 1930s. They can be reserved at **ReserveCalifornia.com**. You can also enjoy a meal or cocktail at the popular Beachcomber at Crystal Cove.

Huntington Beach hosts the US Open of Surfing.

Elegant terns are among the many shorebirds at Crystal Cove and Bolsa Chica.

• **Take a long beach walk** - After exploring the historic district, you can take a beautiful beach walk either north or south. You can't go wrong in either direction, although the south offers tide-pools at low tide.

Laguna Beach - It's no wonder that plein-air artists put this town on the map. Tall coastal hills reach almost to the shore where 10 secluded coves are surrounded by rugged cliffs and rocks. Highlighting your adventure, stop at any of three coastal parks:

• **Crescent Bay Point Park** - Arguably the most beautiful view in Orange County, this park is just off PCH in north Laguna. The views are stunning, with the crashing waves on **Bird** and **Seal Rock** and secluded coves to your left affording excellent chances to see whales, seals and dolphins.

• **Heisler Park** - This is Laguna's most popular attraction, with a cliffside walkway passing **three beautiful coves** - **Diver's**, **Picnic** and **Rock Pile** - and a plethora of public art. The park ends at Las Brisas Restaurant with gorgeous views of the downtown shoreline. **The Laguna Art Museum** is on the corner.

• **Treasure Island Park, Montage Resort** - Two miles south of downtown Laguna, you'll find another stunning park with extraordinary Mediterranean landscaping. It wraps around the luxury hotel, providing public access to the secluded coves below. In return for approval to build, the resort agreed to help maintain the park in perpetuity!

Dana Point - This coastal town has a popular marina, coastal trails and a famous (and gentle) surf spot - **Doheny State Beach**. It was named after the nineteenth-century sailor, author and lawyer Richard Henry Dana who landed here in 1835.

• **Blue Lantern Historic Overlook** - A great view of the marina is from the gazebo near 34343 Street of the Blue Lantern. You can see the rugged **Dana Point Headlands** to the north and Doheny State Beach to the south. Find the historic marker describing a pirate attack here in 1818.

• **Explore the Dana Point Harbor** - A recent revitalization of the harbor has created new hotels, restaurants and better pedestrian connections. Favorite activities are whale watching excursions, trips to Catalina Island, and a visit to the **Ocean Institute**, a marine educational organization.

San Clemente - Finish your coastal adventure at this lovely town at the southern end of Orange County. Founded in the 1920s as a **"Spanish Village by the Sea,"** you'll immediately notice the red-tile roofs and white-plaster walls of the Spanish Colonial style.

• **Savor the downtown** - **Avenida Del Mar** starts at PCH and descends three entertaining blocks toward the beach. Lots of fun restaurants and shops await.

• **Cruise the beach, San Clemente Pier and Casa Romantica** - Follow Avenida Del Mar south and you'll arrive at the Pier Bowl area. You can walk out on the San Clemente Pier or eat at the popular Fisherman's Restaurant. Just to the north is the Casa Romantica Cultural Center (casaromantica.org), the historic home of San Clemente founder, **Ole Hanson**.

OUTING #52: THE BIRTHPLACE OF A PRESIDENT

Richard Nixon Presidential Library and Museum

There are only two National Historic Landmarks in Orange County, and the Richard Nixon's birthplace in Yorba Linda is one of them. The 1917 home is part of the Richard Nixon Presidential Library and Museum, which is one of the County's best attractions. This outing recommends two to three hours to explore the library's many excellent exhibits as well as the surrounding home, gravesite and gardens. Complete your day with a visit to the Anaheim Packing District, OC's first food hall, located in a 1919 Mission Revival former fruit packing house.

Tour Nixon's 1917 birthplace home - a National Historic Landmark.

Get your picture taken in the Oval Office!

Background: There are currently 16 Presidential Libraries found throughout the US. Many start out as private foundations, but federal laws dictate that the **National Archives and Records Administration** oversee the exhibits to ensure historical accuracy. In the case of the Nixon Library, which was founded in 1990, the National Archives took over in 2007 and produced a new Watergate exhibit. The Archive Research Room has millions of pages of documents, the recorded "White House Tapes" and two million hours of film.

Museum Highlights - A visit to a presidential library is a great educational opportunity.

1. Watch the short, excellent orientation film on the life of our 37th President.

2. Walk through the permanent exhibits with their multimedia displays:
   - **a.** "Kitchen Debate" with Soviet leader Khrushchev; Presidential Debate versus John F. Kennedy.
   - **b.** Foreign Policy: Detente with China; Middle East; Vietnam War.

3. Study Domestic Policy: fighting inflation; environmental milestones - Environmental Protection Agency, Clean Air Water Acts.

4. Sit at the desk in the **Oval Office**.

5. Explore the evidence of Nixon's demise in the **Watergate Gallery**.

6. Visit the beautiful recreation of the Federal-style **East Room**.

7. Tour Nixon's birthplace home; board **Army One** - the helicopter used by Presidents Kennedy through Ford; and see the grave sites of Richard and Pat Nixon.

Lunch or early Dinner: Visit Orange County's first food hall - **Anaheim Packing District** (440 S. Anaheim Blvd.). This lively, two-story venue was converted from a historic 1919 citrus-packing house. You'll find 26 creative vendors and even a secret speakeasy. Next door is Farmer's Park with more creative cuisine and a craft brewery. Check out the website before you visit. Otherwise, you may be overwhelmed!

OUTING #53: RUSTIC RETREAT

Helena Modjeska Home and Irvine Regional Park

Modjeska's beloved home - Arden - sits in the forest she loved so much.

California's first regional park in 1897 was a gift from James Irvine.

This outing takes you to the rustic canyon home of a world-renowned Polish Shakespearean actress - Madame Helena Modjeska. After a tour of her home and gardens in the foothills of the Santa Ana Mountains, take a short drive to spacious Irvine Regional Park where you can enjoy a picnic, visit a small zoo and even take a train ride.

Background: Deciding to seek a better life in California, actress Madame Helena Modjeska came to the Anaheim Colony in 1876 to take up farming. When that proved unsuccessful, she returned to the stage in the US to great acclaim. She purchased a home among the oak and sycamore trees in **Santiago Canyon**, which she called **"Arden"** after the forest setting of Shakespeare's play *As You Like It*. Remodeled by New York architect Sanford White, Modjeska and her husband lived here from 1886 to 1906. After her passing, the house changed hands and was eventually sold to the County of Orange. It was declared a National Historic Landmark in 1990.

Itinerary:

AM: Book a **docent-led tour** of Arden at 10:00 AM on Wednesdays or Saturdays, or do a self-guided visit Wednesday through Saturday, 10:00 AM to 2:00 PM. The historic home contains rustic furnishings and a large photo gallery, and you'll hear many stories about Helena's amazing life in the late 1800s.

Lunch and Afternoon: Make the short ride to the historic **Irvine Regional Park**, a 495-acre beauty that was opened in 1897. The park is Orange County's most diverse with beautiful groves of oak and sycamore trees surrounded by hiking and equestrian trails. With so much space, it's a wonderful venue for groups and families. Download a brochure and map to choose your activities at: www.ocparks.com/irvinepark. Here's a summary of park highlights:

1. Fishing and paddleboat rentals.
2. **Orange County Zoo** - Specializing in local wildlife in the natural habitats; includes a petting zoo.
3. **Irvine Park Railroad** - A miniature railroad fun for kids and adults.
4. Pony rides, bike rentals, bandshell and food concessions.

Nearby Attractions:

- **Tucker Wildlife Sanctuary** - 12 acres in Modjeska Canyon
- **Whiting Ranch Wilderness Park** - 2500 acres with OC's most scenic rock formations, including Red Rock Canyon

OUTING #54: FOOD HALLS ROCK!

Anaheim Packing District, Rodeo 39, Mercado Gonzalez and the Source OC

Food halls are just plain fun, and Orange County has some great ones. As the county has become more culturally diverse, its food offerings have naturally followed suit. This outing introduces you to four wonderful food halls. Pick the ones that tempt your taste buds and pique your curiosity!

Background: Think Grand Central Market or Farmers Market in LA, the Ferry Building in San Francisco, Quincy Market in Boston. The concept of food halls started out as "festival marketplaces" on the East Coast to help revitalize downtowns. The idea was to employ local tenants, not chain stores or franchises, to celebrate an area's specialties. In addition, many folks wanted an alternative to the sameness of a mall food court. Orange County started embracing the food hall movement in the mid-2010s and hasn't looked back. With an increasingly diverse Asian, Latino and Middle Eastern population, the OC is clearly a "foodie" destination.

Anaheim Packing District: (anaheimpackingdistrict.com) - When a food hall can be located in a building with local history, it has even greater appeal. **Developer Shaheen Sadeghi** found the perfect structure in the heart of Anaheim - a 42,000-square-foot, century-old citrus packing plant, truly representing the county's agricultural past. Opened in 2014, this was Orange County's first big food hall. Walk inside and your senses come alive with sights, smells and choices.

Enjoying Korean BBQ at The Source OC in Buena Park.

This restored, 1919 Mission Revival Packing House in Anaheim holds 25 creative merchants.

There are 25 merchants, most of whom are original, and even a speakeasy! Clearly, the theme is "citrus," but the choices are diverse: Cajun, Indian, Syrian, Japanese, Mexican, Thai, Soul Food, Korean and more. Make sure to explore the area just north of the Packing House - the 2-acre Farmer's Park and the historic **Packard Building** (with a craft brewery). Just south you'll find the Make Building (with a craft brewery and stillhouse).

Rodeo 39 Public Market: (rodeopublicmarket.com) - 12865 Beach Boulevard, Stanton - Located in back of a large parking lot on a busy arterial, Rodeo 39 seems inconspicuous. But once inside, you'll be impressed. The interior design is sharp and hip, with 20 types of tile, hundreds of finishes, and sparkling murals. Rodeo contains 16 creative food vendors, 8 retail shops and a brewery. The food options tend toward Asian cuisine, with Japanese, Vietnamese and Korean offerings, but there are tacos, seafood, pizza and more.

Colorful graphics and creative food merchants welcome you to the Rodeo!

Educational side trip: After your meal, you might want to explore the nearby civil rights monument - the **Mendez Tribute Monument Park** - at 7371 Westminster Boulevard at Olive Ave. This small, linear park with statues and plaques commemorates the end of forced segregation in California schools in the 1947 Supreme Ct. case - *Mendez v. Westminster.*

Mercado Gonzalez Northgate Market: (northgatemarket.com/mercado) - 2300 Harbor Boulevard, Costa Mesa. This stunning market is a 70,000-square-foot celebration of Mexican food. It's a combination of 12 delicious food stands with a supermarket, bar, specialty produce, Mexican curios, and a sit-down restaurant. It's also an immigrant success story. The founder, Miguel Gonzalez, emigrated from Jalisco, Mexico, in the early 1960s to Southern California where he converted a liquor store to a grocery store. And he never stopped. There are now **44 Northgate Markets**, and Mercado Gonzalez is their flagship.

This is a true Mexican market. As you walk in, you'll see colorful graphics announcing the food offerings, often with signs explaining the origins of the dishes. You'll have a hard time choosing between **tortas**, **tacos**, **tamales**, **pozoles**, **carnitas**, **sushi** and **ceviche**. But don't worry. You can bring home fresh tortillas, mole, produce, Mexican pastries and flowers. The murals by local artists add to the ambience, and you won't be able to resist the **churros**!

The Source OC: (thesourceoc.com) 6940 Beach Boulevard, Buena Park - This three-story dining and entertainment destination mall follows the growth of the Korean American community in Orange County. In 2023, the City of Buena Park designated the northern section of the City as **"Koreatown"** and The Source OC is its hottest destination. Don't be fooled by the rather bland exterior of the center - it packs a culinary wallop inside. There are 35 food vendors from Korean BBQ, street food, hot dogs, noodles, boba teas, and desserts. There are classy sit-down restaurants and an informal food court, with a movie theater, virtual reality, K-pop, karaoke, and a kid's indoor playground. The open-air, third floor is particularly nice at sunset with great food, sitting areas and views.

The Anaheim Packing House is two stories of tasty food, colorful sights and people watching.

OUTING #55: MASTER-PLANNED PERFECTION

Planned Communities of Orange County

The Jeffrey Open Space Trail has excellent history exhibits.

Artificial lakes are key focal points in many master-planned communities.

The Spectrum has a beautiful imitation of the Patio of the Lions from The Alhambra in Granada, Spain.

Can you build the perfect city from a master plan? This outing will try to answer that question by exploring the popular planned communities of Irvine, Rancho Santa Margarita, Ladera Ranch and Rancho Mission Viejo. The adventure starts at the earliest village - Woodbridge, Irvine - and ends at the County's last planned community. After your outing, what's your opinion of the design of planned communities compared to more traditional towns?

Background: Southern Orange County has one of the nation's largest concentrations of planned communities in the nation. From the 1960s on, community planners were given a blank slate since large swaths of the area were basically unpopulated. This is because the area was originally huge Mexican ranchos that had been purchased and slowly converted to agriculture following California statehood in 1850. When the demand for housing grew, the community builders soon followed. The first master-planned community was **Irvine**, designed in the 1960s to counteract the relentless sprawl of LA. Then came **Mission Viejo**, **Rancho Santa Margarita**, and **Ladera Ranch**. Finally, by 2020, with the development of **Rancho Mission Viejo**, Orange County had run out of open space.

Itinerary: AM

1. Woodbridge Village (4500 Barranca Parkway, Irvine) - Irvine is one of the largest and highest rated planned communities in the nation. Of its 24 villages, Woodbridge (1975) is one of the oldest and most famous. Its loop road surrounds **two artificial lakes**. Stop at the Village Center's open-air lakeside plaza, grab a bite, and take in the views.

2. Jeffrey Open Space Trail - This 3.5-mile trail is actually a beautifully landscaped outdoor museum. It runs along the east side of **Jeffrey Road from the 5 Freeway to Portola Parkway**. The best access point is from Cypress Community Park (255 Visions, Irvine). As you walk north, you'll trace the history of California and the Irvine Ranch with trailside exhibits. The landscaping is varied with meadows, forests, riparian and parkside environments. No wonder this history trail won several design awards!

3. Great Park and Neighborhoods (8000 Great Park Boulevard) - After fits and starts, the Great Park has taken shape. With a total of 1300 acres built on the site of the former Marine Corps Air Station El Toro, it could become one of the nation's premier metropolitan parks. The park includes a **Cultural Terrace**, **Grand Meadow**, **Amphitheater**, two lakes, **Wild Rivers**, **Grand Promenade** and sports complex. Surrounding the Park are some innovative Great Park Neighborhoods, each with a mix of housing densities and styles. Ride the **Great Park Balloon** up 400 feet, visit the Farm and Food Lab and ride the Carousel. Great for kids!

4. Lunch - Spectrum Center Irvine (400 Spectrum Center) - Opened in 1995, this center is truly one of Southern California's most popular shopping centers. In a region known for Mediterranean-style architecture, Spectrum goes a step further with Moorish-inspired designs from Southern Spain and Northern Africa. Although surrounded by over 2300 parking spaces, the center's internal design is stunning with intimate "pedestrian" walkways, sitting areas, fountains and lush landscaping.

Irvine's Woodbury Village (2005) has a more formal urban design plan than earlier villages.

PM:

5. Rancho Santa Margarita (22112 El Paseo, RSM) - The next phase of planned community design was in the mid-1980s. The goal was to create a more walkable "urban village" with higher densities, internal pedestrian walkways, and more accessible and prosocial public space than earlier communities such as Mission Viejo. The focal point of RSM is an artificial lake and Town Center with its Mission and Spanish Colonial architecture. Too bad that many of the stores face the large parking lot rather than addressing the street. Take a beautiful walk around **Lago Santa Margarita** (21472 Avenida de Los Fundadores) - it's a 1.1-mile loop trail with subtle changes in elevation and great views of the Santa Ana Mountains.

Spectrum's 3- to-5-story, Tuscan-style apartments frame large, landscaped greens.

6. Ladera Ranch - Designed in the late 1980s and opened in 1999, this innovative community is connected both spatially and digitally. It has a hierarchy of open space that connects people - a **Town Green**, community parks, pocket parks, a 4-mile walking park, and nature trails - and an intranet that connects residents, businesses and community groups. Its nine villages have their own architectural theme, every home is within two blocks of a neighborhood park, and the shallow front setbacks make for more intimate streets. Explore this community from the Town Green, on **Sienna Parkway**, just south off Crown Valley Parkway. To see some of the neighborhoods, walk south using the trail along Sienna Parkway.

With artificial lakes, a grand meadow, promenade, and a cultural terrance, the Great Park will live up to its name.

7. Rancho Mission Viejo - Orange County's last planned community celebrates ranch life as it builds 14,000 new homes with Ranch and Early California styles. It continues the planned community tradition of providing abundant resident amenities - neighborhood hubs, community farms, fitness centers, pools and a 20,000-acre **Nature Preserve** - as well as operating its historic ranching operations at the **Cow Camp**. The community's newest villages will be sited on hilltops in order to preserve canyons and riparian habitats. Check out life on The Ranch at the Hilltop Club - 75 Escencia Dr., Rancho Mission Viejo.

OUTING #56: PICK YOUR LANDMARKS!

Preserving Orange County

*If you like historic buildings and places, this outing invites you to choose and explore your favorite landmarks. A new historic preservation group - **Preserve Orange County** - has created a great website and interactive map - OC Historic Interactive Map (which you can scan at the bottom using the QR code) - that helps you refine your search. Once you've picked your landmarks, combine your adventure with a nice lunch and a history walk. Consider this outing the Orange County equivalent of Outing #19 - Preserving Los Angeles. You can also sign up for a tour on the website - Preserve Orange County.*

Newport Harbor High School Murals (1937): Artwork funded through Works Progress Administration; Art Deco style.

Background: Although Orange County is a newer county (1887) than Los Angeles (1850), it has historic resources that date from the late 1700s. Its **oldest cities** - **Anaheim**, **Santa Ana** and **Orange** - incorporated between 1876 and 1888. From that point on, Orange County became a major citrus producer, shipping its products nationwide. After World War II, demand for housing skyrocketed, and the orchards gave way to housing tracts. Between 1950 and 1970, suburban growth was a massive 600% - expanding from 216,000 residents to over 1.4 million! Needless to say, much of this growth was car-dependent with wide arterials and strip commercial centers dominating the landscape. Nevertheless, interesting pockets of historic architecture remain, and the County and private-sector advocacy groups are working hard to preserve and promote these areas.

In terms of historic designation, Orange County has **two National Historic Landmarks** - Richard Nixon's birthplace and Helena Modjeska's rustic home, Arden - and numerous buildings on the National Register of Historic Places - such as Mission San Juan Capistrano, the **Old Orange County Courthouse** in Santa Ana, and the **Casa Romantica** in San Clemente. The best concentrations of historic commercial architecture are found in downtown Santa Ana, Orange and Fullerton. There are also county and city-designated landmarks and hundreds of historic buildings that have yet to receive recognition. So, enjoy your explorations and look for those plaques!

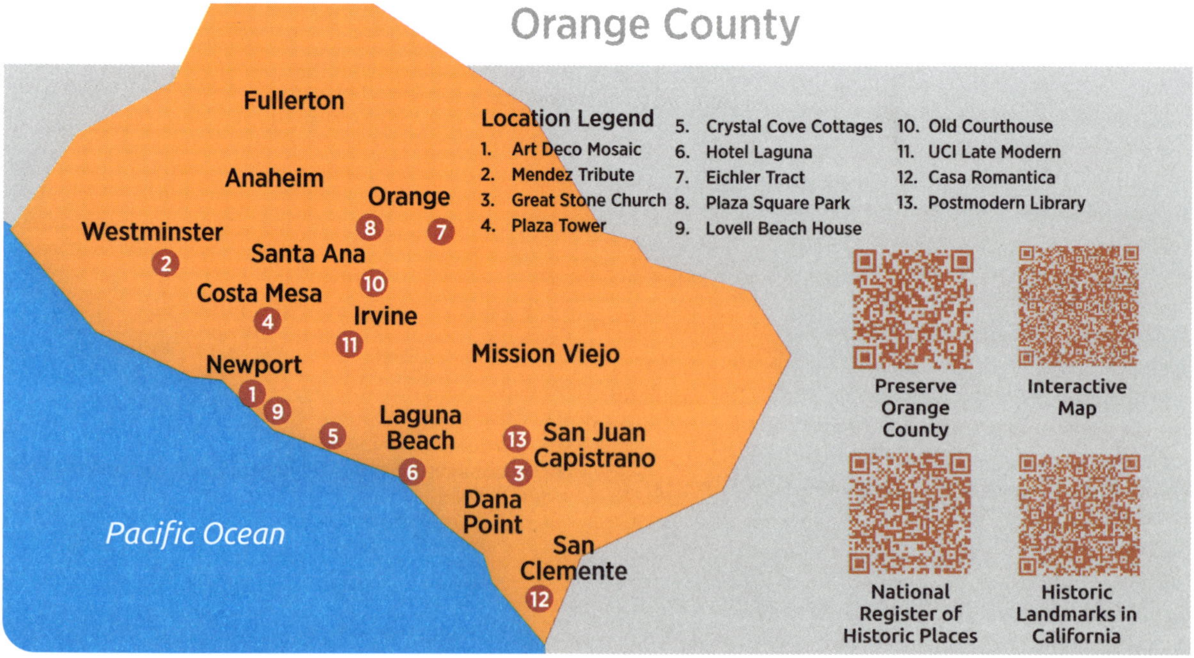

Orange County

Fullerton
Anaheim
Orange
Westminster
Santa Ana
Costa Mesa
Irvine
Newport
Mission Viejo
Laguna Beach
San Juan Capistrano
Dana Point
San Clemente
Pacific Ocean

Location Legend

1. Art Deco Mosaic
2. Mendez Tribute
3. Great Stone Church
4. Plaza Tower
5. Crystal Cove Cottages
6. Hotel Laguna
7. Eichler Tract
8. Plaza Square Park
9. Lovell Beach House
10. Old Courthouse
11. UCI Late Modern
12. Casa Romantica
13. Postmodern Library

Preserve Orange County
Interactive Map
National Register of Historic Places
Historic Landmarks in California

Mendez Tribute Monument Park (2022) in Westminster celebrates a landmark civil rights case.

Ruins of the "Great Stone Church" in Mission SJC - felled by an earthquake in 1812.

Plaza Tower (1990): OC's most graceful skyscraper. Shimmering stainless steel.

You can rent one of the 46 vernacular beach cottages (1920—1940) in Crystal Cove State Park.

Hotel Laguna (1930) - Mission Revival style right on the sand!

Mid-century Modern tract home (1960) in Orange by noted developer Joseph Eichler.

Plaza Square Park in Old Towne Orange was named one of "America's Great Places."

Modernism on the Beach: Famed architect RM Schindler's design on Balboa Peninsula.

Orange County Courthouse (1901) - Great stories inside this Richardsonian Romanesque-style beauty.

UCI's Krieger Hall (1965) - Famous example of futuristic Late Modern architecture by William Pereira.

Famous Spanish Colonial home (1927) of San Clemente founder Ole Hansen; now a cultural center.

San Juan Capistrano Library (1982) - One of the nation's finest examples of Postmodern architecture; Michael Graves architect.

OUTING #57: HISTORY, ART & FOOD

Discover Santa Ana

This outing celebrates the history, diversity and creativity of Santa Ana - Orange County's second largest city and county seat. The City has a vibrant and historic downtown, diverse architecture, an excellent food scene, lots of art, several museums and even a zoo. History buffs will love touring the Old Courthouse, foodies will enjoy 4th Street Market, and art lovers can check out the many Chicano murals and galleries. Santa Ana has a different and more urban feel than the rest of the County.

Background: As the original County seat from 1886, Santa Ana is known as "Orange County's Downtown." Fortunately, its downtown wasn't demolished during the 1960s, a period when "urban renewal" ruined many urban centers. Santa Ana therefore has the largest concentration of historic commercial buildings in Orange County, a whopping 683 buildings on its Register of Historic Buildings and a wonderful smorgasbord of architectural styles. It also has **three National Register Historic Districts** – Downtown Santa Ana (1984), French Park (1999) and Floral Park (2023).

Downtown 4th Street, built before parking requirements, is one of the county's best urban streets, teeming with constantly evolving stores and restaurants. Nearby **Artists Village** hosts a monthly Art Walk and features an attractive promenade. The Old County Courthouse showcases special exhibits, historic maps, the County archives, and a beautifully restored courtroom. Finally, the Bowers Museum, the county's oldest, has excellent permanent and rotating exhibits.

Santa Ana is a city of many murals.

Itinerary - AM: Visit the **Old County Courthouse** (211 W. Santa Ana Blvd.) – This beautiful landmark, completed in 1901 shortly after Orange County broke from Los Angeles, is a breath of fresh air surrounded by huge camphor and palm trees. Before going inside, walk around the perimeter and you'll experience one of the West Coast's best examples of **Richardsonian Romanesque architecture** - decked out in red Arizona sandstone on a granite base.

You'll step back in time as you enter the Courthouse. Start at the ground floor with its small **OC History Center** of old maps and rare photographs - including original maps of Disneyland and Knott's Berry Farm! You can visit the **County Archives** to browse rare books and ask questions of the archivists who can research almost anything. Archivist Chris Jepsen has an informative history blog at *OC History Round Up*. On the second floor, you may see couples getting their marriage licenses! On the third floor, you'll find the original courtroom restored for tours and filming. You can arrange a tour at ocparks.com.

Lunch - There are plenty of food options downtown. Your best bet is the **4th Street Market**, an innovative food hall at the corner of 4th and Bush Streets. **Alta Baja Market** on the corner has unique products from both sides of the border including wines from Guadalupe Valley in Baja and signature "micheladas." If you're a taco lover, try the gourmet **Lola Gaspar** on the Artist's Promenade or, further afield, **La Super Birria** on First Street or **El Gordito** on Main. For evening dining options, there are many great choices in the area bordered by 4th and 2nd Streets from French to Broadway.

Nature's most perfect food - the taco - is found in abundance in Santa Ana!

Santa Ana celebrates Saturday Art Walk on the Artist Promenade.

PM: Explore Historic Downtown Santa Ana (DTSA) - 4th Street, Murals and Artists Village

1. Creative 4th Street - 4th Street is your key to downtown. Over the years, it's seen decline, redevelopment, and reinvestment, and today it seems to be transitioning from a primarily Latino shopping street to a gentrified mix of new restaurants and specialty retail. Start from French Street and go west five blocks to Broadway. You'll pass the Yost Theater, 4th Street Market, and an interesting variety of shops. Notice the four-story, Classical Revival **Spurgeon Building** (1913) at Sycamore with its distinctive clock tower.

2. City of Murals - Everywhere you look in this creative downtown, you'll see murals. The best concentration is located in the alley behind Fourth Street between Main and Bush streets. Here you'll find the *Viva Santa Ana* mural collection by the Artist(a) Coalition depicting Chinese immigrants, street vendors, agricultural workers, traditional Mexican dancers and more. Check out the AAA's webpage on 10 murals in Santa Ana that celebrate Chicano culture by Sarah Rafael García.

3. Artists Village Promenade - Two blocks south of 4th Street at Broadway and 2nd Street, you'll find this beautiful pedestrian street of galleries and restaurants. Anchored by the Spanish Colonial **Santora Building**, it is one of the most beautiful urban spaces in the county. Take in the exhibits at the Grand Central Art Station sponsored by Cal State Fullerton. The **DTSA Art Walk** is held on the first Saturday of the month from 5:00 to 10:00 PM complete with live music, vendors and lots of art on display.

Nearby Attractions:

- **Bowers Museum** - One of Orange County's oldest museums; excellent collection of plein-air paintings and Early California exhibits.
- **Historic Floral Park** - A beautiful neighborhood of 600 vintage homes (1920 - 1950) in the northern tip of Santa Ana.
- **Santa Ana Zoo** - A 20-acre park focusing primarily on animals and birds from Central and South America.
- **Discovery Cube** - An educational science center with over 100 hands-on exhibits for kids.

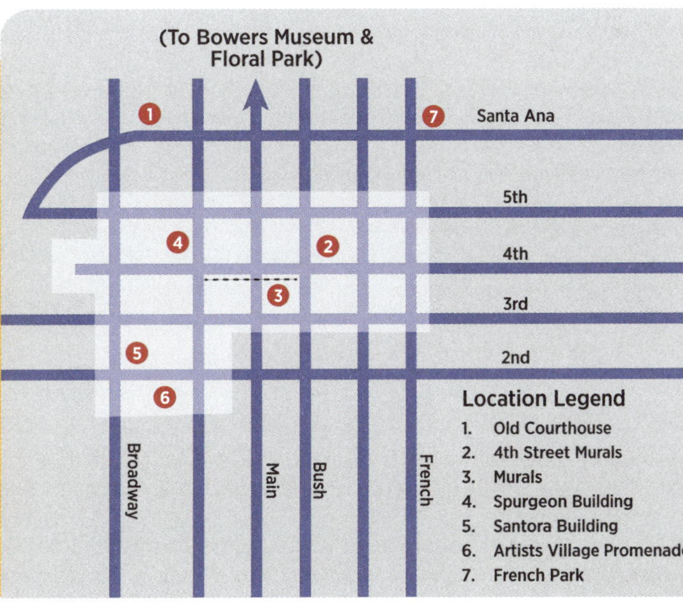

OUTING #58: PRIME COASTAL WALKS

Dana Point, Laguna Beach and Crystal Cove

Dana Point has proudly embraced its interesting history. *Sea stars seem to be making a comeback in Laguna's fragile and beautiful tide pools.* *This young visitor has discovered how kelp attaches to sea bottom.*

The beautiful coast of Southern California has attracted explorers, trading ships, developers, artists and surfers. This outing combines the dramatic history of Dana Point and the County's most beautiful coastal trail in Laguna Beach. Crystal Cove State Park is a more secluded beach walk starting from the park's Historic District. Expect great views and lots of fresh sea air!

Dana Point History Walk: Dana Point's beautiful location on the coast gave it a prominent role in California history. Visited by Yankee merchant ships and pirates in the early 1800s, chosen for development by one of Hollywood's original founders and home to early surfing legends, Dana Point now boasts an innovative mixed-use town center - the **Lantern District**.

1) Start your walk at the **Blue Lantern Gazebo Overlook** (34343 Street of the Blue Lantern). You'll have a great view of the Marina and the rugged Headlands. Find the California Historical Landmark plaque describing the arrival of **Richard Henry Dana** in 1835 and a pirate who raided Mission San Juan Capistrano 17 years earlier.

2) Walk towards PCH and turn right on Del Prado just past the Coastal Kitchen Inn (1926). Stop under the **street-spanning arch** and observe the historic paintings and markers.

3) Continue south one block on Del Prado to the corner of **Street of the Ruby Lantern**. Notice the historic lantern street sign with its "ruby" light atop. These lanterns were originally used by ships in the harbor 200 years ago to advertise their products. They were brought back in the 1920s by developer **Sydney Woodruff** - of Hollywood Sign fame - as marketing symbols to sell homes in the new town.

4) As you proceed south on Del Prado, you will notice the results of the **Town Center Plan** adopted by the City in 2006 - wider sidewalks, benches, landscaped medians, and, to the left, three-to-four-story mixed-use buildings. The ground-floor retail of restaurants and shops is complemented with residential units above. Approving this higher density and contemporary architecture in a laid-back surf town was not easily won! By the way, there are great coffee shops and restaurants on the Street of the Amber Lantern.

5) Turn right on the Street of the Violet Lantern and walk two blocks to the lookout and the **Bluff Top Trail**. Descend the trail and stop at the statue of the **Hide Drogher** (1990) - a replica of the 19th-century sailors (RH Dana was one!) who tossed cowhides off these cliffs to the merchant ships below. Continue down the trail to the cement foundations of the Dana Point Inn. As the plaque notes, Woodruff stopped construction in 1939 due to the Great Depression.

6) Follow the trail to its end at the overlook on the Street of the Amber Lantern. Look south beyond the Marina towards **Doheny State Park**. The land was donated to the state in 1931 by oil tycoon Edward Doheny in honor of his son Ned who was found dead in the Greystone Mansion in Beverly Hills in 1929.

Cowhides, thrown down from the cliffs, floated in the wind " like a kite with a broken string." - R.H. Dana

The Laguna Beach Coastal Trail in Heisler Park is a must-see!

7) Walk one block and make a left on Santa Clara. On your right, you'll soon see the landmark Spanish Colonial home of **Sydney Woodruff** whose dream to create a romantic Mediterranean-style resort town was dashed by the Great Depression. It's a pleasant two-block walk back to your car on the **Street of the Blue Lantern**. As you've seen, Dana Point has lots of stories to tell!

Laguna Beach Coastal Walk: Heisler Park to Downtown - This walk combines natural beauty with well-placed public art. Heisler Park, the town's most popular attraction, is an oceanfront park hugging a stunning, rocky shore with walking trails, gardens, a marine refuge with tide pools, picnic tables, barbecues, surfing, and even lawn bowling. The walk then descends to Main Beach and Laguna's fun compact downtown with its restaurants and shops.

1) Start your walk on the beach side of the **Laguna Beach Lawn Bowling Club** (455 Cliff Dr.) where you find the 9/11 Monument and the **Veteran's Memorial on Monument Point**.

2) Walk south along the trail and stop at the "Breaching Whale" sculpture and "Lunar Tides" mosaic at the base of the amphitheater.

3) Continue to the **Gazebo**, past Las Brisas Restaurant (nice place for a drink!), along the bluff-side trail, and down the steps to the Main Beach Boardwalk.

4) Stroll the Boardwalk past the landmark **Lifeguard Tower** and enter Laguna's compact downtown at the Forest Avenue Promenade.

Crystal Cove State Park - Just north of Laguna, you'll find one of the best beach walks in the County - three miles of secluded, flat beaches. You can walk on top of the coastal bluffs, but the shoreline is much more fun. Park your car in the **Los Trancos parking lot** off PCH, walk through the tunnel and you'll enter the Historic District. You can go either north or south from here - both directions are beautiful. Look for shorebirds, sea lions, and dolphins; at low tide, there are great tide pools and plenty of shells. But, please remember, California's fragile marine life is protected by the **Marine Life Protection Act of 1999** - no collecting allowed.

OUTING #59: CALIFORNIA HISTORY WALKS

Irvine History Trail and Downtown San Juan Capistrano

It's nice to combine a little exercise with some learning! Both of these walks share tremendous variety, but are quite different. The Jeffrey Open Space Trail, opened in 2015, is a beautiful walk in a linear park with lots of great history exhibits and varied landscapes. The San Juan Capistrano Walk is an interesting downtown loop in the birthplace of Orange County.

Jeffrey Open Space Trail (JOST) - Planned communities provide an abundance of recreational open space, and the **Irvine Company**, which developed the City's Master Plan, is an industry leader. The JOST, about five miles long (and being expanded), is one of the most interesting history trails in Southern California. It's a linear park that meanders through meadows, creek beds, woodsy trails, stone tunnels, public art displays and botanical gardens. The variety of surfaces, landscaping, seating options and historic markers is truly impressive. From the 5 Freeway, go north on Jeffrey and park in the shopping plaza on the corner of Trabuco and Jeffrey. Cross the street and join the trail.

1) The Walk - Along the trail are markers describing 500 years of local history. From the Trabuco Rd. entry point, going north will lead you back in time with exhibits on the **founding of the Irvine Ranch** and the growth of the citrus industry. Crossing the steel bridge at Irvine Boulevard, markers describe the birth of California and the Mexican Rancho Period. As you approach **Portola Parkway**, you enter the period of Spanish exploration going back as far as **Cabrillo's exploration** of the **California coast** in **1542**! The earliest period described is that of Native American heritage. Walking south from Trabuco, the trail traces the transformation of the ranch into the City of Irvine and the founding of UC Irvine.

You'll be struck with the tremendous attention to detail and quality materials along the trail, not surprising since the Irvine Company and its villages are among the most successful in the nation. Even the restrooms look like solid rustic architecture from the National Park system! **Separating pedestrians from roadways** has a long tradition in American planned communities. The garden suburb of Radburn, New Jersey, set the standard back in 1926. The trail is being extended and is an important link in the open space corridor from the Santa Ana Mountains to the Pacific Ocean.

Downtown San Juan Capistrano History Walk - SJC is Orange County's oldest settlement, and the City has done an admirable job blending old and new. The Mission, built in 1776, is the biggest attraction (described in Outing #46). This adventure includes areas outside the Mission grounds, including Los Rios Historic District and the River Street Market.

1) Start in front of the Mission at the corner of Ortega Highway and Camino Capistrano. Notice that all the buildings in this beautiful town are brick, stone, wood, or plaster.

2) Walk one block east to El Camino Real and cross the street to the south side. Look back at the Capistrano Inn with its blend of ranch and Spanish Colonial styles - a clear result of the City's architectural review process and height initiative. Walking south you'll see the **Camino Real Playhouse** and next to it the **Blas Aguilar Adobe** (1794) - one of several adobes built to house soldiers and Native Americans from the Mission. Find the prickly pear cactus in the small area south of the adobe. The white scales on the surface of the cactus pads are "cochineal" insects and when crushed produce a red dye.

Large, barnlike structures surround River St. Market's impressive gathering spaces.

This tile display explains how California got its name - from a mythical island!

3) Continue down El Camino Real as it curves around and ends at Camino Capistrano. To your left at the corner is the 1883 **Judge Egan Home**. This Italianate Victorian beauty has been reborn as Ellie's Table Restaurant. To your right is the 1938 **Eslinger Building** - a Streamline Moderne office building placed on the National Register. This modern style certainly doesn't fit with early California history, but it's a beauty nonetheless.

4) Turn right and continue up **Camino Capistrano**. Across the street is a line of transformed adobe buildings, the most famous of which is **El Adobe Restaurant**, built from the town's historic jail and, more recently, a favorite of former President Richard Nixon.

5) Turn left at **Verdugo Street** and walk down one block to the railroad tracks and the **historic Depot** (Mission Revival – 1886). Cross the tracks and enter the Los Rios Historic District - the oldest continuously-lived-in street in California.

6) Los Rios Historic District - Turn right and you're back in early California. The board-and-batten homes on the right have become restaurants and shops. Enter **Los Rios Park** on the left with its **Montanez Adobe** (1829), native plant Butterfly Garden, and History Wall. You might even find the 200-year-old pepper tree! Once back on Los Rios Street, go south and follow the signs to River Street Market.

7) River Street Market - This popular commercial center, opened in 2024, has brought even more buzz to downtown. It combines restaurants and shops, designed in a California Agrarian Modern style, around an open-air, central gathering space. With native oak and sycamore trees, rustic materials, decomposed granite walkways, and movable seating, River Street embraces SJC's agrarian roots. The upscale restaurants and bars are beyond most cowboys' budgets however!

The History Wall in Los Rios Park tells the story of California's oldest street.

Painted Lady in Los Rios Park Butterfly Garden.

Nearby Attractions:

- Ecology Center
- Casa Romantica
- Dana Point Marina and Doheny State Beach

OUTING #60: FOLLOW THE WATER!

Orange County Water District and San Joaquin Marsh Reserve

This outing could be called "follow the water!" It visits the world's largest water recycling facility - the Orange County Water District - followed by a visit to a 300-acre wildlife sanctuary for bird-watching. With a hard hat and OCWD vest, you'll see firsthand how clean water is produced from wastewater in this state-of-the-art facility. You'll have to book a tour online - OCWD Tours - for a group of 10 or more. With smaller groups, you can join the district's quarterly tours. For lunch, this outing recommends nearby Mercado Gonzalez - a colorful 70,000 square foot Mexican food hall and supermarket in Costa Mesa. Then, it's a short drive to the San Joaquin Marsh Wildlife Sanctuary adjacent to UC Irvine.

From "toilet to tap!" Would you take a drink? In the future, millions will.

Author Hoffman at the "reverse osmosis" stage of the water treatment tour.

Background: It's easy to take our infrastructure for granted, but, in our semiarid region, water needs to be managed carefully. Since 1933, the OCWD in Fountain Valley has been monitoring ground water levels. As demand increased, it discovered that natural recharge from the **Santa Ana River** was not enough. Importing water from distant sources like the Colorado River or the Sacramento Delta became impractical. Then, in 2008, an ingenious solution was devised.

In 2008, the **District's Groundwater Replenishment System (GWRS)** (initial cost - $481 million!) facility began to use treated wastewater from the neighboring **Orange County Sanitation District**. It might sound scary to reuse sewer water, but technology came to the rescue. This prepurified wastewater undergoes further treatment at the OCWD. Although the resulting water exceeds federal standards for drinkability, the water does not go directly to homes but rather is injected into recharge basins so that local water districts have adequate supplies. Interestingly, the District also injects this "final product" water into wells near the ocean to provide a barrier from seawater intrusion.

Itinerary: AM - Tour the Ground Water Replenishment System at OCWD

1) This 90-minute tour starts with a slide presentation about how the Water District manages a **groundwater basin** that provides 85% of the drinking water to 2.5 million people in Orange County. Then it's time to put on the hard hats!

2) Touring the GWRS Facility - It's hard to imagine that this huge, modern facility with its tanks, pipes and huge machinery even exists in the middle of suburban Orange County. The tour visits the three steps in the purification process before the water is injected back into the County's groundwater basin:

a) Step 1 - **Microfiltration** - Bundles of minute (0.2 microns) fibers filter out particulate contaminants.

b) Step 2 - **Reverse Osmosis** - Water fed through semipermeable membranes encased in long, pressure cylinders. Resulting water is so pure that minerals have to be added back.

c) Step 3 - **Ultraviolet light** with hydrogen peroxide, followed by lime treatment - After water is exposed to these treatments, its pH levels are checked and it's ready to be released.

d) Final Step - Taste the Water! Although the purified water does not go directly to homes, the tour guide will invite you to drink the product water. This water is pure and tasty - **"from toilet to tap!"**

Lunch - Mercado Gonzalez, Northgate Market, Costa Mesa - Only a seven-minute drive from the OCWD, this is a wonderful lunch choice (fully described in Outing #54). As you enter the huge market/food hall, you'll be delighted by the colorful graphics and lively atmosphere. The food stalls ("puestos") are on your right. Warning! You will not be able to resist the churros!

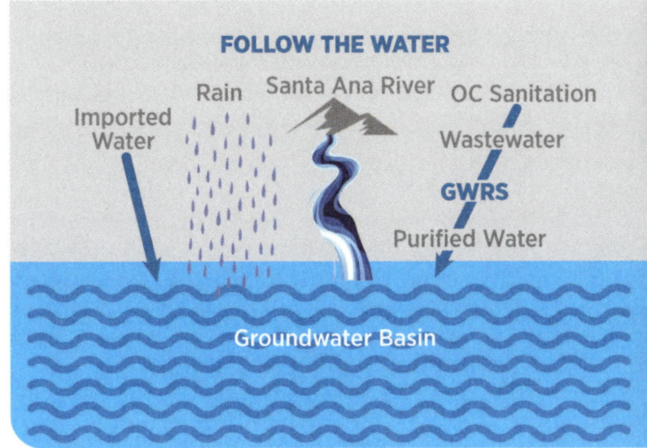

Solo egret in Pond E.

PM - Visit the San Joaquin Marsh Wildlife Sanctuary (5 Riparian View, Irvine) - This "wetland of distinction" is a true hidden gem for bird watchers and nature lovers, and it matches the important theme of the day - "follow the water." The wetlands naturally clean the urban runoff from **San Diego Creek** before it flows into the environmentally sensitive Upper Newport Bay. The bulrush and other marsh plants clean much of the harmful nitrogen from the water. This **Natural Treatment System** is a lot different from the reverse osmosis of the OCWD, but it helps the nearby Irvine Ranch Water District meet its environmental goals.

Visiting the Marsh - You can call ahead to the **Sea and Sage Audubon Society** (949-261-7963), which operates the Visitor's Center and can often arrange a bird guide. And plan to bring binoculars! You'll have a chance to see some of the over 200 species of birds that visit the marsh, 100 of which are part of the migratory Pacific Flyover.

1. Turn into Riparian Way from Campus Drive. After a short drive along San Diego Creek, make a left into the parking lot.

2. Visit the yellow **Audubon House**, the Visitor's Center run by the Sea and Sage Society. Here you can get a trail map, find out what birds are visiting, study the exhibits and buy a bird guide.

3. Enjoy the trails and the birds - There are many trails to choose from, but a good start is the **Fledgling Loop Trail** - only .5 miles long, but you'll go by six major ponds. Catch the trail just to the right of the Visitor's Center and take the counterclockwise loop. After you pass the two big ponds on your left, turn left and left again to view Pond 1 with its island. Here you may see white pelicans, terns, egrets, cranes, and many other avian friends. Follow the path back through the **Marsh Campus** with its demonstration garden, Duck Club (the area used to be part of a gun club complex), the **Visitor's Center**, and your car. You have followed the water today and the birds!

Wow! Is that a White Pelican? It's great to have a bird guide with a good scope!

OUTING #61: DOWNTOWN RIVERSIDE, WOW!

Historic Mission Inn and the Cheech Center for Chicano Art

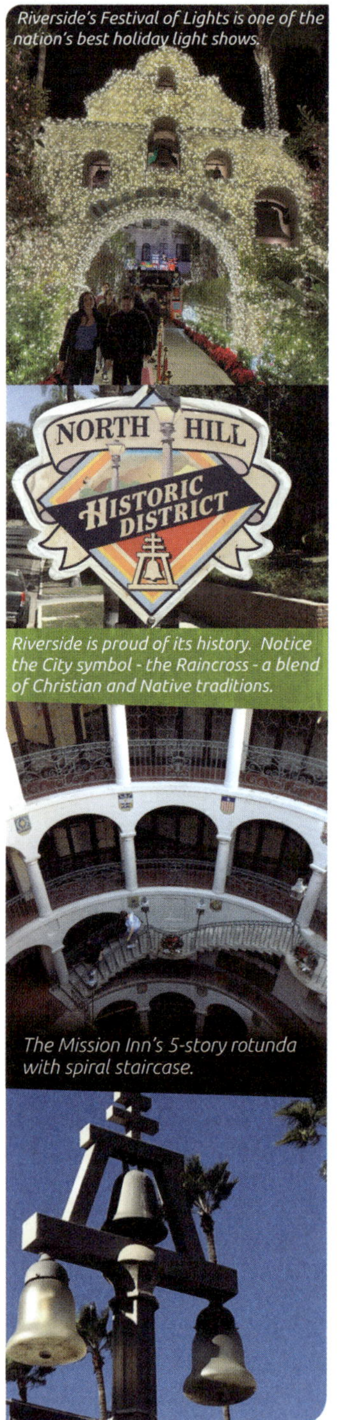

Riverside's Festival of Lights is one of the nation's best holiday light shows.

Riverside is proud of its history. Notice the City symbol - the Raincross - a blend of Christian and Native traditions.

The Mission Inn's 5-story rotunda with spiral staircase.

Spend a day in beautiful and historic Downtown Riverside. The attractions are literally right next to each other, so park your car and enjoy. This outing includes a docent tour of the famous Mission Inn, lunch at Tio's Tacos, and an afternoon visit to the Cheech Marin Center for Chicano Art. It's particularly fun to visit during the holiday's Festival of Lights when the Mission Inn is decorated with thousands of lights inside and out.

Background: Downtown Riverside is a historic gem. The City became one of the wealthiest in the US in the late 1800s due to the growth of its citrus industry. With refrigerated railroad cars and improvements in irrigation, **Riverside's navel oranges** were shipped to the East Coast. The town attracted wealthy visitors and investors as beautiful churches, commercial buildings and homes sprang up. Many homes from this era still exist, and the City has designated 13 historic districts.

A walk along Mission Inn Avenue between Lime and Market Streets is an architectural showcase, with excellent examples of Mission Revival, Spanish Colonial, Beaux Arts and Gothic styles from the early 1900s. The famous and fanciful **Mission Inn** (built between 1902 and1932) was declared a **National Historic Landmark** in 1977. It attracted movie stars and presidents and is still the city's biggest tourist draw. Currently, the Inn & Spa has 238 rooms, including 27 suites.

In June 2022, comedian **Cheech Marin**, the **world's largest collector of Chicano Art**, formed a public-private partnership with the **Riverside Art Museum** to open a new, engaging museum - "the Cheech." It is considered the world's best collection of Chicano Art and aims to be a catalyst for Latino artists in the Inland Empire.

Itinerary:

AM: Tour the Mission Inn and Downtown Riverside: Book a docent-led tour of the Mission Inn through the **Mission Inn Foundation** (missioninnmuseum.org), a nonprofit education and preservation organization. The tour will provide the fascinating backstory of how the landmark was saved from ruin several times, most recently in 1992 by businessman Duane Roberts, inventor of the frozen burrito. You will explore the exuberantly detailed **Mission Revival hotel** with visits to the Cloister, Spanish and Rotunda Wings, and Moorish-inspired Alhambra Court. Original owner Frank Miller decorated the Inn with treasures such as Tiffany-stained glass windows and 19th-century oil paintings depicting California historic landscapes. A definite show-stopper here is the St. Francis of Assisi wedding chapel. This tour is a classic Southern California experience.

Take some time to explore the downtown. You can book a walking tour with the Mission Inn Foundation or download a **Downtown Riverside Historic Walking Tour>** The best concentration of historic buildings is found between Lime St. and Market, along Mission Inn and University Avenues. Riverside also one of the few cities that created a pedestrian street in its downtown. It extends along Main Street from the Convention Center to City Hall, past the Mission Inn and lots of fun stores and restaurants.

Chicano Art often depicts the urban experience.

Bronze heart sculpture will have donor names on cactus leaves.

The De La Torre brothers' lenticular art is a showstopper at The Cheech.

Lunch - Restaurants abound but a trip one block down Mission Inn Ave. to **Tio's Tacos** is more than entertaining. The owner has decorated his large property with folk art, ceramic tile and everyday objects in a way that is reminiscent of Watts Towers in Los Angeles. Another option is the **Riverside Food Lab**, a lively food hall next door to the restored Fox Theater on Mission Inn and Market Streets. Of course, you could eat inside the Mission Inn or at the **Spaghetti Factory** (3191 Mission Ave.) in a restored 1912 fruit packing house. How cool is that!

PM: Visit the Cheech Marin Center for Chicano Art and Culture - Conveniently, the "Cheech" is located just east of the Mission Inn. Cheech appreciates the Riverside community and its love for art and culture, so he decided to donate over 500 pieces of his collection to the **Riverside Art Museum**. The result is a rotating collection of beautiful and engaging works of art - some from his collection, some from contributing Chicano artists from throughout the Southwest. It's a good idea to call ahead and see if you can arrange a brief tour. The friendly staff gives a good orientation by discussing several of the permanent pieces on display.

The two-story museum is just the right size, with the **visiting exhibitions** located upstairs. As you enjoy the artwork, look for symbols and themes common to Chicano Art - Aztec and Mayan images, religious icons, cultural heroes, issues of immigration, urban life, and Mexican murals. One permanent piece in the lobby is particularly intriguing - a 26-foot, LED-backlit lenticular mural by Einar and Jaimex De La Torre. This 3-D mural is transformed as the viewer walks by. This is one "muy suave" museum!

Hoffman with a lifelike Cheech at The Cheech.

Nearby Attractions:

- **California Citrus State Historic Park** - Over 225 acres of many types of citrus; informative, small museum; tours Friday - Sunday
- **Redlands** - Great college town. Smiley Library with Abraham Lincoln Museum; Kimberly Crest Mansion (1897)

OUTING #62: INLAND EMPIRE GOLD

Redlands and Citrus State Historic Park

This outing focuses on that famous and vanishing Southern California fruit - the orange! It includes a visit to the Citrus State Historic Park where you can still see acres and acres of citrus and learn about its history. Then, you visit another Inland Empire town that grew rich from oranges - Redlands. If you like vintage architecture and US history, this will be an excellent outing. You can visit a famous library with an Abraham Lincoln Museum and tour the 1897 chateau-style Kimberly Crest Mansion and Gardens. Redlands' walkable downtown offers numerous options for lunch. Finally, this is a great town for an architectural driving tour as you "follow the palm trees" to the vintage neighborhoods.

Background: Incorporated in 1888 and quickly growing wealthy from navel oranges, **Redlands** was known as both "the City of Millionaires" and **"the City of Beautiful Homes."** Although the economy changed, the City preserved many of its stately homes and maintained a small-town feel along its tree-lined downtown State Street. Its adjoining **University of Redlands**, founded in 1907 and designed in a Mediterranean Classical style, adds a collegiate feel to this already proud town.

Itinerary:

AM: Visit the California State Historic Park (9400 Dufferin Ave., Riverside): In a region of vanishing groves, it's refreshing and somewhat nostalgic to explore this park with over **250 acres of citrus trees**. The park is open daily affording visitors the opportunity to walk the trails, have a picnic, or simply drive through in your car. If you want to learn more, **visit Fridays through Sundays** when grove tours are offered at 10:00 AM, and the **Visitor Center** is open. It has excellent exhibits on the history of the California citrus industry. Make sure to call ahead if you want to join a grove tour or bring a group.

The Citrus Park is truly a breath of fresh air. Once in the groves, you will see varieties of citrus you never knew existed. There are QR Code Taghunts throughout the park to share history and facts. Finally, if you visit from January to March, much of the fruit will be ripening, and the park often hosts fruit tastings in the Visitor Center.

Lunch in Redlands - Redlands has a pedestrian-friendly, hometown downtown where you'll find a cluster of good restaurants on and around **State Street** and Citrus Ave. between Orange and 7th. A traditionally popular choice is Martha's Greens and (with bakery!) on Citrus.

PM: Explore Redlands - There's more to do than one afternoon allows, but check out these suggestions:

1. A great place to start is the landmark **A.K. Smiley Library**, built in 1898 in a unique Moorish/Romanesque style. One of California's oldest libraries, it is listed on the National Register and contains important research archives.

2. Visit the adjoining Lincoln Memorial Shrine - The only museum and archives dedicated to the study of Abraham Lincoln and the American Civil War west of the Mississippi River. So, what's an Abraham Lincoln Museum doing so far from his roots? It was the dream of local **philanthropist Robert Watchorn**, a great admirer of President Lincoln. He hired noted **architect Elmer Grey** who designed the octagonal entrance in 1937.

The interior is a treasure of art, murals and exhibits. Upon entering, you'll immediately notice the murals of heroic female figures painted by New York artist Dean Cornwell. Enjoy the collections in this small but powerful museum. You may even find a painting by Norman Rockwell.

3) Tour the beautiful Kimberly Crest Mansion - This is a 1897 chateau- style house museum with **Gilded Age furnishings** and **Italian-style gardens**. The 7,000 sq. ft. mansion was donated by heirs of the Kimberly Clark Corporation and sits on a small hill with great views of the San Bernardino Mountains. The gardens are open daily; tours are Thursdays, Fridays and Sundays, and begin at 1:00 PM and last about 45 minutes. Another great home to check out is the **Morey Mansion** (190 Terracina Blvd.) - an exuberant Queen Anne Victorian home dubbed "America's Favorite Victorian Home" and seen in numerous TV commercials.

4) Architectural Driving Tour - Before you leave delightful Redlands, take some time to explore the neighborhoods with vintage architecture. You can often find the oldest parts of a town by finding the tallest trees. So **follow the tall palm trees** and cruise the stately homes on Olive, Highland and Fern Avenues. You'll see numerous well-preserved early "period revival" styles such as Craftsman, Mission, Spanish, Colonial and Norman. The nearby Redlands Bowl Amphitheater in **Smiley Park**, built in 1929, hosts summer concerts. What a town!

The Kimberly Crest Mansion is one of Southern California's best examples of the "Châteauesque" style.

Lincoln Museum at Smiley Library: a gem!

Everywhere you look, Redlands embraces its orange history!

Nearby Attractions:

- **Downtown Riverside** - Mission Inn or Cheech Marin Center for Chicano Art
- **Oak Glen**- Apple picking in the fall; a short drive from Redlands

OUTING #63: MID-CENTURY MODERN HOLIDAY!

Palm Springs Renaissance

The Kaufmann House (1946) by Richard Neutra became the leading model for postwar, residential Modernism.

Marilyn is back in front of the Art Museum; not everyone is pleased!

Palm Springs relaxation zone!

Palm Springs is so hip and cool that you may want to stay several days. This day-long outing will introduce you to the most famous Mid-Century Modern neighborhoods as well as other fun attractions. Of course, it's exciting to visit during Modernism Week (in February and October), but it gets quite crowded and expensive. As this outing will show, Palm Springs is more than famous architecture. It has a world-class museum, a newly opened Native American Cultural Center, and dramatic nature hikes in the mountains and palm canyons. In few places in the world can you find a dramatic mountain backdrop, stunning desert and cultural mecca all in one.

Background: Palm Springs has the greatest variety of mid-century modern homes in the nation, and their preservation sparked the city's renaissance. Starting in the 1920s and '30s, the Hollywood elite discovered this desert resort. After World War II, **pioneering modernist architects** designed landmark homes and **"desert modern" neighborhoods**. Between 1947 and 1965, the Alexander Construction Company built 2,200 homes. The City's popularity, however, got out of control in the 1980s with rowdy "spring break" crowds, and the downtown began to decline. But, starting in the 1990s, the City and its strong preservation community designated many buildings and neighborhoods as historic landmarks, and the boom was on! Palm Springs is also a city of many distinctive neighborhoods, each with their own specialized street signs. **Modernism Weeks** are bigger celebrations than ever, drawing architectural enthusiasts from all over the world.

Itinerary - AM: A Mid-Century Modern Neighborhood Driving Tour

1. Start your tour at the **Visitor's Center** at the historic **Tramway Gas Station** (1965) at the corner of N. Palm Canyon Dr. and Tramway Road. Pick up the small brochure – **A Map of Modern Palm Springs** – and be on your way to beauty. Maps of stars' homes are available, but walls and hedges make viewing difficult!

2. Start with the Little Tuscany neighborhood high among the boulders in northwest Palm Springs. Plug in 1030 W. Cielo in your navigator to the famous **Edris House (1953)**. See how **architect E. Stuart Williams** blended the home into its desert environment.

3. Close by is the famous **Kaufmann Desert House (1946)** by **Richard Neutra** at 470 West Vista Chino. With its open floor plans, floor-to-ceiling glass and sleek horizontal lines, it is the most photographed and quintessential home of the mid-century style in Palm Springs.

4. Follow Monte Vista to the **Vista Las Palmas** neighborhood built in the 1950s. Most famous is the **House of Tomorrow** (1350 Via Ladera), aka **Elvis Presley's Honeymoon Hideaway**, but the best part is cruising this gorgeous neighborhood butted against the mountains. Look for the famous "Swiss Miss" homes (where the A-frame touches the ground) and the classic butterfly roofs.

5. Follow Palm Canyon Drive through downtown to **Twin Palms Estates** (turn right on El Camino Real) – the City's first modern housing tract (1957—1959). Originally built as a Jewish enclave due to restrictive covenants in other parts of the city, Twin Palms sold quickly. Although there are only two floor plans here (both of 1,600 sq. ft.), the open car ports, exposed concrete block, clerestory windows, breezeways, varied colors, and butterfly roofs made each home seem distinct. And, of course, each home had two palms!

Lunch and Exploring in Downtown Palm Springs –

The 3-block stretch of E. Palm Canyon Drive between Baristo and Tahquitz Canyon is abuzz with restaurants, shops and historic buildings. In addition to your lunch, you'll find some fun exploring: the **Palm Springs Historical Society** (221 S. Palm Canyon); **La Plaza**, one of the first outdoor shopping centers (1936); the Spanish Colonial La Plaza Theater; and the **Palm Springs Walk of Stars** embedded in the sidewalk.

PM: So much to see! Choose your activity:

1. The Palm Springs Art Museum is conveniently located downtown and has an excellent permanent collection as well as rotating exhibits.

2. Agua Caliente Cultural Museum and Plaza - Opened in 2023, this tribal museum, spa and outdoor oasis trail is one of the largest in the US. The museum with its five galleries tells the story of this tribe - the **Agua Caliente Band of Cahuilla Indians** - from their perspective. The exhibits are excellent with 3-D graphics and lots of video displays. It's located right downtown, at the site of the hot mineral spring that the tribe has held sacred for millennia. This is a must see!

3. Take a beautiful hike in Indian Canyons – Only four miles south of downtown, you can hike one of the most beautiful areas of the Western US, where native palm trees grow amid mountain springs (hey, is there a name here?). The area is run by the Agua Caliente Band of the Cahuilla Indians, and, for a small fee, you have access to trails of varying difficulty. **Andreas Canyon** is a good choice if you have limited time. Watch your step for rattlesnakes or rosy boas, and you'll find blooming cacti in the spring. Closer to town is another great hike: **Tahquitz Canyon Loop** - a steep, 2-mile loop trail to a waterfall.

4. Desert plant lovers? – A fun stop at 1701 South Palm Canyon Drive is the **Moorten Botanical Garden**. Established in 1938, this private arboretum of desert plants is quirky and wonderful.

Nearby Attractions:

- **Sunnylands** - Highly sought-after tour of mid-century Annenberg estate in Rancho Mirage
- **Palm Springs Aerial Tramway**- Exciting ride from desert floor to mountaintop at 8,516 feet
- **Living Desert Zoo and Gardens**- Beautiful zoo and botanical gardens in Palm Desert

How many "Swiss Miss" rooflines can you find in the Las Palmas neighborhood?

All the mid-century rooflines - gable, shed, butterfly, flat, and accordion - are shown on this street sign.

OUTING #64: NATIVE LAND

Agua Caliente Cultural Museum and Indian Canyons

This outing includes the new Agua Caliente Cultural Museum in downtown Palm Springs followed by a beautiful hike in nearby Indian Canyons. The Agua Caliente people share their history and culture in five, state-of-the-art exhibition areas. With an adjoining Outdoor Oasis Trail, Cultural Plaza, and a spa created from an ancient mineral spring, this facility is the second largest of its kind in the US. It's inspiring that this band of the Cahuilla Nation tells their story of resilience in such a beautiful facility.

Andreas Canyon is a short, dramatic hike along a stream.

Background: The history of Native Americans in California is one of dramatic and often devastating change. At the time of the Spanish arrival in 1769, there were an estimated 300,000 native peoples in California living in scores of autonomous hunting and gathering cultures. Tragically, the Spanish Mission system, along with epidemic diseases, decimated the native population. The invasion by American settlers, California statehood and the Gold Rush depleted their numbers even more. Finally, by the late 1800s, the federal government, by Executive Order, granted millions of acres to native tribes, and lawsuits in the mid-1950s granted more land. Currently in California, thirty native reservations operate gaming businesses. The casinos are seen as an interim step to more economic independence.

Itinerary: AM - Visit the Agua Caliente Cultural Museum - As you enter the Cultural Plaza area, notice the beautiful **Oasis Trail** with native fan palms winding through the property. The five exhibition areas in the museum are done in order:

1. Our Home - Introduces visitors to the lands occupied by the Agua Caliente and eight other bands of Cahuilla Indians.

2. Creation and Migration - This timed visit tells the band's creation story in a theatre setting with 360-projection and immersive digital animation.

3. Our Land - Contains replicas of the band's Indian Canyons (which you can explore later) along with its **sacred mineral hot spring - Sec-he** - found here. Examples of basketry, clothing made from agave fibers, a ceremonial house, and other examples of art are found here. The tribe was organized around small clans, with marriage outside of the group encouraged for both health and harmonious relations.

4. Change, Adaptation and Self-Determination - Show the Tribe's more recent history, beginning with the arrival of Euro-American settlers in the 19th century all the way to the present day. Don't miss the **3-D animation of the Coachella Valley** as it has changed from a sparsely-populated area with an abundant aquifer to its present population of over 350,000 with over 130 golf courses. The struggle for land and political rights is well documented here, culminating in the election of an All Women Tribal Council in 1954.

5. Into the Future - This final exhibition area looks both forward and back in time, displaying artifacts such as metates and projectile points found during the excavation for the **Cultural Plaza** that are over 8,000 years old. This long-standing occupation of the region is juxtaposed with interviews of Tribe members expressing pride in their traditions and customs but looking to a future of sustainable growth and opportunity.

Lunch - The Agua Caliente Cultural Plaza faces Tahquitz Canyon Way, one block from S. Palm Canyon Drive and its many downtown restaurants.

The third museum gallery - Our Land - recreates the mountain canyons so vital to the Cahuilla people.

If you're lucky, you'll see a Rosy Boa! These salmon-colored beauties are not venomous.

Take the trails above Palm Canyon. Hugging barrel cactus not recommended!

PM: Hike Indian Canyons - The Agua Caliente Band owns and runs this portion of their ancestral home with its mountain canyons and hiking trails. Drive south on Palm Canyon Drive (Highway 111) and follow the signs to the canyons. For a small fee, you can access some breathtaking canyon and mountain trails where fan palm oases thrive from the year-round springs. The best hikes are:

- **Andreas Canyon Trail** - Offers the shortest loop trail (1.1 miles) that enters the canyon along the stream and fan palm forest.

- **Palm Canyon Trail** - A longer hike that starts from a Trading Post and parking area. The deep canyon winds south along the palms and links up with other loop trails that climb the adjoining mountains for expansive views.

Further Exploration: There are growing resources, museums and cultural centers for those interested in the fascinating history of native peoples of Southern California. The varied climate and geography helped shape the distinct cultures of the Chumash, Serrano, Tongva, Alliklik, Luiseno, Acjachemen, and Kumeyaay tribes. You may also consider:

- **Palm Springs Art Museum** - Located downtown, this museum has a strong permanent collection of traditional and contemporary Native American art.
- **Autry Museum of the American West, Griffith Park, Los Angeles** - Has the nation's second largest collection of Native American art after the Smith sonian Institution National Museum of the American Indian.
- **Coachella Valley Preserve** - For desert lovers, this 20,000 acre preserve of critical habitat has two fan palm oases, the largest being the **Thousand Palm Oasis**. You'll find this hidden gem just north of Palm Desert off Interstate 10.

OUTING #65: DESERT WONDERLAND OF ROCKS

Joshua Tree National Park

This amazing high desert park of huge boulders and surreal Joshua trees can be seen in one well-planned day. The one major road - Park Boulevard - winds through the most scenic spots. Bring lots of water, snacks, and a picnic lunch - this is wilderness and there are no concessions inside the park. It's fun to visit in the spring to see the desert bloom, but Joshua Tree is beautiful any time of the year. Consider a two-day adventure by camping in the Park, renting an Airbnb in Joshua Tree, or booking a room in the quaint 29 Palms Inn located in a palm tree oasis.

Background: We can thank a determined **community activist** and **desert lover**, **Minerva Hoyt**, for this glorious park. She lobbied President Franklin Delano Roosevelt in the 1930s, and it was declared a National Monument in 1936. Then, as part of the **California Desert Protection Act**, it was declared a National Park in 1994.

The huge 792,000-acre Park encompasses **two different deserts – the Colorado** and **the Mojave**. The former, with elevations less than 3,000 feet, comprises the eastern portion of the park where you will find the spiderly ocotillo, jumping cholla cactus, and lots of creosote bushes. The latter, at elevations above 3,000 feet, makes up the western portion of the park. Here you will find the dramatic boulder stacks and oddly shaped Joshua Trees, named by Mormon settlers in the mid-19th century. At these higher elevations, it's often cooler than you think, and you'll see juniper, scrub oak and pinyon pines. This outing includes the western Mojave portion of the park with its Wonderland of Rocks and forests of Joshua trees.

The wild-armed Joshua Tree is not a tree but a species of yucca.

Itinerary: A Beautiful Drive Through the Park - I recommend starting at the **North Entrance Station** in **29 Palms** and looping back westward along **Park Boulevard**. You'll exit at the West Entrance Station in the town of Joshua Tree. Here are six scenic stops along the way:

1) Start your adventure at the new **Visitor Center** (6563 Freedom Way) in downtown 29 Palms. Here you can get information from the rangers, get a park map, and enjoy the exhibits and new museum.

2) Ascend into the park through the entrance kiosk. The landscape gets more rugged and beautiful as you gain elevation. (Do not take the left turn for **Cottonwood Springs** unless you want to see the **Cholla Cactus Garden**.) The first stop is **Skull Rock** with its ample roadside parking and nice trails on both sides of the road.

3) Continue west on Park Boulevard past Jumbo Rocks and Sheep Pass. Just past **Ryan Mtn.**, make a left at the turnoff for **Keys View** and immediately turn into the parking lot on your left at **Cap Rock**. Here you'll find a little picnic area and a nice three-quarter mile, flat nature loop around the rocks. Don't worry! Cap Rock will not slip off its boulder!

Be very careful exploring the Wonderland of Rocks. You can get hopelessly lost quickly!

4) As you leave the parking lot, turn left to ascend to Key's View at an elevation of 5,185 feet. As you climb, you'll drive through a forest of Joshua trees that is gradually replaced by junipers and scrub oak. At the end of the road you'll be treated to an amazing view of Coachella Valley, including Palm Springs, the **San Andreas Fault** and the distant **Salton Sea**.

The Hidden Valley Loop Trail is a stunner!

Keep your eyes peeled for the desert's largest lizard - the chuckwalla.

Jumping cholla cactus - beware of segments that break off!

Cap Rock's Loop Trail is a level 1-mile walk.

5) Drive back to Park Boulevard admiring the views and turn left at Park Boulevard. In only five minutes, turn left into the large parking lot for **Hidden Valley** – the most crowded spot in the park. This is a wonderful place to enjoy your picnic lunch under the impressive boulders. When you're ready, walk across the parking lot and up a steep little path to the Hidden Valley nature loop trail (about 1.2 miles in total). Many consider this **one of the most beautiful desert hikes in the Southwest**. This "valley," where cattle rustlers hid away, is a gorgeous treasure of rocks and plant life of all sizes and types. Don't miss this trail!

6) Optional hike - Barker Dam - Another popular, one-mile loop trail to a small reservoir surrounded by huge boulders. Its access is straight across Park Boulevard from Hidden Valley. Great place to see rock climbers and birds.

7) Continue west along Park Boulevard for more gorgeous vistas. Soon you will notice the **"Wonderland of Rocks"** on your right – improbable, massive mountains of cream-colored granite boulders that began eons ago underground. For your last stop and good views of the rock formations, stop at **Quail Springs** (parking lot on your left).

8) Descend into the town of Joshua Tree as you leave the park. Lots of fun, hip shops to browse. You did it!

Hidden Gems:

49 Palms Oasis – A strenuous, 3-mile hike to a fan palm oasis.

Cholla Cactus Garden - Big concentration of the "jumping cactus" in the eastern part of the park on the way to Cottonwood Spring.

Indian Cove - Stunning campground on the northern end of the Wonderland of Rocks.

Pioneer Town - A fun, short, scenic side trip on the way to or from Joshua Tree NP; a 1940s movie set with quaint, false-front Western architecture. Visit the hip **Pappy's & Harriet's** for great BBQ and really good live music. Follow the signs north from Highway 62 in Yucca Valley.

Integratron - White-domed structure designed by a UFO-ologist for rejuvenation and time travel; popular as sound bath; reservations required.

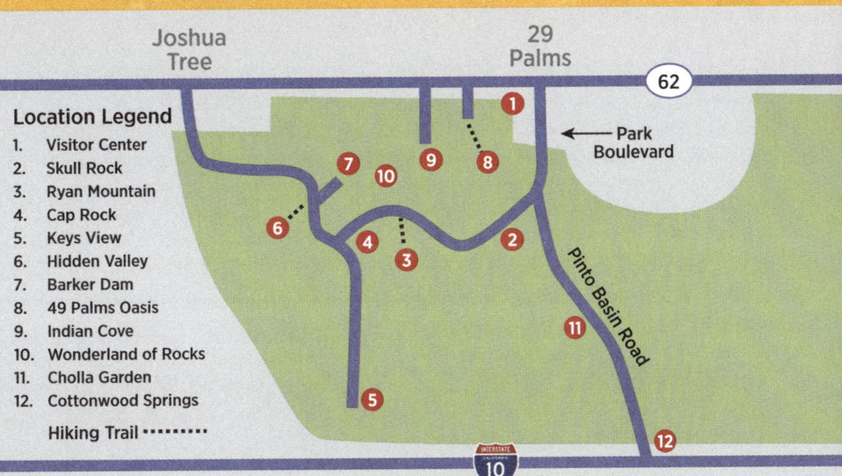

OUTING #66: AMERICA'S FINEST CITY

San Diego Harbor Tour, Little Italy and Old Town

There's so much to do in America's "finest city" that we created four downtown outings. The first is a nice introduction to San Diego that includes the harbor, the most popular urban village and the city's birthplace. San Diego's mediterranean climate is so ridiculously nice that you can comfortably visit any time of the year. It's recommended that you start with a harbor cruise, have lunch in Little Italy, and then explore California history in Old Town San Diego.

Piazza della Famiglia, in the heart of Little Italy, is Southern California's most beautiful urban space.

San Diego Harbor is home to several nuclear-power aircraft carriers.

The "Kissing Sailor Statue" (aka Unconditional Surrender *and* Embracing Peace*) is a crowd pleaser!*

Background: **San Diego Harbor** - California's long 700-mile coastline only has three major natural harbors - San Francisco, Humbolt and San Diego. San Diego's harbor is where the Spanish began their **colonization of California in 1769** and where the US Navy set up base headquarters for their major ships. The harbor is still home to several aircraft carriers and three naval bases, but also serves the tourist public with sightseeing boats and ten museum ships, including the popular **USS Midway Aircraft Carrier Museum** and the **Maritime Museum** of San Diego with its vintage ships.

Little Italy - San Diego prides itself as a **"City of Villages"** and Little Italy is its gold standard. Originally home to Italian immigrants drawn to the tuna industry, the area declined after WW II due, in part, to the construction of the 5 Freeway. But, due to enlightened urban planning, an active Little Italy Association, and weekly farmers markets, Little Italy is now San Diego's most vibrant urban neighborhood.

Old Town State Historic Park San Diego: California's Birthplace - In 1769, this was the site of the first Spanish settlement in California with its Mission and nearby Presidio or fort (the Spanish built four presidios along the California coast). In the 1820s, Mexico took over "Alta California" and officially declared San Diego a chartered "pueblo" or town. In 1850, California was admitted to the Union, and much of San Diego's expansion migrated toward the harbor. Old Town today has an eclectic mix of historic buildings (many of which are small museums), specialty stores, and lots of restaurants - something for all ages.

Itinerary: AM - On the Waterfront

San Diego has done an excellent job showcasing and promoting its lovely harbor. Park your car along Harbor Drive and stroll south along the Embarcadero from Grape Street.

1. Stroll the Embarcadero: On your left is **Waterfront Park** with its landmark **"The Serpent Tree"** sculpture, creative play areas and fountains. You can walk all the way to Seaport Village, past historic ships and the **"Kissing Sailor Statue"** just south of the USS Midway Museum aircraft carrier.

2. Maritime Museum of San Diego - This floating museum of nine historic ships, includes the ***Star of India***, the oldest active sailing ship, and the ***San Salvador***, the restored galleon of Spanish explorer Juan Cabrillo. You can buy a ticket to explore the ships or even book a harbor cruise aboard a high-speed Swift Boat.

3. Harbor Cruises - There are several cruise companies that dock along the Embarcadero. It's great to see the skyline, Point Loma and Coronado Island from the water. If you want to stay inside the harbor, use Flagship Cruise Lines. They offer one-hour, narrated tours of either the north or south harbor. For an open sea adventure, book a tour with Hornblower for a 3.5-hour whale and dolphin excursion.

In the "City of Villages," Little Italy sets the standard.

California's first mission inspired generations of architects.

It's fun to get out on the water for a narrated cruise of the north or south harbor.

Lunch in Little Italy - This colorful urban village has over 70 restaurants, patio cafés, delis, and great shopping, mostly along India Street between Cedar and Grape Streets. Start with a coffee at the Little Italy Food Hall on **Piazza della Famiglia**, a beautiful 10,000 square foot plaza between Columbia and India Streets. There are tons of restaurants in either direction on India St., but turning right is the best move.

PM: Explore Old Town State Historic Park - There's much to explore here, but a nice walking tour starts at the corner of San Diego Avenue and Twiggs Street where the pedestrian walkway begins. On your right is San Diego's largest adobe - **La Casa de Estudillo** (1829), a National Historic Landmark and an authentic example of early California living during the Mexican period. Turn right for the Historic Carriages and Stable Museum. Straight ahead is the **Plaza de las Armas** - the original town square laid out by the Spanish. In the far corner is a fun courtyard of Mexican shops and crafts - **Bazaar del Mundo**.

Very Nearby Attractions:

- **Heritage Park Victorian Village** - Beautiful pre-1900 homes one block north at Juan and Harney Streets
- **Serra Museum** (1929) - Just up the hill on the site of the original "presidio," a stunning Mission-revival building with commanding views. Open Friday through Sunday
- **Mission San Diego de Alcalá** (1813) - A few miles up the road in Mission Valley (10818 San Diego Mission Road.). This is California's first church and the first of its 21 Missions, symbolizing the arrival of Catholicism and the end of the Native American way of life

OUTING #67: EXPLORERS & GAS LAMPS

Cabrillo National Monument and Liberty Station

National Monuments are special places protected by the federal government, and this outing visits a very dramatic one - Cabrillo National Monument at the end of Point Loma. You'll learn about the first visit by a European to California in 1542, walk to a lighthouse at the end of a dramatic peninsula, and then have lunch at Liberty Station - a restored 1923 Naval Training Center converted to restaurants, museums and art galleries. You'll finish your day by exploring downtown San Diego's lively heart and soul - the Gaslamp Quarter - where Victorian-era buildings mix with the new.

Commanding views from the Cabrillo Statue.

Background: Cabrillo National Monument - Established in 1913, this is one of 390 parks in the **National Park System**. It is dedicated to telling the story of Juan Rodriquez Cabrillo, the first European to set foot on the West Coast of the US. Although he stayed only six days, he and his men were the first to have contact with coastal indigenous tribes. As you will learn, his voyage to find the mythical "Northwest Passage" to Asia faced many hardships. The Monument also has opportunities for nature hikes, tide pools and a visit to the **Old Point Loma Lighthouse** - all with expansive views high above the Pacific.

Liberty Station - Once a **Naval Training Center** built in **1923**, Liberty Station has been reborn as a creative hub of restaurants, art galleries, local businesses, and museums. Here you'll find over 300 acres in a formal, rectangular plan with Spanish Colonial architecture enclosing long grassy areas. Liberty Station closed in 1997 after training over 2.75 million Navy recruits and sailors. It has 38 historic buildings and was placed on the **National Register of Historic Places** in 2001. San Diego is a navy town that values its history and architecture, and Liberty Station is a prime example. Use the website - **libertystation.com** - to help you plan your visit.

Cabrillo entered San Diego Harbor in 1542 - the first European to set foot on the West Coast.

Gaslamp Quarter - This is where San Diego's "New Town" developed in the late 1800s as "Old Town" grew out of favor. Gas lamps were installed in 1867, and the area became known as **"Stingaree"** - a rough area with a popular Red Light District. The famous **lawman, Wyatt Earp**, even ran several gambling halls here. In the 1980s, as historic preservation and its tax incentives became popular, the district was placed on the **National Register**, and the City widened the sidewalks and brought back replicas of the gas lamps. Soon, the Gaslamp Quarter became the most popular downtown area. Use the website - **gaslamp.org** - for more info.

Itinerary: AM - Visit Cabrillo National Monument

1. The drive to the Monument along Cabrillo Monument Drive passes through **Fort Rosecrans National Cemetery** where over 120,000 military personnel are buried, the earliest from the Mexican American War in 1846.

2. After getting your bearings at the Visitor Center, walk down to the **Cabrillo Statue** and its dramatic views of the San Diego Harbor, skyline and North Island Coronado. Visit the small museum detailing the Cabrillo Expedition and see the short film - ***The Voyages of the San Salvador.*** The life of a 16th century sailor was fraught with danger.

3. Take the short path up the hill to the Old Point Loma Lighthouse. Here you'll also find the **Kelp Forest Overlook** with exhibits on migrating gray whales. If the tide is low, consider visiting the tide pools located at the end of a steep access road near the entrance station.

Lunch at Liberty Public Market (2820 Historic Decatur Rd). This will put you in the lively Arts District section near the northern end of the Liberty Station complex. The market is a lively food hall with over a dozen creative, international food stands and several craft stores. After lunch, get to know the rest of Liberty Station.

1. Explore the Arts District - Walk west along the interior courtyard and explore the many art galleries and shops. At the north end you'll find Stone Brewing Bistro and Gardens, just one of the many craft breweries of San Diego.

2. Further Exploration - Continue walking west to the NTC Command Center with its history displays. Here you'll also find several museums, including the Women's Museum of California. Farther west is **The Quarter District** with more shopping and public places.

PM: Gaslamp Quarter - The heart of the Gaslamp is 5th Avenue between Harbor Dr. and Broadway. Start at the south end by the **Convention Center**, turn onto 5th and go under the wonderful, Victorian style street-spanning arch. **Petco Park**, home of the San Diego Padres, is just two blocks east. As you head north, there are restaurants galore and over 90 historic buildings, mostly from the Victorian era (pre-1900s), many of which have been repurposed as shops, entertainment venues, and bars.

For history buffs, you can book walking tours at the **Davis-Horton House** Museum (410 Island Avenue). There are Thursday and Saturday tours and even Ghost Tours. Since the Gaslamp likes to walk a bit on the wild side, you can also find pub crawls and Brothels, Bites and Booze Tours!

Liberty Station is bursting with art and creativity.

Liberty Public Market is a lively food hall in the Arts District.

Nearby Attractions:

- Little Italy
- USS Midway Museum
- Balboa Park
- San Diego Zoo
- Hotel Del Coronado

Harbor Drive
5th Ave.
Broadway
San Diego Bay

Location Legend

1. Cabrillo Nat'l Monument
2. Rosecrans Nat'l Cemetery
3. Liberty Station
4. Coronado
5. Convention Center
6. Petco Park
7. Gaslamp Quarter

OUTING #68: A TALE OF TWO PARKS

Balboa and Chicano Parks

The outing combines two very different parks - both National Historic Landmarks, but with very different stories. One is a magnificent urban park over 100 years old; the other, a park born of protest, under a freeway, in the 1970s. Since Balboa Park is much bigger and has over 15 museums, plan at least three hours there. You might visit Chicano Park in the morning, have lunch in Barrio Logan and then head up the hill to Balboa Park for the afternoon.

Background: Chicano Park is the largest concentration of Chicano murals in the world, located in the oldest Mexican American community in San Diego - **Barrio Logan**. The park was born when the community stopped construction of an unwanted development after having been promised a park under the Coronado Bridge. Negotiations followed and local artist Salvador Torres proposed turning the massive freeway pylons into expressions of art in the tradition of the **Mexican Mural Movement**. The Chicano Park was born in 1971!

Balboa Park, on the other hand, was born from years of careful planning. As early as 1868, the City set aside 1400 acres of open space for a park. After hiring numerous famous designers, **Bertram Goodhue** was chosen to deliver a **"Spanish Dream City"** to celebrate the opening of the Panama Canal in 1915. Goodhue created a series of ornate Spanish Renaissance-style buildings along the east/west pedestrian walkway - **El Prado** - that is the key attraction today. The **1915 Panama-California Exposition** drew over 3 million visitors and created a lasting legacy.

In **1935**, San Diego held another exposition - the **California Pacific International Exposition** - to boost the City's economy during the Great Depression. **Architect Richard Requa** expanded the architectural theme beyond Spanish Colonial to include styles of the greater Southwest, including Pueblo, Mayan and Aztec symbols. These fascinating buildings can be found around the **Pan American Plaza** at the southern end of the Park.

Balboa Park has the most beautiful concentration of Spanish Colonial buildings in the nation.

Itinerary:

AM: Visit Chicano Park (1949 Logan Avenue) - This amazing collection of murals is located in a very unlikely place - beneath the **San Diego–Coronado Bridge** in Barrio Logan, a predominantly Chicano or Mexican American community. The murals are painted on the pillars supporting the freeway above and the 7-acre park has a small museum and cultural center where you can obtain a mural map. The website - chicano-park.com - provides excellent background.

Exploring the Park - Start near the Cultural Center on National and walk in a clockwise loop to the northwest. As you walk through the park, you will see many of the themes so prominent in Chicano Art:

1) **references to "Aztlan"** - ancestral home to the Aztec people
2) **pre-Colombian societies** - Aztecs and their deities
3) **agrarian roots** - United Farm Workers (UFW) and Cesar Chavez
4) **Mexican revolutionaries** - Pancho Villa, Emiliano Zapata
5) **Lady of Guadalupe** - Mexican national symbol of hope & salvation
6) **famous Mexican muralists** - Rivera, Orozco, Siquieros
7) **unity and pride** - references to La Raza, the Barrio and original protest

Chicano Park was born from protests in the 1970s.

You will find a breadth of creativity in this incredible place (declared a **National Historic Landmark** in 2016). Some of the original murals from 1974, such as "Renacimiento Rebirth of La Raza," have been restored.

Lush ornamentation along El Prado pedestrian walkway.

Lunch - There are lots of nearby restaurants in **Barrio Logan** just north and west of the Park. **The Gaslamp Quarter** is only a five-minute drive away.

PM - Architectural Walking Tour of Balboa Park - You could spend several days in this wonderful park with its many museums and gardens, but let's do a walking tour to get you started. Your adventure starts in the center of Balboa Park at the fountain just north of the statue of **El Cid**. Before you begin, check in at the Information Kiosk for a map and information on museum exhibitions and openings.

1. Start at the central fountain. Looking both west and east, you can appreciate the formal axis plan of Goodhue's original design. Most of the original 1915 buildings are found along this axis. In any direction you walk, there's plenty to see.

2. Walk east along the Promenade - This is one of the most beautiful architectural walks in California. To your right is the ornate **House of Hospitality** (1915-1935) with its beautiful interior courtyard and **El Prado Restaurant**. Just ahead on the left beyond the Lily Pond is the **Botanical Building** (1915) - one of the largest wood lathe buildings in the world containing exquisite plants. Just ahead on both sides you'll see some of the most ornate Spanish Colonial facades in California - the
Casa del Prado and **Casa de Balboa**.

Turn left to see the Spanish Village center of Arts and Crafts or go straight to the end of the promenade to the **Natural History Museum** (1933)- a monumental building somewhat out of scale and style with the rest of the park - and the **Fleet Science Center**.

Artist paints Aztlan - mythical homeland of Aztecs.

3. Walk west toward the California Tower - This ornate tower is the signature building of the park and symbol of San Diego. You can climb to the top for great views and visit the **Museum of Man** within. Continue walking and you'll cross the **Cabrillo Bridge** - a dramatic, Roman-aqueduct-style entrance to the park.

4. Walk south toward the Organ Pavilion - Immediately on your right is the Mingei International Museum containing folk art and a fancy restaurant. Straight ahead is the **Spreckles Organ Pavilion** (1915) with its grand arch and 4,445 pipe organ. To the left is the **Japanese Friendship Garden** (1999) located in a deep canyon. Farther south are buildings added to the park in 1935 with styles beyond Spanish Colonial - the **Air & Space Museum** (Streamline Moderne); the **Automotive** and **Comic-Con Museums** (Pueblo and Aztec/Mayan Revival).

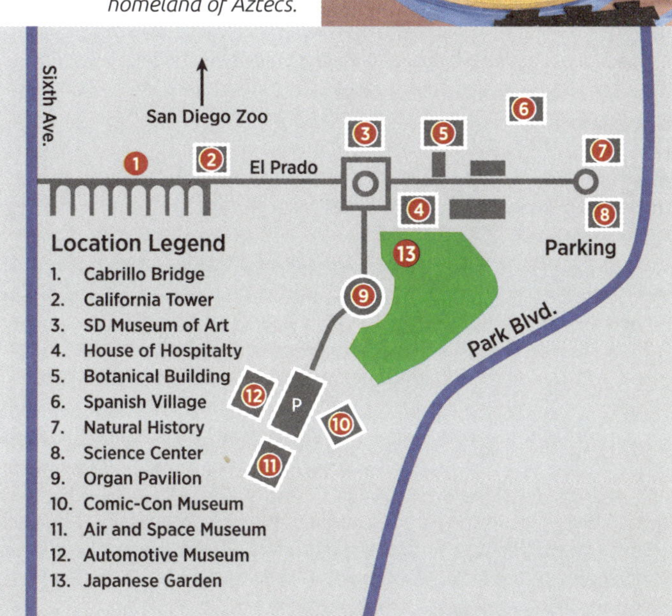

OUTING #69: ANCHORS AWAY!

USS Midway Museum and Hotel Del Coronado

In a navy town, it's not surprising that an aircraft carrier would be one of San Diego's top attractions. Come abroad this massive ship, talk to the veterans who flew its planes, and walk the flight deck with views of San Diego Harbor and skyline. After a morning visit to the Midway, enjoy lunch at nearby Seaport Village and then take the Coronado Bridge to the attractive city of Coronado and its famous landmark - Hotel del Coronado, the last of the great 19th-century resort hotels.

The "shooter" is the final check before launch.

The USS Midway had a crew of 4,500 and was the 41st aircraft carrier commissioned by the Navy.

Midway's *flight deck contains restored aircraft from 1942 to the present day.*

Background: By the 1930s, San Diego was the dominant West Coast base for navy planes and their floating airports. World War II and the Korean and Vietnam Wars added to the City's military presence. Despite base closures and military downsizing in the 1990s, San Diego is still the principal homeport of the **US Pacific Fleet** on the West Coast, including three aircraft carriers.

The **USS *Midway*** is the longest-serving aircraft carrier of the 20th century. Named after the climactic Naval battle of WW II, it was commissioned in 1945 and actually missed the war by one week. The Midway, which could hold 120 planes, served in the Atlantic Fleet during the Cold War and then saw combat duty in the Vietnam War in 1965. In April 1975, it served as a floating base for helicopters that evacuated refugees during the Fall of Saigon. In 1990, Midway served in the Persian Gulf during Operation Desert Storm where it launched 3,000 missions with no losses. The carrier was **decommissioned in 1992** and opened as the USS Midway Museum in 2004.

Itinerary:

AM: Visit the USS *Midway* - This is a massive vessel with lots to see. The main action is on the **Hangar** and **Flight Decks**, and wherever you go, take the time to talk to the volunteer docents who share their stories of military service.

1. Explore the Hangar Deck - As you enter the *Midway* on the massive Hangar Deck, grab either a standard Audio Tour or the Family Audio Tour geared to children. Turn right and go to the Battle of Midway Theater to see the short movie - ***Voices of Midway*** - which plays at 25-minute intervals. It's an inspiring story of how a torpedo plane squadron, against incredible odds, helped the US win this decisive battle in the Pacific. The Hangar Deck has many exhibits, World War II aircraft, flight simulators, and access to the tight quarters of the enlisted sailor's bunks.

2. On the Flight Deck - Here in the fresh air, with beautiful views of the San Diego Harbor and skyline, you can walk up, touch and sometimes board 20 different aircraft. A highlight is to learn from veteran pilots what it takes to launch and land jet airplanes on the world's smallest airport. There are also special tours of the **Ship's Island/Bridge** and **Navigation and Flight Control areas** - the true command center of this enormous craft. Below deck exhibits include the Engine Room, Wardroom, Chapel and Chowline/Galley.

Coronado has a plethora of vintage homes from Victorian (pictured above) to Mid-Century Modern.

Further Adventure: For naval enthusiasts, consider taking the **Flagship Cruise's South Harbor Tour** - a 1-hour narrated cruise that includes the US Navy Surface Fleet, Naval Amphibious Base (home of the Navy Seals) and the **Coronado Bay Bridge**. The ships dock just north of the *Midway*.

Lunch - Just south of the USS *Midway*, right on the water, is The Fish Market Restaurant in Tuna Harbor Park by "The Kiss" statue. Just a few minutes south on foot is **Seaport Village** - a 14-acre development with both casual and fine dining options, and plenty of unique shops.

PM: Cross the Bridge to Coronado - It's a quick and scenic ride across the Coronado Bay Bridge to the City of Coronado (founded in 1890). It's a beautiful coastal town connected to the mainland by a thin strip of land called the Silver Strand. After crossing, turn left on **Orange Avenue**, the town's lovely "Main Street." Here you'll find lots of specialty shops and restaurants, wide sidewalks and a lushly landscaped median. For architecture aficionados, you can book a heritage walking tour with the Coronado Historical Association at the **Coronado Museum** and check out the monumental fresco murals by Mexican artist and art teacher Ramos Martinez in the **Public Library**.

Originally advertised as "Mission Style," the Hotel Del *is really a massive Queen Anne Victorian beauty!*

Visit the "Del" - The main attraction here is Hotel Del Coronado (1888), a **National Historic Landmark** and one of the nation's best surviving examples of wooden Victorian architecture. Its signature red-roof turret, almost ten stories tall, served as a nautical landmark for decades. The hotel was visited by scores of prominent personalities, over 12 Presidents, and many movie stars - most famously Marilyn Monroe during the filming of *Some Like It Hot*.

You can spend the whole afternoon at the Del. The Victorian-style, two-story lobby with its intricate woodwork, hand-painted silk wall coverings, and birdcage elevator have been carefully restored. The new **Ice House Museum** contains behind-the-scenes exhibits, guided history tours, and audio guides. Stroll the 26-acre grounds with its gorgeous, south-facing beach and views of **Point Loma**. Surf lessons and cruiser bike rentals are available. Book a room at The Del for an unforgettable California experience!

Nearby Attractions:

- **Little Italy**
- **Chicano Park**
- **Maritime Museum**
- **Balboa Park**
- **Gaslamp Quarter**

OUTING #70: PACIFIC COAST HIGHWAY CRUISE

Oceanside to Torrey Pines

Get off the Interstate and cruise the coast! This outing is a beautiful drive south on the Pacific Coast Highway (Highway 101) in north San Diego County, ending in a scenic hike at Torrey Pines State Natural Reserve. You'll drive through five towns - each with its own character - with optional stops along the way. On your right, you'll see crashing waves and surfers galore; on your left, you'll pass several large lagoons and wetlands. No strip malls, huge parking lots, or chain restaurants here. Instead, plenty of surf shops, funky boutiques and specialty retail to capture your attention. This a classic SoCal cruise!

Itinerary:

Oceanside - Start your coastal cruise in Oceanside from the 5 Freeway – the first exit going south after Camp Pendleton. The opening of **Camp Pendleton**, the country's largest Marine Base, was a major impetus to growth. Oceanside is a big town (over 170,000 people) with a newly redeveloped downtown and beautiful, long sandy beaches. Possible stops:

1. **Longest wooden pier in California** - 1,941 feet to be exact.
2. **California Surf Museum** - Preserving the legacy of California's state sport.
3. **Oceanside Harbor Village** - Great for picnics, casual dining, seal watching and beach access.

Carlsbad - An attractive coastal town originally famous for its spalike water and lots to do (see Outing #71). The center of the walkable downtown is at the corner of State Street and Carlsbad Village Road. You can catch the Coaster trains at nearby **Carlsbad Village Station** (2775 State Street).

4. **Carlsbad Sea Wall Trail** - Easy hike (1.4 miles) right on the beach just south of Village.
5. **Flower Fields** (ranunculus, by the way) - A burst of spring color just east of the freeway.
6. **LEGOLAND** (most creative of amusement parks!)
7. **Batiquitos Lagoon** - Flat 1.6 mile trail along a coastal estuary; small Nature Center.

Encinitas - Famous as a great surf town and known as a **"floral capital,"** Encinitas also has an excellent, compact downtown. Northern part of town - known as **Leucadia** - has laid-back, funky, surfer vibe.

8. **Leucadia Donut Shoppe** (1604 N. Coast Highway)- Popular stop after checking out the waves!
9. **Self-Realization Meditation Gardens** - Tranquil gardens above famous **Swami's** surf break.
10. **San Elijo Lagoon** - Large estuary with excellent loop trails, bird watching and Nature Center.

Solana Beach - Small community with very contemporary design. The award-winning **Transit Station** (architect Rob Quigley, 1994) is the city's train depot and only two blocks from the cutest park-at-the-beach anywhere - Fletcher Cove Beach Park.

11. **Cedros Avenue Design District** - 2.5 blocks of art galleries, restaurants and retail one block east of Coast Highway. Follow the street-spanning arch!

Del Mar - Cute, small and fashionable, this is your last stop before your hike. Del Mar was developed in the early 1900s, and became "Playground of the Stars" due to the nearby Del Mar Turf Club. Take a self-guided **Historic Del Mar Village Walking Tour** with your smartphone. Just open the link on the silver plaques placed on historically significant buildings.

12. **Del Mar Race Track** - opened in 1937 in a Spanish Colonial/Mission Revival Style. Bing Crosby filed the articles of incorporation and was a frequent visitor.

Torrey Pines State Natural Reserve – Just a 10-minute drive from Del Mar. Parking can fill up quickly here, but the visit is well worth it. The Reserve is home to our nation's rarest pine tree - **the Torrey Pine** - found only here and on Santa Rosa Island. There are about 3,000 of the famous pines inside of the reserve and three main trails to choose from. The scenery is epic - high broken cliffs, red sandstone formations, and deep ravines overlooking the ocean. Don't miss the picturesque **1923 Pueblo-Style Visitor Center** that was once a restaurant and lodge.

Hidden Gem in La Jolla - The Salk Institute for Biological Studies, designed by **Jonas Salk** and **Louis Kahn** in the 1960s, is considered one of the most significant modernist buildings in the world. Tours are available of this stunning research facility overlooking the Pacific Ocean near UC San Diego.

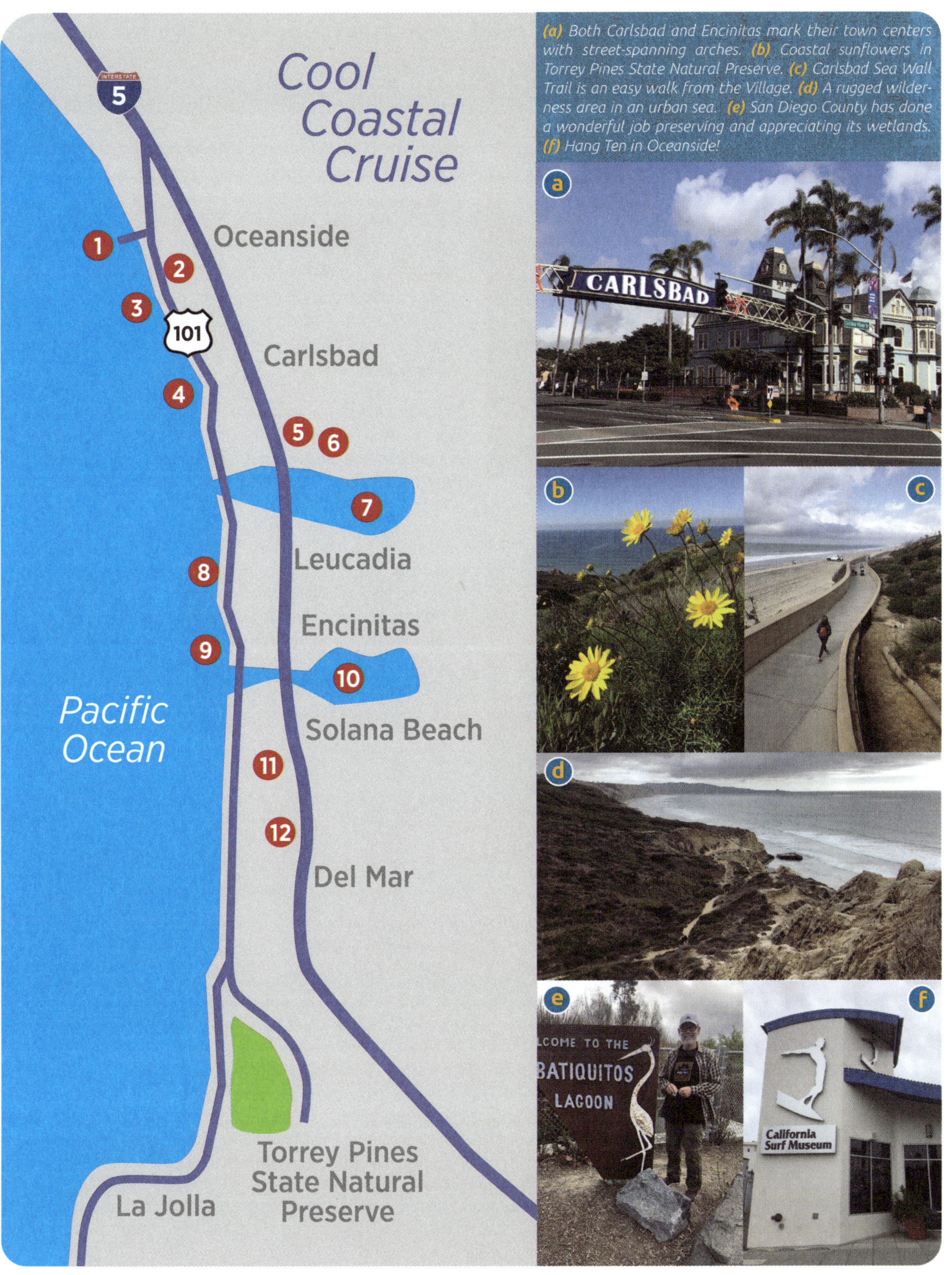

(a) Both Carlsbad and Encinitas mark their town centers with street-spanning arches. (b) Coastal sunflowers in Torrey Pines State Natural Preserve. (c) Carlsbad Sea Wall Trail is an easy walk from the Village. (d) A rugged wilderness area in an urban sea. (e) San Diego County has done a wonderful job preserving and appreciating its wetlands. (f) Hang Ten in Oceanside!

OUTING #71: FLOWERS, GEMS & RANCHOS

Carlsbad Delivers!

Get up close and personal with giant Tecolote ranunculus!

Art Deco accordion on display at the Museum of Making Music.

There's so much to do in this dynamic coastal city that you're going to have to pick and choose! From early March to early May, you can walk through the famous Flower Fields. You can visit the delightful Museum of Making Music and learn more about your favorite band or instrument. For jewelry lovers, you can see precious stones at the Gemology Institute of America. History buffs will enjoy walking the spacious grounds of the Leo Carrillo Ranch Historic Park. If you have children, a great choice is creative LEGOLAND - the theme park with millions of building blocks of fun.

Background: Situated in north San Diego County, water has played an outsize role in Carlsbad history. The earliest residents were Native American **tribes** - the **Luiseno** and **Kumeyaay** - who settled near freshwater streams. Local California Missions, such as **San Luis Rey**, were sited near a dependable water source. The town's name came from an 1880 discovery by early resident John Frazier of water similar in quality to that of a famous spa resort town - Karlsbad - in the Czech Republic. A water company was formed by a German-born merchant, and the town's fertile fields of avocado, citrus and olives fueled growth.

In the heart of the downtown village, you can see Frazier's statue and a replica of a half-timbered German house at the site of the original well. In 1952, Carlsbad incorporated to avoid annexation by its northern neighbor, Oceanside. The town's population grew by an astounding 100,000 residents between 1970 and 2020 and is now the County's fifth largest city. With a bustling **downtown Village**, convenient train station, and wonderful beaches, Carlsbad seems to have it all. And, to complete the theme of water, it is home to the nation's largest **desalination plant**.

Itinerary:

Walk the Flower Fields (visit early March to early May) - Since the 1940s, North San Diego County has a rich history of growing flowers, and this 55-acre site of dazzling **Giant Tecolote Ranunculus flowers** marks the beginning of spring. Located on a gentle hill just east of the 5 Freeway, you can spend two-to-three hours here walking the fields, taking the **Tractor Wagon Ride**, and exploring the demonstration gardens and greenhouses. Kids will enjoy the Sweet Pea Maze, and a top attraction is the Historic Poinsettia Greenhouse. **Fun fact:** The poinsettia's color is actually from the leaves which surround its tiny flowers.

Museum of Making Music - This small but well-curated museum focuses on the making, selling and using of musical instruments. Its galleries trace the evolution of music from the marches and rags of the early 1900s through jazz, folk, rock, pop and cross-cultural genres. Many vintage instruments are displayed, and there are numerous "sit and play" areas where you can create your own sound. Just like the Grammy Museum in downtown Los Angeles, the "MoMM" has lots of interactive touch screens where you can hear various instruments and artists. Group tours for 10 or more guests can be arranged. Rock on!

Modest and rustic, Leo's hacienda is quintessential California ranch living.

Actor Leo Carrillo was named Goodwill Ambassador of California by the governor.

Leo Carrillo Ranch Historic Park - If you like California history and the romance of the old ranchos, you will love this hidden gem in a valley northeast of Carlsbad. The ranch, named "Los Quiotes" for the daggerlike spikes of the yucca plant, was built as a weekend retreat by the **Hollywood actor** and **conservationist**, **Leo Carrillo**. Leo starred in over 90 films and was most famous for his role as "Pancho" on *The Cisco Kid* television series of the 1950s. He was also an ardent **conservationist** and served on the **State Beaches and Parks Commission**, helping to acquire Hearst Castle and supporting the development of the LA Arboretum and Anza Borrego State Park.

Start your historic ramble through the Ranch at the **Wood Barn Visitor Center** with its orientation film and exhibits. Next door is the **Historic Stable**, a stone and adobe structure restored to host weddings and large events. A highlight is the original Spanish-style hacienda, (1882) which Carrillo purchased in 1937 and modified in a California Ranch Style. Its U-shaped plan with a central fountain is classic early California. Another highlight is **Deedie's House**, Carrillo's wife's **Pueblo-style** artistic workspace with its native American artifacts. The ranch grounds are beautiful and hopefully you won't run "afoul" of any of the resident peacocks!

Leo Carrillo played Pancho on TV's The Cisco Kid.

The Enchanting Red Egg *features enamel, precious gems and metals.*

You will be awed by the variety and beauty of gemstones on display.

The Butterfly *by David Zoltan features tourmaline.*

Gemological Institute of America (GIA) - Pardon the pun, but this place is truly a hidden gem! Established in 1931, the GIA is the **world's leading authority on diamonds, colored stones, and pearls**, and there are only twelve campuses worldwide. The GIA Museum introduces the visitor to the vast world of gems with beautiful rotating exhibits throughout the campus. It's amazing to see the tremendous varieties of gemstones in their natural state, and then to see their transformation into jewelry. GIA is open Monday through Friday for guided or self-guided museum tours. Call in advance and make sure to have your photo ID with you.

Fun Fact: In the 1940s, the GIA developed the **"4Cs"** for evaluating diamonds: **cut**, **clarity**, **color** and **carat!**

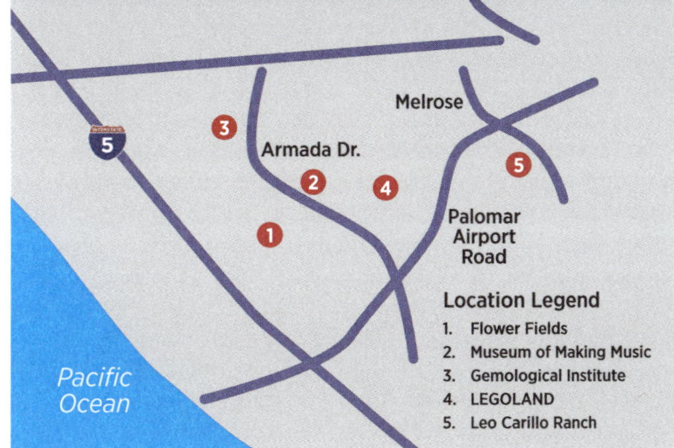

OUTING #72: KING OF THE MISSIONS

Mission San Luis Rey

California's twenty-one Franciscan Missions are reminders of a dramatic and complicated period of history, and Mission San Luis Rey is one of the biggest, best preserved and most beautiful of all. Conveniently located just five miles off Interstate 5 in Oceanside, San Luis Rey has much to offer. It has a well-curated museum, a large and ornate church, an impressive quadrangle, and an active archaeological site - the outdoor "lavanderia" (washing area) and sunken gardens. The self-guided tour is fine, but do yourself a favor and call ahead to arrange a tour by the Museum Director or one of the well-trained docents.

With its sparkling baroque facade and rich history, you can see why Mission San Luis Rey was named a National Historic Landmark.

Background: The Franciscan priests came to **Alta California** in 1769 to convert native tribes to Christianity and to train them for life in a European colonial society. The skills they were taught - farming, construction, cattle raising, weaving, crafts - were to lead the converts (called "neophytes") to life outside the mission system, but this rarely happened. Tragically, exposure to European diseases, to which the natives had no resistance, lead to a 50% decline in population, to about 150,000 by 1848.

Founded in 1798, Mission San Luis Rey was the 18th mission built by the **Franciscans**, and the most prosperous. At its height, it supported a Native American population of almost 3000 with over 50,000 livestock. Here, the native population was less prone to infectious disease since the converts were able to live in their traditional villages rather than in crowded areas near the Mission. It is one of the nine California Missions to be designated a National Historic Landmark. The Mission today is an active **Parish Church** and maintains a large **retreat center** for spiritual renewal.

The SLR Mission Church is one of the largest and most impressive in California.

Itinerary: Exploring Mission San Luis Rey

1. Gorgeous Facade - Admire the bright white facade of the Mission with its distinctive stepped gable and two-story bell tower - a combination of **Baroque** and **Classical styles**. Notice the 32 roman arches and balustrade of brick latticework to the left. At the entrance, find the National Historic Landmark plaque in front. When was the Mission given this designation by the Department of the Interior?

2. Extensive Mission Museum - To provide historical context, this is the best place to start your visit. The period rooms cover each major era - 1) **Native American culture** - displays basketry and artifacts from the original inhabitants; 2) **Spanish Mission period** - religious and secular objects from 1789 to 1834; 3) **Mexican secularization** - Mission falls into disuse after Mexico claims Alta California and Spanish padres flee; 4) **Mission Restoration** - in late 1800s, Mission slowly rebuilt as church services restored. Find the proclamation signed by Abraham Lincoln returning the Missions to the Catholic Church.

3. Inside the Church - Walking inside this huge chapel is definitely stepping back in time! The thick walls are brightly painted with murals and decorative patterns, leading to a neoclassical altar. San Luis Rey is the only surviving mission church laid out in a **cruciform plan**. The nave is over 165 feet long and 30 feet high. A cupola, the octagonal lantern atop the church, has 144 panes of glass and is unique to this Mission.

4. Quadrangle and Cemetery - All mission grounds featured a quadrangle, often enclosed by Roman arches, where most of the work was done. During the mission era, bullfights were held here. It still contains California's oldest pepper tree (originally from Peru, by the way!). The large and still active cemetery to the east of the church is also worth a visit. It is the oldest in North County and contains grave markers of early settlers, crypts of the friars and a monument to the Luiseno Indians. Notice the skull and crossbones over the cemetery gate.

5. Sunken gardens and Lavandería - Every Mission needed access to water, usually in a channel called a **"zanja."** Take a walk to the hollow just south of the Mission, descend 46 fired-tile steps, and find the two springs where water spouted from the mouths of sculpted gargoyles. This is an active archaeological site with more to be discovered. Native plants and traditional crops are also featured. See if you can find the scaly white insect - cochineal - on the cactus near the sunken garden. Scrape it off into your palm and gently crush it against your skin. A marvelous red dye will appear (easily washed off, by the way!)

Lunch - You can arrange to eat lunch in the Mission's dining room or at the nearby **San Luis Rey Bakery and Restaurant** (490 N. El Camino Real). If you're going north to San Clemente, check out the many restaurants on popular **Del Mar Street**!

Nearby Attractions:

1. Going North? - Visit **Casa Romantica Cultural Center**, San Clemente (415 Avenida Granada) - Scenic Spanish Colonial Revival estate (1927) of San Clemente founder, Ole Hansen. Call ahead for scheduling.

2. Going South? - Carlsbad has much to offer (see Outing #71).

3. Going East? - San Diego, called the "Capital of Craft," is famous for breweries. Highway 78 has been called the **"Hops Highway"** and numerous online brewery guides and tours are available.

San Luis Rey's quadrangle is a beautiful architectural space and home to a community of Franciscan Friars serving the parish.

Cochineal, a white scaly insect that lives on the pads of prickly-pear cactus, can be squeezed to produce a bright red pigment used by native peoples as a cloth dye.

The oldest pepper tree in California was planted in 1830.

One of the beautiful interior courtyards of the Mission.

OUTING #73: GRAPES FOR THE SOUTHLAND

Temecula Valley Wine Region

California's best known wine regions are in the northern and central parts of the states - Napa Valley, Sonoma Valley and Santa Inez Valley to name a few. But those of you wishing for a Southern California wine tasting experience need not be disappointed. Temecula Valley is Southern California's biggest wine region. It's roughly a two-hour drive from LA, Orange and San Diego counties through the scenic Temecula Valley. The challenge will be choosing your tastings since there are now almost 50 wineries. Make this outing a full day with a visit to Old Town Temecula, a charming area of historic buildings and boutique stores.

Background: California is a powerhouse of wine making, producing more than 90% of the US production. The tradition goes back to the first vineyards planted by Spanish missionaries in the 1700s. Today the state has over 150 **American Viticultural Areas** (AVAs), with Temecula Valley receiving this distinction in 1984. The warm climate of the valley is best for Italian, Spanish and Rhone varietals such as **Sangiovese**, **Tempranillo**, **Mourvèdre**, **Syrah** and **Viognier**. However, the area's production has expanded rapidly and also includes **Chardonnay**, **Cabernet Sauvignon**, **Zinfandel** and **Sauvignon Blanc** grapes. Varietals that require cool air, such as **Pinot Noir**, don't fare as well here.

Ponte Winery is one of the many choices in Temecula Valley.

Itinerary:

1. Wine Loop Route - The best way to explore the Valley is a clockwise loop where you will drive by all the major wineries. From Interstate 15, exit at Rancho California Road and head east through town. The wine region begins in about 3 miles at **Butterfield Stage Road**. You'll immediately see wineries nestled on both sides of the road. At Glenoaks Road, make a right and then another right on De Portola Boulevard. Now you're heading back towards Old Town and will pass more wineries. At Anza Road, you can turn right to go back to the Rancho California Rd. or continue straight to Old Town.

2. Choosing your Wineries - With 50 wineries to choose from, this can be a problem. You can use the **First Timers Guide**, the **Temecula Winery Map**, or just go for it! One advantage of using the Guide and Map is that they describe the wine specialties of each winery, making your choices easier. As you drive into the winery zone, you'll see Callaway, the Valley's first winery from 1974, on the hill to your left. Just past the roundabout at Anza Road, you'll be in the center of wine country. You can also explore smaller boutique wineries just off the main roads.

Look for the iconic arches at both ends of Old Town Front St.

3. Old Town Temecula - This is a great way to end your wine experience and it's only one block west of the Interstate on **Old Town Front Street**. Here you'll find five blocks of restaurants, specialty retail, and event venues, such as the Old Town Community Theater, all in a rustic setting with Western false front buildings and wooden sidewalks. Temecula is proud of its Old West history dating from1859 with the Butterfield Overland Stage stop and first railroad in 1882. Whether its olive oil tasting, craft breweries, or country music at the Temecula Stampede, Old Town Temecula is great fun.

NAME THE WINE QUIZ

1. CHARDONNAY	**A.** Dry French wine traditionally made from Pinot Noir grapes
2. CHAMPAGNE	**B.** Sparkling wine from Spain
3. PINOT GRIGIO	**C.** Its grape is used to make champagne; grown internationally; dry wine often oaky with lemon and apple flavors
4. ASTI	**D.** Powerful, yet refined; dry with a biting finish; often bold flavors; black pepper, blackberry; smooth, round mouthfeel
5. PINOT NOIR	**E.** Most common sparkling wine in the world
6. CAVA	**F.** Dry red grown in cool climates; grown in small crops making it rare and expensive; high acidity; sensual; made famous in movie *Sideways*
7. REISLING	**G.** Smooth red wine grown almost exclusively in California; varies from sweet rose to port wine
8. MERLOT	**H.** The sparkling wine of Italy
9. ROSÉ	**I.** White wine from grayish/blue fruit
10. CABERNET	**J.** Made by discarding the skins when the grapes are pressed
11. MALBEC	**K.** Dry red wine known for its deep tannins; France and Argentina
12. SYRAH	**L.** Approachable dry red wine; soft plum, cherry and floral aromas
13. ZINFANDEL	**M.** A dry white wine with crisp herbal flavors and often high acidity; origins in Germany's Rhine region
14. BURGUNDY	**N.** Powerful and sharp red wine, but smooth as ages; basis of wines from Bordeaux region of France

YOUR SCORE _______ **Answers on page 173**

13 - 14 - Future Sommelier! **10 - 12** - Wine Lover! **6 - 9** - Palate Pleaser. **0 - 5** - Keep Drinking!

Snobby wine phrases - Give a prize to the most flowerly description of a wine!

"Fruit forward and assertive with a hint of pomegranate and Interstate 15!"

Final Question: What is the largest winery in California and, in fact, the largest family-owned winery in the world? (answer on page 173)

OUTING #74: APPLE PIES & BIGHORN SHEEP

Anza Borrego Desert State Park and Old Town Julian

No outing showcases California's diverse geography more than this adventure. You will explore California's largest state park and a delightful mountain town that turned from gold to apple pies. The drive from Julian to Anza Borrego is quite dramatic - dropping almost four thousand feet in elevation and trading pine trees for barrel cacti! Due to the driving involved and the many beautiful hikes, plan to spend at least one night in Borrego Springs or in a state park campsite.

Background: Julian's earliest settlers came to the area after the Civil War, and the **discovery of gold** in a nearby creek in 1870 started San Diego's first and only gold rush. While hard rock mining began to decline by 1900, apple trees that were brought to the area thrived in the cool climate. They became the town's true **"Mother Lode"** - the source of the famous Julian apple pies. In the 1970s, the town began preserving its Victorian architecture, requiring that all buildings on Main Street predate 1913. The town is an official California Historic Landmark and, to enhance star gazing, an **International Dark Sky Community**. With its historic charm, Apple Days Festival, and beautiful setting, Julian is a great day trip one hour east of San Diego.

Anza-Borrego Desert State Park is enormous. At more than 600,000 acres, it represents 1/2 the land total of the other 278 California State Parks. Its geographic diversity is also impressive, with mountains, canyons, badlands, palm oases, washes, and valleys. Its name derives from **Juan Bautista de Anza**, the Spanish explorer who passed through in 1774, and **"borrego"** - the Spanish word for **"lamb,"** but referring, in this case, to the resident bighorn sheep. The park is famous for its brief spring bloom, at times spectacular, but whose timing is difficult to predict. Deer, kit foxes, iguanas, rattlesnakes, roadrunners, eagles, and the endangered Peninsular bighorn sheep are found in the park.

Itinerary:

AM: Exploring Julian: Julian is a tiny town, and the main attractions are on or near **Main Street**. You can stroll the three-block area with its quaint stores, restaurants, bakeries and, of course, pies. Hard cider is also one of the specialties. Consider a **self-guided walking tour**. You can obtain a map at the Julian Historical Society or even download the Drives and Detours App on your smartphone and open the "Pies and Pickaxes" Walking Tour. **The Julian Pioneer Museum** has a great storehouse of historic artifacts and is open Friday through Sunday. After lunch, you must treat yourself to apple pie! Other popular attractions:

Apple and cherry pies have replaced gold ore in this former gold rush town.

Strawberry hedgehog cactus in bloom.

Bighorn sheep are the largest mammals in the California desert.

1) Visit a Gold Mine - Experience a slice of 1870s mining history at **Eagle & High Point Mines**. The one- hour tour includes 1000 feet of underground mines, museum, rock shop, and gold panning.

2) See endangered wolves - **The California Wolf Center** is dedicated to wolf conservation. You can visit the education center downtown and book a tour of the center's conservation facility to see two resident wolf packs.

PM: Exploring Anza Borrego Desert State Park

1) Scenic Descent into the Park - Highway 78 from Julian to Anza-Borrego is a windy, spectacular drive, going from pine trees to cactus-covered canyons. A good first stop to stretch your legs is at **Tamarisk Grove Campsite** and its two easy hikes - the **Cactus Loop Trail** and the **Yaqui Well Nature Trail**. Continue north on S3 into the small town of Borrego Springs. At the Christmas Circle roundabout in the center of town, head north to explore the fantastical metal sculptures of **Galleta Meadows**. You'll see dozens of animals by artist Ricardo Breceda, the most unique being the 350-foot-long serpent crossing the road and a huge scorpion facing off with a giant grass-hopper. Continue west on Palm Canyon Drive to the Visitor Center.

2. Visitor Center & Borrego Palm Canyon - You'll enjoy a stop at the Visitor Center where you can talk to a ranger, get a good map, take the mini-nature loop, and see the exhibits. The park is so vast that you'll need to plan your time carefully. A great first hike starts at the campsite - the **Borrego Palm Canyon Nature Trail**. It's 3 miles round trip with a gentle slope into a canyon with native fan palms. Big-horn sheep are often seen drinking from the stream.

3. Further Afield - There are so many hikes and sights that you'll have to choose carefully. Here are some suggested guidelines:

Follow the flowers - The most intense spring blooms - carpets of purple, yellow and white flowers - are located just north of town near the **Desert Gardens** picnic area and east on S22.

Badlands to the east - This wrinkly, parched landscape is accessible only by dirt roads, some of which require 4W drive. The view from **Fonts Point** is spectacular and has been called "California's Grand Canyon." Another popular hike is **Slot Canyon** - a 2.8-mile, round trip through a narrow wash with amazing rock walls going straight up. If you have time, an excellent option is to book a Jeep tour with California Overland Desert Excursions.

Southern Anza Borrego - Explore this part of the park only if you have another day. Top sights are the Pictograph Trail, Box Canyon, scattered palm groves, and the **Carrizo Badlands**. Highway S2 joins Interstate 8 at the town of Ocotillo.

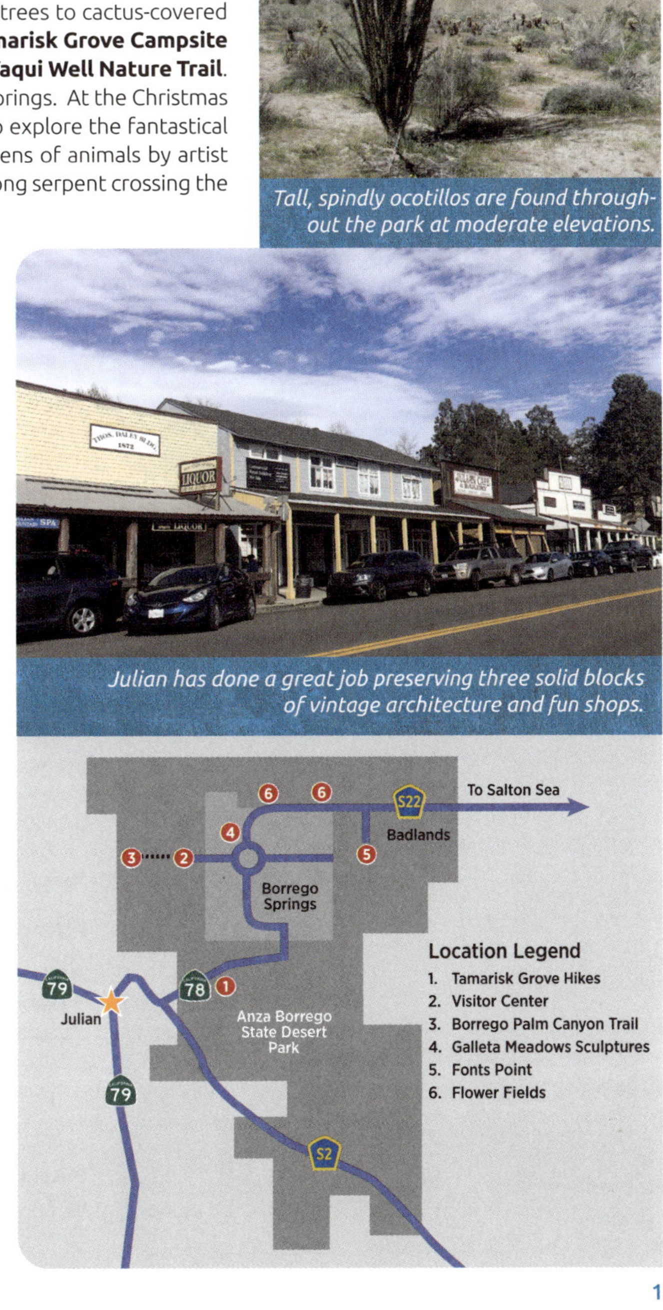

Tall, spindly ocotillos are found throughout the park at moderate elevations.

Julian has done a great job preserving three solid blocks of vintage architecture and fun shops.

OUTING #75: SPAIN ON THE COAST

Stunning Santa Barbara

Founded in 1786, Old Mission Santa Barbara is still home to Franciscan Friars.

For its architecture, art, landscaping and history, the Santa Barbara County Courthouse is a must see!

Docent-led tours of the Mural Room are available weekdays at 10:30 AM and every day at 2:00 PM.

The Spanish began settling California in 1769, and nowhere did they leave their mark more than in beautiful Santa Barbara. This tour takes you to the Queen of the Missions, a Spanish-Moorish castle courthouse, a restored fort, and a beautiful Red Tile Walk through a town that preserved its history in meticulous detail.

Background: The beauty of Santa Barbara resulted from an act of nature and a bold vision from its citizens. After a devastating earthquake in 1925, civic leaders decided to create a downtown true to its Spanish Colonial history, not one with the prevailing architecture of the time such as Victorian, Romanesque, Colonial, or Greek Revival styles. Inspired by its Old Mission and historic adobes, it also became the first city in America to set up a municipal **Board of Architectural Review** and one of the first to require a unified architectural theme – in this case, **Spanish Colonial Revival**. But how would the City attract business? It was the site of a large film studio from 1912 to 1921, but was soon eclipsed by Hollywood. The first airport was closed in 1931 due to noise and safety concerns. So, from that point on, Santa Barbara's leaders decided to focus on being beautiful, thereby attracting tourists, artists, architects and writers.

The result is a downtown where no details are left to chance. The City created a romantic version of Spain with white walls, red tile roofs, paseos, courtyards, and fountains. In 1924, it sponsored its first annual **"Old Spanish Days Fiesta,"** a 5-day celebration in August still popular today. The City's **General Plan** has a **Historic Preservation Element** creating design guidelines for historic districts. They cover signage, lighting, windows and landscaping are all intended to enhance the pedestrian experience. For example, to strengthen the Spanish theme, wrought-iron lanterns are encouraged, and the City adopted a custom font, called "Mission," on all street signs. Santa Barbara has designated over 100 historic landmarks and five historic districts, the largest being **"El Pueblo Viejo" (Old Town)**, which is the focus of this outing.

Itinerary:

AM: Explore the Santa Barbara Mission – the **"Queen of the Missions"** - This is the 10th of the 21 Franciscan missions and the only one that has stayed under the leadership of the Friars since its founding in 1786. Take Garden Street north from downtown and enjoy the short drive through some wonderfully preserved neighborhoods of early 1900s, period revival architecture. See if you can spot the rounded gables of **Mission Revival homes** just south of the landmark. The view of the Mission – on high ground just beyond a large park with the Santa Ynez Mountains as backdrop – has to be one of the most beautiful sights in Southern California.

Paseos and courtyards are meant to capture the romance of Spain.

Lovely senoritas on El Paseo during Fiesta Days.

The Mission itself has so much history that it was declared a National Historic Landmark – the highest designation that a building or site can have. Its neoclassical, twin-towered façade is the result of reconstruction after the 1926 earthquake. The nine-room museum features exhibits on the **Chumash** – the large and prosperous native tribe that built the Mission, explored the **Channel Islands**, and also revolted in 1824 - as well as religious art and artifacts from the Spanish and Mexican period. The Cemetery and Mausoleum are particularly fascinating with the burial stone of **Juana Maria** – the Lone Woman of San Nicolas Island - who survived there alone for 18 years before being brought back to the mainland in 1853. Her story inspired the novel ***Island of the Blue Dolphins***. Sadly, she died shortly after returning to Santa Barbara and no one was able to speak her native tongue.

Lunch – Keeping to the historic theme of this outing, consider lunch at the famous El Paseo Restaurant - built in 1922 in a beautiful courtyard next to the **"Street of Spain."** Enter **El Paseo** at the wooden sign halfway down Anacapa Street between Canon Perdido and De La Guerra Streets. There are also numerous restaurants on State and Anacapa Streets as well as in the hip district south of Highway 101 called **"the Funk Zone."**

PM: Take the historic Red Tile Walk in downtown Santa Barbara: This exploration will showcase the highlights of Santa Barbara's "El Pueblo Viejo" (Old Town) with 17 possible stops over a five-block route. You can find the walk online at "Red Tile Walking Tour." The tour begins at the magnificent Santa Barbara County Courthouse and from there you work your way south to the quaint El Paseo complex for a glass of wine or snack.

1. Santa Barbara County Courthouse – This is the "Grand Dame" of the Spanish Colonial style, and one of the most beautiful courthouses in the US. Declared a **National Historic Landmark**, this 1926 structure is a **blend of Spanish Colonial and Moorish styles** – called the "mudejar style." With its sunken garden, clock tower, irregular plan and dramatic entry, it could definitely be a castle if it weren't an active courthouse for the county. Before entering the Courthouse, take in the botanical treasure of the surrounding gardens, with exotic plantings from more than 26 countries. The Spanish missionaries brought over the Canary Island Palm and, since then, **over 40 varieties of palms** have been planted.

Fun Fact: The only native palm in California is the **Desert Fan Palm** found in **150 oases** in Southern California deserts. As you enter the Courthouse from Anacapa Street, grab a guidebook at the kiosk and take the tiled stairs to the second floor. These Tunisian tiles are an excellent example of Moorish-Islamic designs with their intricate, geometric patterns. Look up at the painted ceiling with its eight-point star modeled after a 14th century synagogue in Toledo, Spain. Irregular pointed arches and squat columns seen throughout are other examples of the "mudejar" style of northern Africa and southern Spain. At the top of the second floor, notice the Spanish "farole" or lantern, patterned after those that hung in Spanish galleons. Finally, check out the Romanesque rose window so prevalent in early European Christian churches. Find the entrance to the **Mural Room** on the second floor.

This incredible room was formerly the seat of the County Board of Supervisors and is now used for tours and weddings. The 360-degree **murals by Dan Groesbeck** were finished in 1928 and depict key moments in Santa Barbara history: the landing of Spanish explorers, the building of the Mission, and the arrival of Major General Fremont in 1846, signaling the transition from Mexican to American rule. The muralist also took some artistic license. See if you can find Errol Flynn and Peter Pan on the back wall!

Now take the elevator or stairs to the fourth floor and examine the unusual **Clock Gallery**. You'll find drawings depicting the history of time, and the inner working mechanisms of the Seth Thomas Tower Clock. If you time it right, you'll get an earful of bell ringing! Continue up to the **Observation Deck** where you'll get a 360-degree view of beautiful Santa Barbara in all its red-tile glory! Take in the Mission to the northeast and, on a clear day, you'll see the Channel Islands to the south. No wonder Santa Barbara is called **"The American Riviera!"**

The Funk Zone evolved from a former industrial area.

Red Tile Walking Tour.

What's the best way to create a pedestrian street that helps business and residents?

2. El Presidio (Fort) de Santa Barbara State Park – Walk two blocks south on Anacapa to Canon Perdido Street and you'll see the flagpole and chapel of the Santa Barbara Presidio. Of **California's four presidios**, this is by far the best preserved. Enter the Visitor's Center and the small museum to see the exhibits on the fort's history. The self-guided tour takes you to the back courtyard where you'll find some active archaeological digs, restored adobe walls of the original fort, and a statue of King Carlos III of Spain. The reconstructed Chapel is beautiful inside. See if you can find the only object from the 1700s.

Fun fact: The Presidio was never attacked although the Argentine pirate Bouchard anchored off the coast and may have been dissuaded when the Spanish soldiers and townspeople changed clothing and marched along the Presidio's walls to make their numbers seem larger!

3. Casa de la Guerra and El Paseo – Walk half a block south on Anacapa and enter the passageway marked "El Paseo" on the overhead wooden sign. You are entering a winding passageway created in 1922 to create a "Street in Spain." This historic walkway, placed on the National Register, goes all the way to State Street and represents an important part of the revival of Spanish Colonial architecture in Santa Barbara. El Paseo winds by Casa de la Guerra – the nineteenth century adobe home of Jose de la Guerra, the 5th Spanish Comandante of the Presidio. Under Mexican rule, the house was a social hub and one of its three-day wedding "fandangos" is immortalized in **Richard Henry Dana's** *Two Years Before the Mast.* The New Englander couldn't believe how long the Californios could party! And Santa Barbarans continue the tradition to this day with their weeklong August "Spanish Fiesta Days." Check out this historic house museum before wine tasting along El Paseo.

4. Stroll State Street - The City's "Main Street" cuts 10 blocks through downtown all the way to Stearns Wharf. Once one of the most iconic streets in Southern California, it has recently experienced much change. Due to the COVID-19 pandemic, the City decided to close eight blocks to car traffic. The results have been mixed. Some legacy businesses have closed, partly due to the competition from online retail. Revitalizing downtowns and creating truly vibrant urban spaces is a challenge facing many cities. Santa Barbara certainly has the experience to succeed.

Of California's four presidios, Santa Barbara's is the best preserved.

El Paseo and "The Street of Spain" (1922) was an inspiration for the revival of Spanish Colonial architecture in Southern California.

Design guidelines encourage new development to complement historic elements.

Nearby Attractions:

1. **Santa Barbara Botanical Gardens** - showcases California native plants and habitats. Reservations required.

2. **The Funk Zone** - a hip, 13-block area at lower State Street and the waterfront. Here you'll find creative collectives, small restaurants, breweries and boutiques.

3. **Lotus Land** - a world-famous garden located on 37 acres in nearby **Montecito**. Exotic and rare plants in creatively designed groupings. Reservations required.

4. **Ojai** - small, artistic, historic community with New Age vibe; surrounded by Topatopa Mountains.

OUTING #76: DANISH DELIGHT & BUCOLIC MISSION

Solvang and La Purisima Mission

The spacious Santa Ynez Valley is only two hours from Los Angeles and here you'll find over 100 wineries, two California missions, and the Danish capital of America - Solvang. This outing describes the major attractions, from east to west, inviting you to plan your day. You'll even have the chance to feed the world's largest birds at Ostrichland!

Background: Solvang, meaning "sunny fields,"was founded by Danish settlers in 1911. When the Lutheran Church (1928) incorporated traditional Danish architecture, residents began following suit. The town's popularity grew due to visits by Danish royalty and a 1947 article in the *Saturday Evening Post*. Solvang incorporated in 1985 and adopted design guidelines to enhance its **"Old World Danish Village"** theme. The result is one of the most beautiful town centers anywhere, with colorful, half-timbered buildings, steeply pitched rooflines and overhanging second stories.

Traditional Danish building colors are deep reds and ochre yellow.

Mission La Purísima is the most completely restored of all California's 21 missions and was declared a National Historic Landmark in 1970. And, unlike other missions, it is part of a **2,000-acre State Historic Park**, which gives it an authentic and rural atmosphere. La Purisima was founded in 1787, and, by 1803, it had a population of 1500 Chumash people and over 24,000 sheep and cattle.

Solvang was built with the pedestrian in mind - wide sidewalks, big windows and sittable space.

Itinerary:

Explore Solvang - Immerse yourself in this "old world" pedestrian village. Try to spot the Danish icons - **the Little Mermaid Fountain**, **the Round Tower**, the windmills and the **giant red clog**. You probably can't resist visiting one of the many bakeries to sample the famous "aebleskiver" - a rounded Danish doughy delight! But Solvang is more than quaint streets; it has some excellent museums as well. Consider visiting the Hans Christian Andersen Museum above the Book Loft, the **California Nature Art Museum**, the **Solvang Vintage Motorcycle Museum**, or the Viking Museum. **Mission Santa Ines** (1804) is located one block east of the Solvang Windmill.

Feed an Ostrich or an Emu! - **Ostrichland** is located just west of Solvang on your way to La Purisima Mission. It's fun to get close to these enormous birds with their big eyes. Be careful when you hold the feeding dish. These birds are strong!

Mission La Purísima State Historic Park (Lompoc) - A visit to this complete mission complex is like stepping back in time. Start your visit at the excellent Visitor Center with exhibits on the Chumash people, religious vestments, and the 1930s restoration by the **Civilian Conservation Corps**. As you tour the extensive grounds, you will see recreations of mission life in the 1820s with crafts and skills such as weaving, blacksmithing, candle making, farming and animal husbandry.

New Attraction:

- **The Chumash Museum and Cultural Center, Santa Ynez** - This thriving nation tells its story across a stunning 3.5-acre facility.

OUTING #77: WINE AND DINE IN SANTA YNEZ VALLEY

Los Olivos and Los Alamos

Is there a more relaxing town center in Southern California?

The rustic setting along Foxen Canyon makes great wines taste even better.

A small town with a Western flavor and modern appeal.

A more relaxing outing you may not find. Here we will explore two small, historic towns in Santa Barbara's Wine Country and take the Foxen Canyon Wine Trail through a scenic valley. You could add part of this adventure to Outing #76 (Solvang) or make it a stand-alone visit of several days. Either way, you'll be taken in by the beauty of the countryside and its charming towns. Maybe the movie Sideways *had it right. The meaning of life is a little Pinot Noir!*

Itinerary:

Exploring Los Olivos - Hidden just off Highway 101, a cuter little town you may never find. When you drive in, you'll immediately see a flagpole in the middle of the intersection. This is the center of town, and all the numerous wine tasting, shops and restaurants are within two walkable blocks. Download the **Los Olivos Town Map** or just explore on your own. The town, created in 1887 from a land auction for the Pacific Coast Railroad, was named for a nearby ranch of 5,000 olive trees. Much of the Victorian architecture still remains, and you can download a Historical Walking Tour for a deeper look. For wine enthusiasts, you can follow the **Los Olivos Sparkling Wine Trail**. This town is so relaxing and beautiful that you may never leave!

Take the Foxen Canyon Wine Trail - Just north of Los Olivos and east of the 101, you'll find the start of this 30-mile wine route that highlights 16 excellent wineries and ends in Santa Maria. You needn't take it that far, of course, as you follow your palate and enjoy the rustic beauty. Along the warmer, southern end of the route you find more **Rhone varietals** such as Grenache, Syrah and Viognier. At the cooler northern end, you'll find more **Pinot Noir** and **Chardonnay**. Use the wine map online - **FoxenCanyonWineTrail.net.**

Enjoy Los Alamos - Whereas Los Olivos has a leafy Victorian atmosphere, Los Alamos is a town of Old West heritage and modern appeal. The town was a popular stop first for a **stagecoach** starting in 1861, and then for the **California Pacific Railway** from 1882 to 1940. Today, most of the town's attractions are found along the seven tiny blocks of **Bell Street**. Start the day at the legendary bakery - **Bob's Well Bread** - for artisan breads or pastries. After some wine tasting, head over to the **Depot Mall**, an antique emporium located in the original train depot. Despite a population of under 2,000, Los Alamos is quite a foodie town with options from casual to haute cuisine. Accommodations range from the historic 1880 **Union Hotel** to the mid-century modern **Skyview Los Alamos**.

OUTING #78: UNCOVERING TREASURES ON THE COAST

Ventura

Ventura is a great stop along the coast on your way to Santa Barbara. Just one minute off Highway 101, you will find a California Mission, a walkable Main Street, an abundance of historic architecture, a boat harbor with connections to Channel Islands National Park, and one of the most beautiful city halls in Southern California. I also recommend checking out the Depression-era, post office murals and giant Moreton Bay Fig Tree in a nearby park. From there, take a walking tour of the town and if time permits, enjoy the ten-minute walk to the Ventura Pier where you can catch ocean breezes and watch the surfers at Seaside Park. And when hunger strikes, grab lunch from one of the excellent restaurants on Main Street.

Background: The Ventura area was inhabited by the Chumash people for over 10,000 years before the **City of Buenaventura** was founded by Franciscan padres in 1782. After Mexico won independence from Spain in 1821, mission lands were divided into large land grants. This **Mexican Rancho Era** lasted from 1833 to 1848 until the US victory in the Mexican-American War of 1848. California became the **31st state in 1850**, and the City of Ventura was incorporated in 1866. A major oil boom in the 1920s fueled growth in the downtown area. Today, the City has a population of just over 100,000 and is known for its coastal setting, walkable downtown and historic buildings.

Itinerary:

Take the **California St**. exit, drive two blocks and park your car near Main Street. In a four-block area you'll be able to walk to all the attractions!

1. Ventura City Hall - Built in 1912 by LA architect Albert Martin, you can see this Beaux Arts beauty at the end of California Street. This axial sightline was no accident - it was part of the **City Beautiful Movement** of the early 1900s where important public buildings were sited at the end of straight-line vistas. Take a self-guided tour of this landmark with its neoclassical columns, Italian marble foyer, and stained glass domes. Find the 24 terra cotta busts of friars along the outside of the building. The sweeping stairway will lead you up to a second floor Municipal Art Gallery.

2. Main Street Stroll - Take in one of Southern California's best main streets with a **Historic Walking Tour Guide**. Walking west from California Street, there's some outstanding early 20th-century commercial architecture - Hotel Ventura (487 E. Main; 1926 - Spanish Colonial Revival); First National Bank (21 California St.; 1926 - Renaissance Revival); El Jardin Patio (451 E. Main; 1926 Spanish Colonial courtyard); Bank of Italy (394 E. Main St.; Renaissance Revival - 1924).

Downtown Ventura has one of Southern California's most beautiful street signs.

Closed to cars since the pandemic, comfortable Main Steet has history, shopping, dining and great public space.

Ventura's gleaming Beaux Arts city hall is a treasure to explore.

3. San Buenaventura Mission (211 E. Main St.) - This is the 9th of the 21 Spanish Missions and the last one personally founded by **St. Junipero Serra** in 1782. The church's adobe, stone and tile walls are 6 1/2 feet thick. The Mission Museum's artifacts include basketry from the native Chumash tribe and unique wooden bells only used during Holy Week. The two **Norfolk Island Pines**, planted in the 1880s, were designated **California Millenium Landmark Trees** in 2000. **The Museum of Ventura County**, with collections on art and history, is just across the street.

4. Gordon Grant Murals (Post Office, 675 Santa Clara St.) - One block east of California, you'll find some beautiful murals painted by Gordon Grant in the **Regionalist painting style**. Funded by the Federal Arts Project under the New Deal's Works Progress Administration, these murals celebrate Ventura's agricultural past. Across the street in Plaza Park, you'll find the giant **Moreton Bay Fig Tree**, planted in 1874. This type of tree was popular in plazas, train stations and public parks around the turn of the century. Look south and you'll see the **Historic Mitchell Block** of eight homes representing several architectural styles from Victorian to Craftsman.

California's 9th Mission is right on Main Street.

During the Mexican Rancho Era, Raymundo Olivas was granted 2,250 acres in 1837.

Nearby Attractions:

- **Ventura Harbor** - A medium-sized boat harbor with restaurants and shops, access to the beach and the Robert J. Lagomarsino Channel Islands National Park Visitors Center (1901 Spinnaker). Here you can book your boat ride to the islands aboard Island Packers Cruises - the Official Boat Concessionaire for the national park. Santa Cruz Island is only 19 miles across the channel and is a wonderful site for kayaking, hiking, wildlife viewing and snorkeling.

- **Olivas Adobe Historical Park** - One of the largest Mexican Rancho-era adobes built in 1847 in the Monterey Style.

- **Patagonia Original Store** Opened in 1972 and originally called Great Pacific Iron Works. 235 W. Santa Clara.

- **Carpinteria** - Attractive coastal town whose fun "Main Street" - Linden Avenue - ends at the "world's safest beach" along the State Park.

OUTING #79: HOLISTIC VALLEY TOWN

Enchanting Ojai

People claim that there's something special in the air in Ojai. Maybe it's the famous "pink moment" at sunset. Maybe it's the beautiful valley nestled below the Topatopa Mountains. Whatever it is, folks have flocked to Ojai for health, art, music, relaxation and spiritual fulfillment for more than a century. This outing offers a walking tour of the small, historic downtown with suggestions for further exploration.

Background: The valley was once inhabited by the **Chumash people** and it is from their word for moon - "Awhay" - that the name Ojai is derived. The original 1873 town was named after Charles Nordhoff, an author who promoted California for its health and pleasure. Then, a devastating fire in 1917 allowed for a new start. Enter **Edward Libbey**, a wealthy glass manufacturer, who assembled a team of famous architects to create a cohesive, **Spanish village**. The town took its new name, and the resulting Mission Revival architecture survives today. Ojai has a vibrant arts scene and is known for its many festivals, including the popular **Ojai Music Festival** in the outdoor **Libbey Bowl**.

Itinerary:

Downtown Walking Tour - All the action is on and around four blocks of Ojai Avenue. We'll go west to east.

1. Start at the Ojai Valley Museum (130 W. Ojai) for some excellent background. The museum is housed in a former Catholic Church built in 1919. Next door is the El Roblar Hotel, another Mission Revival beauty, with its beautiful mosaics.

2. Cross the street to the landmark Ojai Post Office Tower and Portico (1917). This tower is the focal point for downtown and was modeled after a cathedral in Havana. Find the National Register Plaque at its base.

3. Explore Libbey Park - Enter this lovely park where oak and sycamore trees abound. You'll pass a wonderful Tot Lot, eight hard courts for the annual Ojai Tennis Tournament, and, in back, the renowned **Libbey Bowl**, a sunken, outdoor music venue with 973 seats. Double back to the front on the park, pass under the archway, and enter the Arcade.

4. Walk the Ojai Arcade (built 1917) - Early Spanish laws from 1573 required arcaded main streets in their colonial cities, and the Ojai Arcade provides this unifying architectural theme. The shopping and food choices are great. Find the historical plaques under an arch, and take the passageway north to the adjoining and comfortable Arcade Plaza for more specialty retail.

5. Discover More - Around downtown you'll find wine tasting, craft beer and art galleries. Outside of town are hiking trails, olive oil tasting, and the popular **Beatrice Wood Center for the Arts**. Make sure to visit the **Ojai Valley Inn and Spa**, a luxurious resort that began in 1923 as a golf clubhouse designed by noted architect Wallace Neff. No wonder people say - "There's nothing to do in Ojai, and not enough time to do it!"

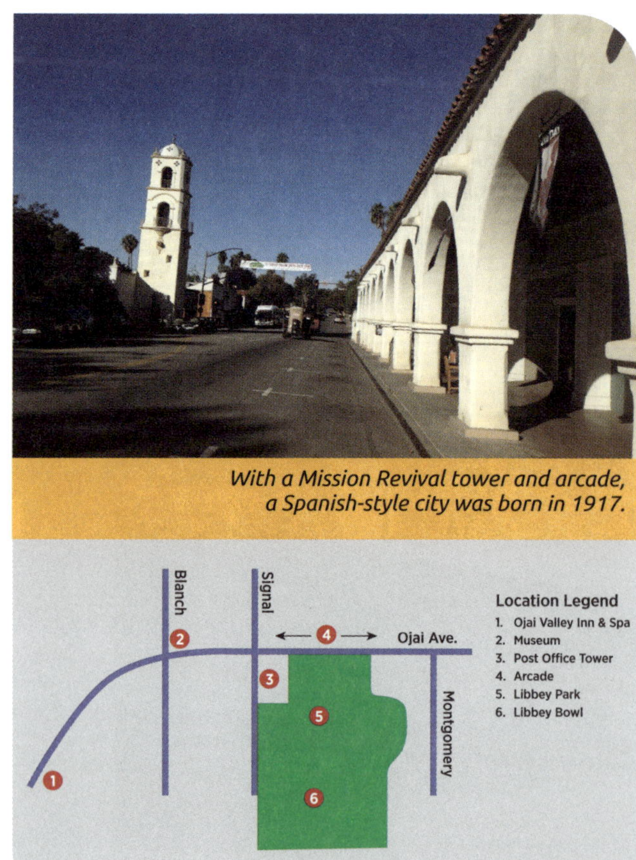

With a Mission Revival tower and arcade, a Spanish-style city was born in 1917.

OUTING #80: PRESIDENT ON A HILL

Ronald Regan Presidential Library & Museum, Simi Valley

This outing will take you to the Ronald Reagan Presidential Library, one of two presidential libraries located in Southern California (the other being the Richard Nixon Library in Yorba Linda - described in Outing #52). Located on top of a hill in the western part of Simi Valley, the Reagan Presidential Library and Museum is the largest in the nation and deserves at least a half day visit. Plan your visit to coincide with one of the Library's excellent special exhibits, and enjoy a nice lunch at the Gipper's Bar and Bistro with its expansive views of the countryside extending all the way to the Pacific Ocean.

Background: There are currently 16 Presidential Libraries from Massachusetts to California administered by the **National Archives and Records Administration**. The Hoover through George W. Bush Libraries have museums with permanent and rotating exhibits. Starting with Franklin Roosevelt, presidential libraries are built with private funding and then transferred to the federal government, ensuring that exhibits reflect the dignity of the presidency and accurately portray events and information.

Itinerary: Exploring the Reagan Library: The library has 24 galleries, the Memorial Site, the Air Force One Pavilion, the Archives Research Room and, of course, an impressive Museum Store. The galleries are organized in two parts - Reagan's life up to the presidency and Reagan's legacy - separated by a visit to the **Air Force One Pavilion** where you can board the presidential plane. The Reagan Library opened in 1991 with a modern Spanish style in keeping with the President's love for the West and consistent with his Santa Barbara ranch.

1. Dramatic arrival - Notice banners of all 46 Presidents, beginning with George Washington, as you wind up the steep Presidential Drive.

2. Start with the Hologram - As you enter the galleries, take in the short film on the history of the White House and a hologram of our 40th President as he speaks about his hopes for America.

3. Enjoy the Galleries - Follow the evolution of the Great Communicator from his days as a sports commentator, actor, Governor of California and then President. The replica of the **Oval Office** is a highlight.

4. Climb aboard the Air Force One - this "Flying White House" is found in a two-story, 90,000 sq. ft. pavilion.

5. Follow Reagan's Presidential Challenges - From domestic issues to foreign policy crises, the final galleries cover the US economy and the ending of the Cold War with nuclear arms treaties and the tearing down of the Berlin Wall.

6. Visit the Gravesite and stroll the Terrace - Nice spot for fresh air and great views. Time for a snack? Enjoy the **Gipper's Bar and Bistro**.

Nearby Attraction:

The Nethercutt Collection - One of the top attractions in the LA area, a two-story museum with over 250 vintage automobiles from 1898 to 1997, rare mechanical instruments and precious antique furniture; a 30-minute drive from the Reagan Library (15151 Bledsoe Street, Sylmar).

APPENDIX A: STREETS FOR THE PEOPLE

SoCal's Best Walking Streets

"The street is the river of life of the city, the place where we come together, the pathway to the center." Thus spoke urban sociologist and author William Whyte in his book **The City: Rediscovering the Center**. *Walkable streets are a treasure, and there aren't enough of them in this vast region of ours, so dominated by automobiles. Here's a fun list of some wonderful, walkable streets to add to your favorites. Now get out and explore!*

Broadway Street, Chinatown

Rodeo Drive, Beverly Hills

Honolulu Avenue, Montrose

Claremont Village, Claremont

Los Angeles

Olvera Street - a colorful gauntlet of Mexican curios, history and food.

Broadway Street, Chinatown - a stimulating, five-block walk from Dragon Gateway at Cesar Chavez Boulevard to Chinatown Plaza and Bamboo Lane.

Larchmont Avenue - charming street with boutique stores and food galore in the heart of Los Angeles; best stretch between Beverly Blvd. and **The Grove LA**.

First Street, the Grove LA - some of the Southland's best streets are in shopping centers; Rick Caruso's creation next to the Farmers Market is perfectly proportioned for the stroller.

Abbot Kinney Boulevard, Venice - hippest three blocks you'll ever walk; palm trees and boutiques.

Ocean Front Walk, Venice - a human carnival of beachside tackiness, movement and color - where the city meets the sand.

Los Angeles County

Rodeo Drive, Beverly Hills - the "Fifth Avenue of Los Angeles," three blocks of elegant retail and glitzy storefronts; Beverly Drive, one block east, is fun, too, with lots of restaurants.

Honolulu Avenue, Montrose - not glitzy but comfortable, this 3-block shopping park exudes down-home comfort with old-style streetlamps, lots of trees, and Mom & Pop charm; five stars!

Manhattan Beach Boulevard, Manhattan Beach - bright, 4-block, downhill stretch past lively restaurants and shops, emptying onto Manhattan Beach Pier.

Claremont Village - this college town sets the standard; friendly merchants, creative stores and pedestrian comfort. Don't miss the Folk Music Center and Some Crust Bakery.

Myrtle Street, Monrovia - from Olive to Palm Drive, a stroller's delight; don't miss Merengue Cuban Bakery.

Colorado Boulevard, Old Town Pasadena - this town center set the standard by repurposing vintage architecture and refurbishing back alleyways; four square blocks of discovery.

First Street, The Grove

Main Street, Ventura

3rd. St. Promenade, Santa Monica

India Street, Little Italy

Orange County

Main Street, Seal Beach - three blocks of "aw-shucks" charm ending at a picturesque wooden pier; small specialty shops make for great lingering and window shopping.

Marine Avenue, Balboa Island, Newport Beach - cross the bridge and you'll find the most colorful of streets; don't pass up a chocolate-covered banana or a stroll along picturesque Newport Bay.

Forest Avenue, Laguna Beach - this artist town delivers a charming, walkable downtown. Forest Avenue has a pedestrian promenade and its iconic eucalyptus trees.

Avenida Del Mar Street, San Clemente - this town of red-tile roofs has a relaxed and beautiful downtown. Start at the corner of El Camino Real and head towards the ocean breezes.

Glassell & Chapman, Orange - this delightful town preserved their beloved Plaza Square and the surrounding historic district. Explore north, south, or west from the plaza.

San Diego County

India Street, Little Italy, San Diego - lively and colorful, this street has tons of restaurants and an attractive square - Piazza della Famiglia - at the corner of India and Date Ave.

Orange Avenue, Coronado - with its beautiful palm and fir tree median, this street is a memorable walk from Eighth Street to Hotel del Coronado.

University Avenue, Hillcrest & North Park neighborhoods - same street, different neighborhoods. Vibrant Hillcrest neighborhood centers near 5th Street; North Park on 30th Street.

Santa Barbara & Ventura Counties

State Street, Santa Barbara - almost regal in its Spanish Colonial splendor, this great street pays attention to detail with wide sidewalks, historic landmarks, and beautiful arcades.

Main Street, Ventura - framed by historic buildings, queen palms, and creative merchants, this street is easy strolling and the pride of the town.

Copenhagen Dr., Solvang - it's like being in a quaint Danish village.

Ojai Ave, Ojai - with its vintage, arcaded Spanish Colonial architecture, adjoining Libby Park, wine tasting and museum, this street is a morning or afternoon of fun.

Riverside County

Palm Canyon Drive, Palm Springs - there's much to see and do along this "Walk of the Stars" stretch between Tahquitz Canyon and Baristo; you'll need a mister during the summer though!

APPENDIX B: WHAT STYLE IS IT?

A Guide to Architectural Styles

If you like architecture, Southern California is a great place to live. Due to its size, history, and creativity, it may have the most diverse architecture in the world. As you travel around different areas, it's fun to spot architectural styles and guess their approximate age. Here are some examples of styles you might see in Southern California, followed by a brief descriptor. Let's go building watching!

EARLY CALIFORNIA (1770 - 1850) - adobes, ranchos, churches, Monterrey style balconies.

QUEEN ANNE VICTORIAN (1880 - 1910) - corner turret; steep roofs.

CHÂTEAUESQUE (1880 - 1910) - busy, steep roof with pinnacles.

BEAUX ARTS (1885 - 1930) - decorative Classical Revival; symmetrical walls of masonry.

MISSION REVIVAL (1890 - 1920) - rounded Mission-shaped roof feature; stucco walls.

GOTHIC REVIVAL (1870 - 1940) - pointed arch windows; steep, cross- gable roofs.

CRAFTSMAN (1905 - 1930) - gable roof; decorative beams; front porch.

SPANISH COLONIAL (1915 - 1940) - red tile roofs; asymmetrical facade.

TUDOR (1890 - 1940) - steeply pitched roofs; decorative half-timbering.

PRAIRIE (1900 - 1920) -overhanging eaves; horizontal emphasis.

PUEBLO REVIVAL (1910 on) - projecting wooden roof beams (vigas); flat roof.

ITALIAN RENAISSANCE (1890 - 1935) - symmetrical; overhanging eaves.

EXOTIC REVIVAL (1914 - 1930) - movie palaces, libraries, estates.

ROMANESQUE REVIVAL (1880 - 1940) - masonry walls; round arches; irregular massing; short columns.

ART DECO (1926 - 1940) - exuberant surface detailing - geometric, organic, thematic.

FRENCH ECLECTIC (1915 - 1945) - roof emphasis; stone walls.

STREAMLINE MODERNE (1930s) - smooth, curved walls; horizontal ribbon windows; nautical themes.

BRUTALISM (1960s) - unpainted concrete and blocky forms.

MODERNISM (1945 - 1960) - open floor plans; large windows; straight line forms.

INTERNATIONAL STYLE (1950 - 1980) - tall, geometric forms of steel, glass and concrete.

POST-MODERN (late 1970s - 1990) - playful historic, cultural references with modern material.

LATE MODERN (1985 - present) - new shapes, new textures; beyond the box.

LYRICAL MODERNISM? (2003) - some buildings defy labels!

DECONSTRUCTIVISM (1985 on) - the parts are more than the whole!

APPENDIX C: MUSEUMS ALL OVER THE PLACE!

Art, Architecture, Science and Culture

Despite its ideal climate for outdoor activities, Southern California is one of the most museum-rich areas in the world. This list is by no means exhaustive, but represents the diversity of these wonderful places of learning.

Getty Villa, Pacific Palisades

The Broad, Downtown LA

Academy Museum of Motion Pictures

Petersen Automotive Museum, Los Angeles

Downtown Los Angeles

The Broad – world-class contemporary art in a stunning building on Bunker Hill; free general admission.

California African American Museum - history, art & culture with emphasis on California and the West.

California Science Center - Samuel Oschin Air & Space Center (including Endeavor Space Shuttle), IMAX Theater, permanent and rotating exhibits; great for kids.

Chinese American Museum - dedicated to the resilient story of Chinese Americans in California; located in El Pueblo de Los Angeles Historical Monument.

Grammy Museum - celebration of many genres of music with interactive exhibits and concert footage; located in LA LIVE sports and entertainment district.

Japanese American National Museum - the national repository of the Japanese American experience in the heart of Little Tokyo.

Italian American Museum of Los Angeles - located right on Olvera Street in former 1908 Italian Hall.

Lucas Museum of Narrative Art - dedicated to storytelling through visual images.

Museum of Contemporary Art (MOCA) - only artist-founded museum in LA; two locations - one on Bunker Hill, the other in Little Tokyo.

Natural History Museum - dinosaur bones, dioramas, nature gardens and new Commons community hub.

Greater Los Angeles

Academy Museum of Motion Pictures - four stories of exhibits housed in former 1930s department store; stunning view terrace and Geffen Theater.

Autry Museum of the American West - tells an inclusive story of the West and its many cultures; largest collection of Native American artifacts in SoCal.

Getty Center - stunning modern architecture overlooking LA with art from Middle Ages to today.

Getty Villa - Greek and Roman antiquities in a recreated Roman country home from AD 79.

Griffith Observatory - beloved Art Deco landmark with expansive views, celestial exhibits, and planetarium shows.

Hammer Museum - contemporary art museum located in Westwood Village.

Hollyhock House - Frank Lloyd Wright's first commission in LA; textile block style from 1921; great views of Hollywood Hills.

Holocaust Museum LA - first survivor-founded and oldest Holocaust museum in the US.

La Brea Tar Pits and Page Museum - showcases ice age fossils in world-famous excavation site.

LA County Museum of Art (LACMA) - West's largest art museum located along Museum Row.

Maritime Museum of Los Angeles - discover the history of the Port of Los Angeles right on the water.

Huntington Library and Gardens, San Marino

Orange County Museum of Art, Costa Mesa

Cheech Marin Center for Chicano Art, Riverside

San Diego Museum of Art, Balboa Park

Museum of Latin American Art (Long Beach) - only US museum dedicated to contemporary Latino art.

Museum of Tolerance - examines racism and prejudice around the world.

Nethercutt Collection - world-class collection of antique automobiles & rare musical instruments.

Petersen Automotive Museum - a celebration of automobiles past and present; rare vehicles in vault; located in Museum Row on Wilshire Boulevard.

Skirball Cultural Center - Jewish educational center with permanent and rotating exhibits.

Reagan Presidential Library (Simi Valley) - hilltop museum & burial site of the 40th President.

Wende Museum (Culver City) - fascinating collection of Cold War art and artifacts.

Pasadena/Claremont/Pomona

American Museum of Ceramic Art - considered one of nation's best collections.

Gamble House - considered the quintessential Craftsman Bungalow (1908) by Greene and Greene architects.

Huntington Library and Gardens - famous research library, British & American art galleries, and 130 acres of themed botanical gardens.

Norton Simon Museum - finest collection of Impressionist and post-Impressionist paintings on the West Coast.

Orange County

Bowers Museum - one of oldest OC museums with popular rotating exhibits and event spaces.

Hilbert Museum of California Art - California Scene paintings spanning the 20th century.

Nixon Presidential Library & Museum - this National Historic Landmark also includes the birthplace home of the 37th President.

Orange County Museum of Art - innovative art in a cutting-edge building in the Segerstrom Center.

UCI Langson ICMA - American impressionistic art depicting the California landscape.

Riverside / San Bernardino

Cheech Marin Center for Chicano Art - houses Cheech's unparalleled collection and rotating exhibits.

Palm Springs Art Museum - contemporary & Native American art; sculptures, paintings, and photos.

Sam Maloof Foundation - workshop, home and galleries of famous 20th-century furniture maker.

Sunnylands - mid-century Annenberg summer estate and gardens in Rancho Mirage.

San Diego Area

Balboa Park Museums - with 18 world-class museums, you may need a week!

Maritime Museum - walk the decks of historic ships, including the *Star of India* and a Spanish galleon.

USS Midway Museum - board the longest-serving aircraft carrier of the 20th century.

Museum of Making Music (Carlsbad) - discover how instruments were made, sold and used.

APPENDIX D: FIND THE PLAQUE!

National Historic Landmarks and More

As you explore the vastness of Southern California, you will occasionally see a plaque or marker on or near a building . This indicates that this place is somehow special, but not all designations are equal (see box below, opposite page). Although there are many levels of designation (city, county, state and national), the highest honor that a building can receive is that of National Historic Landmark (NHL) – a designation by the federal government that the landmark is of exceptional national significance. You may find, however, that state or local designations are more meaningful to your interests. Regardless, finding landmarks makes exploring more fun.

National Historic Landmark Plaque

Jet Propulsion Laboratory, La Cañada/Flintridge

Hollyhock House, Los Angeles

Gamble House, Pasadena

Estudillo House, San Diego

Here's a list of some of the more well-known national historic landmarks in Southern California. Whereas these NHLs are fairly rare, there are over 1,500 additional structures on the National Register of Historic Places, about 1,200 California Historical Landmarks, and over 1,000 Historic-Cultural Monuments in Los Angeles alone. And, yes, a place can have more than one designation. Keep your eyes peeled for these plaques!

Los Angeles

Baldwin Hills Village - best example of the Garden Apartment design with Village Green (1935-1942).

Aline Barnsdale Complex (Hollyhock House) - Frank Lloyd Wright masterpiece on a panoramic hill in Hollywood.

Bradbury Building - famous early office building with stunning interior space and wrought-iron balconies (1893).

Eames House (Case Study House # 8) - progressive, modern home of glass and steel from 1949.

Gamble House (Pasadena) - masterpiece Craftsman bungalow by Greene and Greene (1908) "architecture as art"

Little Tokyo Historic District - Japanese American ethnic district in downtown.

Los Angeles Memorial Coliseum - only stadium to host 2 Summer Olympics, a Super Bowl and World Series (1921).

Los Cerritos Ranch House (Long Beach) - largest adobe home built during Mexican Rancho Period (1844).

Rose Bowl (Pasadena) - 92,000 capacity stadium host to annual Rose Bowl college football game (1922).

Upton Sinclair House (Monrovia) - home of Pulitzer Prize-winning novelist and muckraker.

Santa Monica Looff Hippodrome - on Santa Monica pier; early example of beachside amusement park (1916).

Space Flight Operations Facility (Pasadena) - control room at Jet Propulsion Laboratory where deep space missions are monitored.

Watts Towers - a superb example of nontraditional vernacular architecture and American Native art (1921 - 1954).

Orange

Richard Nixon Birthplace (Yorba Linda) - early home of 37th President; now part of Nixon Library and Museum (1912).

Watts Towers, Los Angeles

Chicano Park, San Diego

Star of India, San Diego

Modjeska House – tucked away in a woodsy canyon, home to famous Polish patriot and Shakespearean actress.

Riverside

Mission Inn – hotel complex; one of largest and most exuberant Spanish/Mission Revival buildings in nation (1902 - 1932).

Santa Barbara

Santa Barbara County Courthouse – one of most beautiful Spanish Colonial buildings in US; historic murals, extensive tiles, and panoramic clock tower (1929).

Santa Barbara Mission – only California Mission where Franciscan Friars have lived continuously since its founding (1820).

Steedman Estate – designed by George Washington Smith, a stellar example of 1920s residential Spanish Colonial Revival architecture.

San Diego

Balboa Park – extensive urban park of museums and gardens built in ornate Spanish Colonial style (1915).

Chicano Park – biggest collection of Chicano murals in the US; began as protest against freeway construction.

Estudillo House – adobe structure in Old Town San Diego considered one of the finest homes in Mexican California (1827).

Hotel del Coronado – one of largest wooden Victorian hotels in US; a beachside icon and haven for celebrities on Coronado Island (1888).

San Diego Presidio - paved the way for Spanish colonization of California in 1769; no structure remains but the museum is part of Presidio Park.

San Luis Rey Mission (Oceanside) – one of largest and best preserved of the California Spanish Missions (1815).

Star of India – oldest iron-hulled merchant ship still floating; docked at San Diego's Embarcadero (1863).

Levels of Landmark Designations

National Historic Landmark (NHL) - exceptional properties significant to American history and culture; managed by National Park Service & approved by Department of the Interior (over 2,600 places in US).

National Monument - protects objects of national significance; often larger properties than NHLs, protecting areas of unique geographic features.

National Register of Historic Places - official list of the nationally significant historic properties.

California Historical Monuments - buildings, sites or places of statewide significance; over 1,200 statewide. Look for the brown bear on the marker.

County Landmarks - each county may have their own program of designating landmarks.

City Historic/Cultural Landmarks - locally designated buildings and places.

APPENDIX E: FUN FACTS

Trivia Quizzes for the Urban Explorer

CALIFORNIA QUIZ

All about our wonderful state!

1. State Freshwater Fish ______________
2. State Bird ________________
3. State Reptile ______________
4. State Motto ______________
5. Third Largest City ______________
6. Lowest Point ______________
7. Highest Point ______________
8. Year of Statehood ___________
9. State Nuts (4) ___________ ___________ ___________ ___________
10. State Flower ______________
11. State Animal ______________
12. State Tree ________________
13. State Fabric ______________
14. State Marine Fish ____________
15. State Fossil _________________
16. State Mineral _____________
17. Largest County (land area) ____________________
18. State Marine Mammal ___________________
19. State Colors _____________________
20. State Nickname _________________
21. State Crab ____________________
22. State Gold Rush Ghost Town ___________________
23. State Sport ____________________

SCORE ________

18 - 23 = Very Stately! **14 - 17** = California Connoisseur. **10 - 13** = Advancing Statehood. **< 10** = Time to Explore!

Answers on page 173

QUIZ ON LANDMARKS & FUN FACTS

Only in Southern California!

1. California's first Spanish mission was built here. ____________________
2. Largest mammal in the California desert. ________________________
3. This facility has built and managed six Mars rovers. ________________
4. At 11,499 feet, this is SoCal's tallest mountain peak. ________________________
5. The second largest city in Los Angeles County. _______________________
6. This native bird is a member of the cuckoo family. ___________________
7. A famous seaman, author and lawyer visited here in 1835 to collect cattle hides, describing it as the "only romantic spot in California." __________________
8. Which Southern California county has the lowest overall elevation? _________________
9. The largest state park in California is in Southern California. Name it. ____________________
10. Grown almost exclusively in Southern California, this is our State Fruit. ___________________
11. Southern California experiences over 100,000 of them every year. _____________________
12. This landmark has hosted two Olympic Games in the 20th century. ____________________
13. Closely related to salmon, it is born in fresh water and then goes out to sea. ____________
14. The second largest Asian group in LA County. __________________
15. These are the four main sources of water for Southern California. ______________________

    _______________ ____________________ ____________________

16. Famous amphitheater built in 1922 and listed on the National Register. ____________________
17. Known as the "City of Trees and PhDs." ________________________
18. This famous landmark has over 2,600 honorific markers. ____________________
19. Most of Southern California has this type of climate. ___________________
20. This city is known as the "American Riviera." _____________________
21. Within two million, what was Southern California's population in 2024? ________________
22. The first navel orange tree was grown here in 1873. ___________________

SCORE ________

20 - 25 = SoCal Gold! **15 - 19** = SoCal Explorer. **10 - 15** = Day Tripper!

Answers on page 173

QUIZ ON SO CAL ATTRACTIONS

So Much to See!

1. It rises 5,873 feet in elevation in about ten minutes. ________________
2. This county has more craft breweries than any other in US. ____________
3. Third oldest major league ballpark in the U.S. _______________________
4. City with twenty-three miles of scenic coastline. ____________________
5. This desert "tree" is actually a plant. _____________________________
6. This landmark commemorates the founding of LA by the Spanish in 1781. ______________
7. Purchased by Long Beach in 1967. ______________________
8. The US National Mammal lives here, 26 miles from shore. __________________________
9. This city is home to the most famous Craftsman Bungalows. ___________________________
10. Desert valley home to Palm Springs and several famous music festivals. ______________________
11. The largest enclave of Vietnamese outside of that country live here. _______________________
12. Largest floating museum in Southern California. ________________________
13. Disney and Warner Brothers Studios are located in this city. _____________________
14. Famous city and zip code surrounded by Los Angeles and West Hollywood. ____________________
15. Called the "Galápagos of North America." ______________________________________
16. The McDonald brothers opened their first burger restaurant here in 1940. ______________________
17. Southern California's wine region. ________________________
18. It ends at the Santa Monica Pier after traveling 2,448 miles. ______________________
19. Biggest natural harbor in Southern California and third largest in the state. _________________
20. It started out with thirteen letters but dropped four. ________________________
21. Named for a Spanish explorer, it has 18 world-class museums. ___________________
22. Starts in downtown Los Angeles, passes through West Hollywood and Beverly Hills, and ends at the ocean in Pacific Palisades. _____________________
23. These "Big Three" burger companies originated in Southern California. __________________________

    ______________________ ___________________
24. Famous Mexican food chain restaurant that opened in Downey in 1962. ______________________
25. Ice Age mastodons, saber-toothed cats and sloths have been unearthed here. ______________________

SCORE __________

21 - 25 = Urban Explorer Royale! **17 - 20** = Outing Master. **11 - 16** = Weekend Warrior!

Answers on page 173

QUIZ ON PRESIDENTS OF THE 20th CENTURY

Southern California has two presidential libraries.
Use this quiz before your outing.

Some presidents may appear more than once, some not at all.

A. Theodore Roosevelt
B. William Taft
C. Woodrow Wilson
D. Warren Harding

E. Calvin Coolidge
F. Herbert Hoover
G. Franklin Roosevelt
H. Harry Truman

I. Dwight Eisenhower
J. John Kennedy
K. Lyndon Johnson
L. Richard Nixon

M. Gerald Ford
N. Jimmy Carter
O. Ronald Reagan
P. George H. W. Bush

Q. Bill Clinton
R. George W. Bush
S. Barack Obama
T. Donald Trump
U. Joe Biden

1. Signed the Federal Interstate Highway Act 1956. __________.
2. Only President to lead a labor union. __________
3. Only President who was also a Supreme Court Justice. __________
4. Cut the corporate tax rate from 35 to 21%. __________
5. Signed Medicare into law. __________
6. Established the Environmental Protection Agency. __________
7. Established the Food and Drug Agency, 150 National Forests & 5 National Parks. __________
8. Signed the biggest welfare reform law in history. __________
9. Sent in federal troops to enforce desegregation of Little Rock Central High School in Arkansas. __________
10. Most recent President born in Massachusetts. __________
11. Turned down offers to play professional football. __________
12. Donated all his Presidential and Congressional salaries to charity. __________
13. Half of the longest married First Couple. __________
14. Withdrew troops from South Vietnam. __________
15. Began working life as a sports commentator. __________
16. Said, "Ask not what your country can do for you, but what you can do for your country." __________
17. Said in his inaugural speech – "The only thing we have to fear is fear itself." __________
18. Two Presidents since 1950 that saw federal budget surpluses. __________
19. President who appointed first Black Supreme Court Justice. __________
20. Grew up in Independence, Missouri; as President, he implemented the Marshall Plan to rebuild war-torn Europe. __________
21. Advocated for the establishment of the League of Nations after World War I. __________
22. President during the onset of the Great Depression. __________
23. Signed the Civil Rights and Voting Rights Acts. __________
24. Signed the largest crime bill in US history in 1994. __________
25. Signed the largest ($1.2 trillion) infrastructure bill in US history. __________
26. Alaska and Hawaii were admitted to the Union during his presidency. __________

SCORE __________

24 - 26 = Very Presidential. **20 - 23** = Civics Star! **16 - 19** = Current History Follower.

Answers on page 173

APPENDIX F: RESOURCES FOR THE URBAN EXPLORER

Books, Websites, Groups

In our age of internet searches and artificial intelligence, finding wonderful places is often as easy as reaching for your phone or computer. For example, you can search "architecture of Pasadena" or "which city has more fun activities - Ventura or Ojai?" and find great links, resources and ideas. But at times, the amount of information can be overwhelming. Here are just a few examples of the most comprehensive resources for the urban enthusiast. Happy exploring!

Books

A Field Guide to American Houses, Virginia Savage McAlester (2015) - definitive guide for identifying domestic architecture and styles; copious photos and illustrations.

An Architectural Guidebook to Los Angeles, David Gebhard & Robert Winter (2018) - known as "the Bible" to Los Angeles architecture scholars and enthusiasts; covers Greater LA area.

Preserving Los Angeles, Ken Bernstein (2021) - comprehensive summary of what LA has achieved in the area of historic preservation.

San Diego Architecture from Mission to Modern, Dick Sutro (2002) - Sponsored by the American Institute of Architects, this guide divides the city into regions with great photos and explanations.

Amazing Websites

Los Angeles Conservancy - From the home page, click the "Learn" link to explore over 800 historic properties throughout LA County; this group sponsors weekly and monthly walking tours.

Los Angeles City Planning - Conducted the largest citywide historic resources survey in the nation - **SurveyLA**. Type in the following search words followed by "Los Angeles":

- **Local Historic Districts (HPOZs)** - see descriptions and photos of over 35 historic districts.
- **Historic Landmark Programs** - locate any of the over 1200 landmarks on a digital map.
- **Historic Themes** - explore nine contexts such as "ethnic-cultural" or "entertainment industry."

Preserve Orange County - Explore over 290 historic sites within the County's 34 cities and unincorporated areas on an excellent interactive map.

Advocacy Groups & City Websites

City of Santa Barbara Historic Preservation - A long tradition of protecting historic buildings.

Congress for New Urbanism - Founded in 1993, a movement to create vibrant urban places; sign up for digital journal Public Square to see case studies.

Los Angeles Conservancy - Founded in 1978 to save the Central Library in downtown LA from demolition, it has the largest membership of any local preservation group in the nation.

Old Riverside Foundation - Civic organization dedicated to preservation of historic resources throughout Riverside and the Inland Empire.

Pasadena Heritage - Protecting this proud city's architectural legacy since 1977.

San Diego - Save Our Heritage Organization - Based in Balboa Park, SOHO manages and operates historic sites throughout the county.

Visit Palm Springs - Pride of Preservation - This official tourism authority of the city believes that historic preservation is good for civic pride, business, and the environment.

ANSWERS TO QUIZZES

CALIFORNIA QUIZ

1. Golden trout
2. Quail
3. Desert tortoise
4. Eureka
5. San Jose
6. Death Valley
7. Mt. Whitney
8. 1850
9. Walnuts, pecans, almonds, pistachios
10. Golden Poppy
11. Grizzly bear
12. Redwood (sequoia)
13. Denim
14. Garibaldi
15. Saber-toothed cat
16. Gold
17. San Bernardino
18. California Gray Whale
19. Blue and Gold
20. Golden State
21. Dungeness crab
22. Bodie
23. Surfing

QUIZ ON LANDMARKS AND FUN FACTS

1. San Diego
2. Bighorn sheep
3. Jet Propulsion Laboratory
4. Mt. San Gorgonio
5. Long Beach
6. Roadrunner
7. Richard Henry Dana
8. Imperial County
9. Anza Borrego State Desert Park
10. Avocados
11. Earthquakes
12. LA Memorial Coliseum
13. Steelhead trout
14. Filipino
15. Sacramento Delta, Colorado River, Eastern Sierra, groundwater
16. Hollywood Bowl
17. Claremont
18. Walk of Fame
19. Mediterranean
20. Santa Barbara
21. Twenty-three million
22. Riverside

QUIZ ON SOCAL ATTRACTIONS

1. Palm Spring Aerial Tramway
2. San Diego
3. Dodger Stadium
4. Malibu
5. Joshua Tree
6. El Pueblo de Los Angeles
7. Queen Mary
8. Bison
9. Pasadena
10. Coachella Valley
11. Little Saigon
12. USS *Midway*
13. Burbank
14. Beverly Hills
15. Channel Islands National Park
16. San Bernardino
17. Temecula Valley
18. Route 66
19. San Diego Harbor
20. Hollywood Sign
21. Balboa Park
22. Sunset Boulevard
23. McDonald's, In-N-Out, Carl's Jr. (also Jack in the Box)
24. Taco Bell
25. La Brea Tar Pits

QUIZ ON PRESIDENTS OF THE 20TH CENTURY

1. I
2. O
3. B
4. T
5. K
6. L
7. A
8. Q
9. I
10. P
11. M
12. J
13. N
14. L
15. O
16. J
17. G
18. L, Q
19. K
20. H
21. C
22. F
23. K
24. Q
25. U
26. I

NAME THE WINE QUIZ

1. C
2. E
3. I
4. H
5. F
6. B
7. M
8. L
9. J
10. N
11. K
12. D
13. G
14. A

FINAL ANSWER: Gallo Winery

INDEX - GREAT PLACES IN SOUTHERN CALIFORNIA

DOWNTOWN LOS ANGELES

GREATER LOS ANGELES

LA COUNTY

Beverly Hills

Burbank

Catalina Island

TOP TEN SOUTHERN CALIFORNIA EXPERIENCES

Top Ten lists are fun, but not to be taken seriously! Regardless, it's great to think about all the many wonderful places in Southern California. Here's my list! What's yours?

Mercado Gonzalez, Costa Mesa, is a celebration of the variety of Mexican food.

Academy Museum of Motion Pictures - don't miss the view from the Dolby Terrace!

Hidden Valley Loop Trail, Joshua Tree NP - impossibly stacked boulders amid desert flora.

Huntington Library and Gardens - where landscape architecture and gallery art come together.

San Antonio Winery - where downtown LA comes together - historic, classy and tasty!

Piazza della Famiglia, Little Italy, San Diego - this is how you create vibrant public space and a fun urban village!

Vista Las Palmas, Palm Springs - one of many beautiful mid-century modern neighborhoods.

Claremont - college town like no other! Fun Village, fascinating art and architecture.

Warner Brothers Studio Tour - so fun to see where movies are made!

Getty Center - where modern architecture steals the show!